Marketing to Family Business Owners

A Toolkit For Life Insurance Professionals

by Russ Alan Prince
and
Karen Maru File

505 Gest Street / Cincinnati, Ohio / 45203-1716

This publication is designed to provide accurate and authoritative information in regard to the subject matter covered. It is sold with the understanding that the publisher is not engaged in rendering legal, accounting or other professional service. If legal advice or other expert assistance is required, the services of a competent professional should be sought. — **From a Declaration of Principles jointly adopted by a Committee of the American Bar Association and a Committee of Publishers and Associations.**

ISBN: 0-87218-149-9

First Edition

Printed in U. S. A.

DEDICATION

Russ Alan Prince

To Sandi, Executive Director Of Our Family Business

Karen Maru File

To Mike, Charlie, and Joe

ABOUT THE AUTHORS

Russ Alan Prince

Russ Alan Prince is one of the foremost experts on the financial and philanthropic behavior of the affluent. He is president of Prince & Associates, Inc., a premier market research and consulting firm dedicated to the upscale market.

Included among his firm's clients are National Life of Vermont, New York Life, Mass Mutual, U.S. Trust Company of New York, Bankers Trust, Dean Witter, Merrill Lynch, and Nesbitt-Burns.

Mr. Prince has been extensively quoted in the media. His comments have been reported in the *Wall Street Journal, Forbes, BusinessWeek, American Banker, National Underwriter*, the *Chronicle of Philanthropy, Institutional Investor* and numerous other publications.

A prolific writer of academic and trade publication articles, Mr. Prince has co-authored *The Seven Faces of Philanthropy: A New Approach to Cultivating Major Donors, The Charitable Estate Planning Process: How to Find and Work with the Philanthropic Affluent, Marketing to the Affluent Investor, Financial Planning for Physicians* and *Marketing to the Affluent.*

Mr. Prince has a master's degree in sociology from the State University of New York (SUNY) at Stony Brook where he was a Lehman Fellow. He also holds an MBA degree from Columbia University where he was a Dean's Scholar. In 1995, Mr. Prince served as an Expert-in-Residence for the W. K. Kellogg Foundation.

Karen Maru File

Dr. File, Associate Professor of Marketing at the University of Connecticut, specializes in the marketing of financial and other professional services to the family business market. In the course of her association with Prince & Associates, she has overseen more than thirty research studies focusing on the buyer behavior of the affluent, including family business owners, with respect to financial services, insurance and charitable estate planning products. As a result of this multi-year research program, she has compiled data from thousands of interviews with wealthy individuals.

In the course of establishing the field of marketing to the family business, Dr. File published some of the first articles on the buyer behavior of the family firm and approaches to segmenting the family firm market. In addition to the research in this publication, her recent studies include a multi-national exploration of relationship marketing and in-depth study of provider-client interactions across four services.

Dr. File has published more than two dozen articles in various journals such as *Family Business Review*, the *Journal of Business Research*, the *Journal of Professional Services Marketing*, *Services Marketing*, the *International Journal of Bank Marketing* and *Industrial Marketing Management*. She was invited by the *International Journal of Bank Marketing* to be a guest editor of its special issue on private banking.

A previous stream of research focused on the interface between financial and philanthropic motivations among the affluent including family business owners. This body of research resulted in two books co-authored with Russ Alan Prince, *The Seven Faces of Philanthropy: A New Approach to Cultivating Major Donors*, and *The Charitable Estate Planning Process: How to Find and Work with the Philanthropic Affluent.*

Before joining a university, Dr. File was vice president and partner at Booz Allen & Hamilton, an international consulting firm. There she directed marketing and market research projects for leaders in the insurance and financial services industries, including AEtna, Colonial Penn, CIGNA, and Fidelity.

Dr. File received her undergraduate education at Cornell University, earned her master's degree at Boston University, and her doctorate at Temple University. She has received teaching awards, an honorary chair for faculty achievements, the directorship of a research institute and has been nominated for *Who's Who Among American Women.*

TABLE OF CONTENTS

Section I

The Family Business Market

CHAPTER 1
The Ten Trillion Dollar Market

Richard Bentley is a successful life insurance professional. Among his clients are small business owners, and they have been good, if demanding, clients.

He has just received an industry newsletter with a headline that reads, "Getting Your Share of the Ten Trillion Dollar Market." The article goes on to emphasize the potential of the family business market. Bentley recalls having recently read other articles about the family business market in insurance newsletters and magazines, but hasn't thought about targeting them specifically in his practice.

He decides that ten trillion dollars, even if there is some hype, might be promising and decides to check out the opportunity further. He gets out a pad and writes:

- *How big is the market, really?*
- *What's the competition?*
- *Do they have different life insurance needs?*
- *Do I sell differently?*
- *What's the potential?*
- *Where does my practice stand now?*

A great many insurance and financial services providers talk about the affluent family business market as if it were something that recently came into existence. They speak of the affluent family business market as if it was a brand new market.

While it is true that the affluent family business market has in recent years been identified as exceedingly profitable, it has always been here and, as long as we have an economy, it always will be here. It will be here when the onslaught of financial services providers targeting the affluent family business market wanes because the providers jumped in without recognizing what it takes to succeed.

The affluent family business market is not new. It is not a market in the making as some in the industry like to profess. What has happened is that in larger numbers, the financial services professionals have realized that affluent family businesses are the most likely means of becoming wealthy. Therefore, if your objective is to market financial services to the wealthy, isn't it logical to consider directing your efforts at affluent family businesses and their owners?

You bought this book because you are interested in the affluent family business market. Like Richard Bentley, take a few minutes to list your objectives for learning about this market and some ideas for how to build a successful practice around it in the Goal Clarification Worksheet located in Figure 1.01.

Figure 1.01

GOAL CLARIFICATION WORKSHEET
Instructions: List your objectives for learning about the family business market and some ideas on how to build a successful practice around it.
1.
2.
3.

Defining the Family Business

Family firms are defined as enterprises in which two social systems, the family system and the business system, intersect. The influence of the family is exerted through ownership, direct participation of family members in the management of the firm, and in the plan to transfer authority and ownership to a successor generation.

These two systems interact as well as intersect. This means that in family firms, the process of making business decisions is affected by family dynamics. The dynamics of family firms are often represented as shown in Figure 1.02 which, for these purposes, also indicates the perspective of the life insurance professional.

Figure 1.02

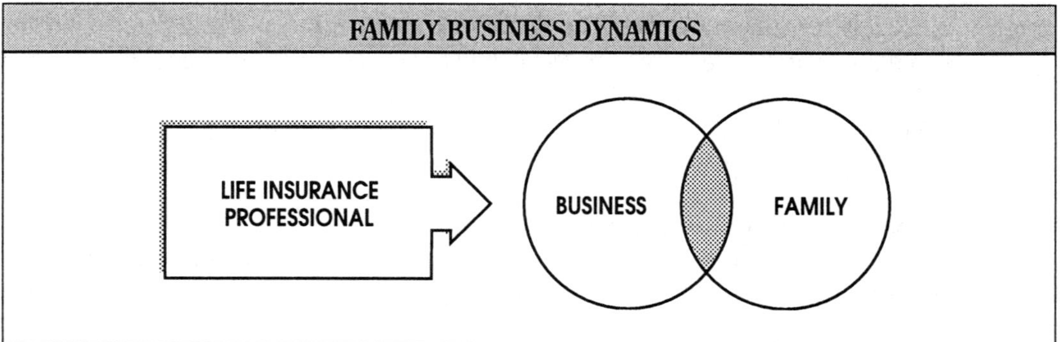

In family firms, business decisions are made by taking into account family factors and dynamics as well as business priorities. For example, purchasing decisions may be affected by individuals who are not part of the formal organizational chart or by family priorities external to the operation of the business. Decisions may also be influenced by criteria specific to a family culture rather than professional managerial practice or by more intense information search and interaction needs motivated by a need to avoid family risk as well as business risk.

All of these dynamics mean that family firms are different from non-family firms in such areas as their management culture, life cycles, priorities, and employee policies. The accumulated weight of all these differences also means that family firms differ from non-family firms with respect to their purchasing of goods and services, including life insurance and financial products.

The Family Business Market

The typical business in America is a family business. The proportion of family firms in the United States has been variously estimated at 90%, 95%, and 96%.

Family businesses include mom-and-pop shops like Kathy's Kitchen. Kathy's markets unsweetened pasta sauces, mustards, and relishes. Her husband Dave is the sales force and her brother Bill is the manufacturing arm. Their son J.B. is the marketing department.

Family businesses also include billion dollar corporations and count among their ranks fully 20% of the Fortune 500. Included here are such corporate giants as Anheuser-Busch and Corning. Family businesses also include successful entrepreneurial firms such as Esprit and Patagonia. Family businesses include interesting niche players, such as Wemco, Inc., the largest single player in the $1.5 billion necktie industry.

The important thing is to not think about "family businesses" as just one type of business. There are many different kinds, and learning the differences is a key to success.

In the first place, as a life insurance professional, you will not target all family businesses. You are not positioned to sell to large incorporated family businesses. On the other hand, you will not want your entire practice to be made up of very small family businesses, either. So you will want to be sensitive to the size of the family businesses you target.

In selecting family businesses to target, you will also want to be aware of where a business is in its life cycle. You will not want to target very young businesses which are usually strapped for cash. Nor will you want to spend time developing relationships with businesses which are in decline and are approaching the end of their life cycles.

You will also want to pay attention to the different reasons family businesses are in existence — what the owners conceive their mission or purpose to be. A major section of this book is devoted to segmenting family businesses based on their objectives.

Being aware of and sensitive to the wide variety within this huge market opportunity is a key to success.

Family Businesses as Purchasers

All family businesses buy goods and services. Family businesses make more than $1 trillion in annual purchases and this is increasing at a rate of more than $100 billion a year. The equity of these family businesses exceeds $2.5 trillion. Indeed, family firms probably account for at least half of all the industrial purchasing in the United States. The question for life insurance professionals is whether family firms buy differently than non-family firms, and if so, how. The field sales experience and an extensive series of research studies done over the past five years by the authors indicates that family businesses do purchase differently than non-family businesses.

When a life insurance professional calls on a small-to-medium-sized business, there is a very good chance he or she is calling on a family firm. But should the fact that a customer firm is a family firm make a difference in the selling strategy? Should it make a difference to those creating marketing strategies of which the salesperson is a part? To begin answering these questions, take a moment to complete the exercise in Figure 1.03.

As you will see, if most of your top clients are family business owners there will be great opportunities to leverage this situation. If your top clients are not family business owners, this book will provide you with the insights and techniques for expanding your practice into this very lucrative market.

In this book, we explore the emerging field of family business studies using a proprietary data base of thousands of family businesses as customers of insurance products. In addition, we draw on the experiences of hundreds of successful life insurance professionals working in this market.

For life insurance professionals, the key implication is that family business owners are frequent purchasers of the products and services you sell. There are many family businesses and they make up a significant market for the sale of insurance and related financial services.

Family Firms Dominate Certain Industries

There are some industries that family firms dominate — construction and real estate are two. Marrion Corporation is a family business with two sons who joined the father and CEO. The business won $324 million worth of new contracts in a recent year.

A number of industries are discovering that their distribution systems are made up of family firms. Included on this list are the distribution systems for liquor, beverages, automobiles, and heating oil as well as supermarkets. The distribution of fuel oil and petroleum is another industry dominated by family firms.

For life insurance professionals, this concentration of family businesses in certain industries means that the potential for networking and cross referrals is enhanced. Also magnified is the ability to target specialties within certain industries.

Family Firms Control Wealth

Although their numbers and concentration are attractive enough, the amount of wealth controlled by family businesses makes them a compelling target for the life insurance professional. Family firms control most of the private wealth in the country.

Figure 1.03

EVALUATING YOUR CLIENTELE EXERCISE	
Instructions: Write the names of your top ten clients. For each one specify the source of his or her wealth.	
Clients	**Sources of Wealth**
1.	❑ Family business ❑ Non-family business ❑ Inherited wealth ❑ Corporate executives ❑ Professional
2.	❑ Family business ❑ Non-family business ❑ Inherited wealth ❑ Corporate executives ❑ Professional
3.	❑ Family business ❑ Non-family business ❑ Inherited wealth ❑ Corporate executives ❑ Professional
4.	❑ Family business ❑ Non-family business ❑ Inherited wealth ❑ Corporate executives ❑ Professional
5.	❑ Family business ❑ Non-family business ❑ Inherited wealth ❑ Corporate executives ❑ Professional
6.	❑ Family business ❑ Non-family business ❑ Inherited wealth ❑ Corporate executives ❑ Professional
7.	❑ Family business ❑ Non-family business ❑ Inherited wealth ❑ Corporate executives ❑ Professional
8.	❑ Family business ❑ Non-family business ❑ Inherited wealth ❑ Corporate executives ❑ Professional
9.	❑ Family business ❑ Non-family business ❑ Inherited wealth ❑ Corporate executives ❑ Professional
10.	❑ Family business ❑ Non-family business ❑ Inherited wealth ❑ Corporate executives ❑ Professional

Figure 1.03 (cont'd)

What percentage of these clients are in each of the following categories:

Family businesses	______%
Non-family businesses	______%
Inherited Wealth	______%
Corporate executive	______%
Professionals	______%
Total	**100%**

Scoring: 70% or more family business = You are excellently positioned in this marketplace. In reading this book, focus on opoortunities for leverage. 50% to 70% = You are well positioned in the family business marketplace. You need to expand on this base and can use the book to do so. Less than 50% = For you the family business market is an exciting new opportunity for expanding your practice. Use this book as a guide.

Simply put, the bulk of privately-held wealth in the United States, and in other countries, is derived from business ownership. Of all the sources of wealth — equity wealth, post-equity wealth, salaried wealth, inherited wealth and flight capital — equity and post-equity wealth derived from business ownership are the most important. Even inherited wealth, if traced back, has its origins in a family owned business. The concentration of wealth in family owned businesses makes them a significant market for providers of financial services. It is estimated that $10 trillion, much of it in the form of family businesses, will change hands over the next few decades.

Principle: Affluent family businesses are the primary source of private wealth throughout the world.

Family Firms are Successful

The reason family firms generate such wealth is that they are the engines of economies. Small businesses create most jobs in a developed economy and are the source of most new technology. Because of business life cycles, today's smaller firms are tomorrow's giants.

The role of family businesses in just one state is a microcosm of their contribution nationally. In recent years, family businesses in South Dakota reported a 111% average sales volume growth per firm with the average sales volume being $5.7 million per firm. They also projected an average 54% sales volume growth over the next six years.

As we will see later, even failed family businesses are successful. Family businesses typically fail because of an inability to pay estate taxes after the death of an owner. Our study of almost 500 such firms shows that most were successful in the five years preceding the bankruptcy, with an average sales growth in excess of 5% per year, as discussed in Chapter 2.

Your Competition

In marketing financial services and products to affluent family businesses, you are competing with almost everyone in the financial services field. Just about everyone, after all, is attracted to wealth.

To begin learning about your competition in this market, take a moment to complete the exercise in Figure 1.04.

As a life insurance professional, you compete against other insurance agents. You might know that if you are working with a family business you should market your services and products differently than you would to a non-family business, but that won't stop other financial service providers from giving you a run for your money. Other insurance agents may know only that they are going after someone wealthy.

As we will see, an understanding of the affluent family business market will enable you to be more effective than your competitors, irrespective of the type of provider they are and whether or not they are as knowledgeable and skilled as you. Nevertheless, other high-quality insurance professionals should not be disregarded as potential competitors.

The same is true if you are promoting investment management services to the affluent family business owner or if you are trying to sell corporate finance services for the business. Affluent family businesses and their owners are prime targets for everyone in the financial services industry. Your advantage will be in your ability to more effectively use your resources to culti-

Figure 1.04

COMPETITION ASSESSMENT EXERCISE

Instructions: For each of the following types of competitors, assign an effectiveness rating in each of the areas shown.

Competitor	Areas		
	Importance to Family Business	*Prospecting & Selling*	*Relationship Management*
Other Insurance Providers	❑ High ❑ Medium ❑ Low	❑ High ❑ Medium ❑ Low	❑ High ❑ Medium ❑ Low
Banks and Trust Companies	❑ High ❑ Medium ❑ Low	❑ High ❑ Medium ❑ Low	❑ High ❑ Medium ❑ Low
Investment Banks and Brokerage Firms	❑ High ❑ Medium ❑ Low	❑ High ❑ Medium ❑ Low	❑ High ❑ Medium ❑ Low
Accountants	❑ High ❑ Medium ❑ Low	❑ High ❑ Medium ❑ Low	❑ High ❑ Medium ❑ Low
Attorneys	❑ High ❑ Medium ❑ Low	❑ High ❑ Medium ❑ Low	❑ High ❑ Medium ❑ Low

vate them because of your better understanding of affluent family businesses and their owners — especially their owners.

Of greater concern are the competitors who are actively positioning themselves to market to affluent family business owners. More and more the large financial institutions as well as smaller, often independent practitioners, are seriously focusing on the affluent family business market.

Principle: The attractiveness of the family business market is drawing numerous competitors.

To get a feel for the growing competitive nature of the business, we will look at what the different competitors in a number of different industries are offering. You must be aware that the very nature of the financial services industry is rapidly changing, so the usual classifications — insurance company, bank — are in flux. When everybody can provide estate and financial planning services, the lines get blurry quickly. Nevertheless, what follows is a brief assessment of the current competitive field.

Insurance Providers

Without question, a tremendous concern of most affluent family business owners is to pass the family business to the next generation. Very often this can best be accomplished by including insurance in the client's portfolio of financial products. This means that insurance providers must be able to provide high-quality business continuation and estate planning services and a significant number of them can.

Other services offered by insurance providers are also in demand by affluent business owners. Retirement programs as well as health and disability insurance are also important.

Leading providers in the life insurance industry have extensively focused on the family business market. Mass Mutual has committed extensive resources in researching and funding academic programs directed at the family business market. And Mass Mutual is not alone in this endeavor. Other insurance providers focused on the family business market include National Life of Vermont, M Financial Group, and Phoenix Home Life.

With respect to your own practice, to be successful locally it's important to understand the abilities of your direct competitors. The exercise in Figure 1.05 will help you look at local competitive conditions.

Even though competition in this area is often intense and challenging, family business owners respond to promoting the benefits of these services. Six chapters of this book are devoted to showing you how to position and sell your services in these areas to family business owners.

At the same time it's important to know what your competitors are emphasizing. Possessing this information can give you the opportunity to take advantage of gaps in your competitor's approach. Remember that it is important to think of the providers of other types of financial services as your competition as well as other life insurance professionals.

Figure 1.05

INSURANCE PROVIDERS COMPETITIVE ASSESSMENT	
Instructions: Write the names of three other insurance providers (individuals, agencies, etc.) that you identify as competing with you for family business clients. Then, check off which types of services they are particularly strong in.	
Name of Competitor	**Services**
1.	❑ Executive Benefits ❑ Retirement Planning ❑ Business Succession and Estate Planning ❑ Asset Protection Planning ❑ Investment Management ❑ Charitable Estate Planning
2.	❑ Executive Benefits ❑ Retirement Planning ❑ Business Succession and Estate Planning ❑ Asset Protection Planning ❑ Investment Management ❑ Charitable Estate Planning
3.	❑ Executive Benefits ❑ Retirement Planning ❑ Business Succession and Estate Planning ❑ Asset Protection Planning ❑ Investment Management ❑ Charitable Estate Planning

Banks And Trust Companies

Many times, the use of trusts by affluent family business owners is essential to achieve their financial and personal goals. Additionally, banks and trust companies are positioned to manage the assets in these trusts as well as the discretionary assets of the wealthy family.

Many banks and trust companies provide high-quality estate planning services as well as other services such as retirement programs and lending services.

With respect to your own practice, to be successful locally, it's important to understand the abilities of your direct competitors. The exercise in Figure 1.06 will help you look at local competitive conditions.

By understanding the services banks and trust companies are most interested in, you are able to compete more effectively against them. Additionally, you may find opportunities to work cooperatively as discussed in Chapters 12 and 13.

Figure 1.06

BANKS AND TRUST COMPANIES COMPETITIVE ASSESSMENT	
Instructions: Write the names of three banks or trust companies that you identify as competing with you for family business clients. Then, check off which types of services they are particularly strong in.	
Name of Competitor	**Services**
1.	❑ Executive Benefits ❑ Retirement Planning ❑ Business Succession and Estate Planning ❑ Asset Protection Planning ❑ Investment Management ❑ Charitable Estate Planning
2.	❑ Executive Benefits ❑ Retirement Planning ❑ Business Succession and Estate Planning ❑ Asset Protection Planning ❑ Investment Management ❑ Charitable Estate Planning
3.	❑ Executive Benefits ❑ Retirement Planning ❑ Business Succession and Estate Planning ❑ Asset Protection Planning ❑ Investment Management ❑ Charitable Estate Planning

Investment Banks And Brokerage Firms

Traditionally, investment banks and brokerage houses have dealt in the buying and selling of family businesses and provided investment management services. In fact, there are some boutique investment banks whose only business is family businesses.

At the same time, their roles have expanded as they seek to offer a wider range of services. More and more of these institutions now have their own trust company subsidiaries. Along the same lines, many of them are focusing on providing high-quality estate planning services.

With respect to your own practice, to be successful locally it's important to understand the abilities of your direct competitors. The exercise in Figure 1.07 will help you look at local competitive conditions.

As you have seen, for the most part investment banks and brokerages will only compete with life insurance professionals in the area of investment management services. They are not directly involved in all the other areas. As with banks and trust companies, this can be an excellent opportunity for you to work cooperatively with them.

Figure 1.07

INVESTMENT BANKS AND BROKERAGES COMPETITIVE ASSESSMENT	
Instructions: Write the names of three investment banks or brokerages that you identify as competing with you for family business clients. Then, check off which types of services they are particularly strong in.	
Name of Competitor	**Services**
1.	❑ Executive Benefits ❑ Retirement Planning ❑ Business Succession and Estate Planning ❑ Asset Protection Planning ❑ Investment Management ❑ Charitable Estate Planning
2.	❑ Executive Benefits ❑ Retirement Planning ❑ Business Succession and Estate Planning ❑ Asset Protection Planning ❑ Investment Management ❑ Charitable Estate Planning
3.	❑ Executive Benefits ❑ Retirement Planning ❑ Business Succession and Estate Planning ❑ Asset Protection Planning ❑ Investment Management ❑ Charitable Estate Planning

Accounting And Law Firms

Accounting firms offer a broad range of services which, like law firms, can be appropriate for the flagship family business and the wealthy family. From the perspective of the affluent family, accountants can and do provide estate and financial planning services.

While not financial services providers per se, law firms are becoming more and more active in the field. They are involved with family businesses in a number of ways. Providing high-quality estate planning is a key activity, especially since law firms are the only ones with the ability to produce the necessary documents.

With respect to your own practice, to be successful locally, it's important to understand the abilities of your direct competitors. The exercises in Figures 1.08 and 1.09 will help you look at local competitive conditions for accounting firms.

Now let's consider attorneys.

As you can see, many accountants and attorneys targeting family businesses will overlap with many of the service areas that you are involved in. However, they work in these areas differently than you. Your services and products are essential in implementing any strategy or plan. Thus, there are great opportunities to work cooperatively with accountants and attorneys.

Figure 1.08

ACCOUNTANT COMPETITIVE ASSESSMENT	
Instructions: Write the names of three accounting firms that you identify as competing with you for family business clients. Then, check off which types of services they are particularly strong in.	
Name of Competitor	**Services**
1.	❑ Executive Benefits ❑ Retirement Planning ❑ Business Succession and Estate Planning ❑ Asset Protection Planning ❑ Investment Management ❑ Charitable Estate Planning
2.	❑ Executive Benefits ❑ Retirement Planning ❑ Business Succession and Estate Planning ❑ Asset Protection Planning ❑ Investment Management ❑ Charitable Estate Planning
3.	❑ Executive Benefits ❑ Retirement Planning ❑ Business Succession and Estate Planning ❑ Asset Protection Planning ❑ Investment Management ❑ Charitable Estate Planning

Figure 1.09

ATTORNEY COMPETITIVE ASSESSMENT	
Instructions: Write the names of three law firms that you identify as competing with you for family business clients. Then, check off which types of services they are particularly strong in.	
Name of Competitor	**Services**
1.	❑ Executive Benefits ❑ Retirement Planning ❑ Business Succession and Estate Planning ❑ Asset Protection Planning ❑ Investment Management ❑ Charitable Estate Planning
2.	❑ Executive Benefits ❑ Retirement Planning ❑ Business Succession and Estate Planning ❑ Asset Protection Planning ❑ Investment Management ❑ Charitable Estate Planning
3.	❑ Executive Benefits ❑ Retirement Planning ❑ Business Succession and Estate Planning ❑ Asset Protection Planning ❑ Investment Management ❑ Charitable Estate Planning

Positioning Yourself

Knowing your competition is important, but it's not enough. You have to understand where you're strong and where you need to enhance your abilities. The exercise in Figure 1.10 will help you evaluate your strengths and weaknesses.

Figure 1.10

SELF-ASSESSMENT EXERCISE

Instructions: For each of the following areas rate your degree of technical expertise in the context of all the competitors we just discussed. (Circle the appropriate number.) In addition, rate your ability to communicate and explain these services to family business owners. (Circle the appropriate number.) Then, write in what you do to add value to your services. Finally, write in how you plan to enhance your abilities in each of these areas.

❑ **Executive Benefits**

Technical Expertise

Beginner **Expert**

1 2 3 4 5 6 7 8 9 10

Communications Effectiveness

Beginner **Expert**

1 2 3 4 5 6 7 8 9 10

Value Added

___

___

___

Steps to Enhance Abilities

___

___

___

❒ Retirement Planning

Technical Expertise

Beginner									Expert
1	2	3	4	5	6	7	8	9	10

Communications Effectiveness

Beginner									Expert
1	2	3	4	5	6	7	8	9	10

Value Added

___

___

___

Steps to Enhance Abilities

___

___

___

❑ Business Succession and Estate Planning

Technical Expertise

Beginner									Expert
1	2	3	4	5	6	7	8	9	10

Communications Effectiveness

Beginner									Expert
1	2	3	4	5	6	7	8	9	10

Value Added

___

___

___

Steps to Enhance Abilities

___

___

___

❑ Asset Protection Planning

Technical Expertise

Beginner									Expert
1	2	3	4	5	6	7	8	9	10

Communications Effectiveness

Beginner									Expert
1	2	3	4	5	6	7	8	9	10

Value Added

___

___

___

Steps to Enhance Abilities

___

___

___

❑ Investment Management

Technical Expertise

Beginner									Expert
1	2	3	4	5	6	7	8	9	10

Communications Effectiveness

Beginner									Expert
1	2	3	4	5	6	7	8	9	10

Value Added

___

___

___

Steps to Enhance Abilities

___

___

___

❑ Charitable Estate Planning

Technical Expertise

Beginner Expert

1 2 3 4 5 6 7 8 9 10

Communications Effectiveness

Beginner Expert

1 2 3 4 5 6 7 8 9 10

Value Added

Steps to Enhance Abilities

What You Can Do

While the larger financial services firms, as well as related service providers such as attorneys and accountants, are taking steps to position themselves with affluent family businesses, the individual financial services professional can be just as competitive. This is a business based on relationships, not size. The larger players admittedly can put more money behind a marketing effort, but this is not always the answer.

The key is being able to meet the needs and wants of the affluent business owners. This includes having the "right" products and services. And, more importantly, it entails having an in-depth understanding of the psychology of the affluent business owner. Our goal is to provide you with these psychological insights.

In the final analysis, the most successful financial services providers with affluent family businesses will be those who have taken the time and made the effort to truly understand the market and subsequently positioned themselves to capitalize on this understanding. It will not necessarily be the larger institutions. The individual life insurance professional can be extremely successful.

However, in order to be successful in targeting the family business market, you will need to adopt a new approach to marketing. With many financial services providers targeting this market, there will be an increasing amount of conflict and competition in the system.

It is going to become harder and harder for you to stand out from the crowd. What you have going for you is that wealthy family business owners are quite astute. They can tell the difference between those who are providing value in the services they offer and those who are pushing products.

To be successful, you have to obtain the knowledge and skills that can enable you to be highly successful in marketing financial services and products to affluent family business owners. Such expertise will enable you to compete (and win) against your competitors whatever their size. Size alone is not the answer. A competitor's size will not, in any way, overshadow your superior understanding and skills.

To review, family business wealth is the principal way of becoming wealthy in the United States as well as in the rest of the world. Thus, the primary affluent market for providers of insurance and related financial services and products is family businesses and wealthy business owners.

As a result, many insurance companies, financial institutions and individual insurance and financial services providers have recognized the profitability and potential of affluent family businesses. Some of them are investing heavily in the field.

It is important to remember that this is not a new market. It has always been here. It is just that the affluent family business market is now being recognized as something special. Thus, the only way to be especially successful is to be well versed in the financial services purchase patterns of affluent family business owners.

Your Action Items

- Decide if you want to be in the family business owner market.
- Make an initial determination about what you need to do to work strategically in the family business market. Plan to revisit this assessment periodically.
- Track your competition, both nationally and locally.
- Follow through on your plans for enhancing your technical and communication abilities.

Richard Bentley looks up from his list of his top five family business clients in some surprise. He hadn't really thought through how much potential was in family businesses and had not organized his practice to go after them specifically.

Bentley decided to learn as much as he could about family businesses, what makes them different and unique, how they buy insurance and what their specific technical requirements are. He decides to go talk to his current clients about what they think the special needs of a family business are. He decides to create a file of industry clippings on the topic and to keep an eye out for seminars on the subject.

Bentley also realizes that the attractiveness of the affluent family business market has not gone unnoticed. It is an area that is becoming highly competitive. What is clear to him is that he needs to learn a great deal more about affluent family businesses and what motivates their owners in order to succeed.

CHAPTER 2
WHAT YOU MUST KNOW ABOUT FAMILY BUSINESS DYNAMICS

Richard Bentley decided to explore the implications of focusing on the family business. He decided to do so by continuing to sell insurance to the owners of small and medium size businesses, but also to make a special attempt to talk with them about their families as well as their businesses.

Bentley ran into trouble on his first call. He had been in the process of working with a non-profit organization on charitable estate planning for some of its wealthy donors. One of his referrals had been to a Mr. Firtrip who owned a printing shop which did a regional business. When he started the meeting by asking Mr. Firtrip how the family was, Firtrip exploded. "I can't tell you how ungrateful they all are. When I told them about this charitable remainder trust we have been discussing, they all objected! Seems as though they oppose my giving the money to a non-profit. They all think it should stay in the family. Even my wife got on my case. She's saying there are nine grandchildren and I have to take care of them all. What ever happened to making it on your own? Anyway, the whole deal is on hold until I get the family thing straightened out."

Bentley shook his head as he left the meeting. "Glad I decided to focus on family dynamics as well as the case," he thought to himself. "Because I did, I had an alternative trust arrangement worked out so that Firtrip could benefit the children and grandchildren more directly."

If you want a rewarding career providing financial services to the affluent, there really isn't much of a choice. As we saw in Chapter 1, family businesses represent a significant portion of the affluent market. Owning a business is the most common way for people to become wealthy, here and around the world.

Moreover, if your goal is not only to provide financial services to the business, but also to the affluent family, then family businesses are the answer. You are positioned to capitalize on the great need for financial services by wealthy individuals as well as the opportunities to provide products and services to the business.

If you are going to work successfully with family business owners you will need to be aware of key family business dynamics. These are aspects of how family businesses run which distinguish them from other business enterprises and which make them unusually challenging to sell to. The three keys to understanding family business dynamics are :

1. Knowing the Hidden Goal of Family Businesses;
2. The Family Business Crisis Point; and
3. Why Family Businesses Fail.

The Hidden Goal of Family Businesses

The hidden goal of a family business is to take care of the family. This is important to know. In a family business, family interests take precedent over business interests. In other words, family goals are more important than business goals.

If there is an overlap, then family and business goals support each other. For example, if the goal of the family is to grow the business in order to provide opportunities for the next generation, and if the market for the firm's goods is strong, business and family goals are mutually reinforcing. This happened for the DeLucas, who ran a well-known regional specialty store. To those who encouraged him to expand, the senior DeLuca would respond "I'd rather keep my eyes on everything right here." However when his son started to ask for more responsibility, the family decided to build a second store for the son to run.

However, if there is a conflict, the family will opt to maximize its own interests over those of the business. For example, when the Davises decided to retire and turn the farm over to the daughter and son-in-law, the family decided to provide the parents with a generous retirement income from the business. This decision resulted in fewer assets available for investment in new equipment or expansion.

Principle: In most family businesses, family goals are more important than business goals.

Later on, we will discuss the various types of family business owners and you will see that there are many ways family goals and business goals can conflict. Remember that family goals will almost always come first in a family business. To illustrate this point, we will look at two types of business insurance: key employee insurance and buy-sell agreements.

Family Goals Come First: The Case of Key Employee Insurance

Let's begin by thinking about how family and non-family businesses differ. Here we will be considering key employee insurance. Take a moment to answer the questions in Figure 2.01.

In order to illustrate the ways in which family businesses differ from other businesses, we conducted a detailed analysis of key employee insurance purchasing. The results of the study provide statistically reliable quantitative evidence that family businesses prioritize family goals.

The first point of comparison between family businesses and other businesses is the benefit these owners sought to achieve with key employee insurance. Typically, key employee insurance is purchased to provide cash flow during the transition after the loss of the employee. That is, during this time of stress, key employee insurance can be a valuable cushion for the business.

Figure 2.01

KEY EMPLOYEE BENEFITS EXERCISE		
Instructions: For each of the following benefits, identify whether the benefit is rated high, medium or low by family and non-family business owners.		
Benefits	**Family Businesses**	**Non-family Businesses**
Keep the business running	❑ High Importance ❑ Medium Importance ❑ Low Importance	❑ High Importance ❑ Medium Importance ❑ Low Importance
Cover the mistakes that the deceased's successor will make until the things the deceased knew from experience have been learned	❑ High Importance ❑ Medium Importance ❑ Low Importance	❑ High Importance ❑ Medium Importance ❑ Low Importance
Assure customers that the business will continue	❑ High Importance ❑ Medium Importance ❑ Low Importance	❑ High Importance ❑ Medium Importance ❑ Low Importance
Continue long-range development programs	❑ High Importance ❑ Medium Importance ❑ Low Importance	❑ High Importance ❑ Medium Importance ❑ Low Importance
Assure creditors that loans are safe	❑ High Importance ❑ Medium Importance ❑ Low Importance	❑ High Importance ❑ Medium Importance ❑ Low Importance
Cover the special expenses of finding, attracting and training a successor	❑ High Importance ❑ Medium Importance ❑ Low Importance	❑ High Importance ❑ Medium Importance ❑ Low Importance

Figure 2.02 shows that both family and other business owners understand and value the benefit of key employee insurance. Most family business owners as well as other business owners say that having sufficient cash to keep the business running is a major benefit of key employee insurance.

In terms of other benefits, however, family business CEOs also seek different benefits. They are especially concerned that the successor to the business may make mistakes which will cost the business. Another benefit of key employee insurance will be to insulate the business against these costs to some degree. As discussed before, many family business owners are skeptical of the abilities of others in the family to run the business effectively. Almost as many family business owners think it is important to protect the business against the mistakes of successors as well as to keep the business running. The third most important benefit family business owners seek is an infusion of cash to assure customers the business will keep going. As shown in Figure 2.02, these benefits are not important to other business owners.

Life insurance professionals selling key employee insurance to family business owners should position the product as providing three strategic benefits:

1. Cash to keep the business running;
2. Resources to cover potential mistakes the successor might make; and
3. Assets sufficient to reassure customers about the continuation of the business.

Figure 2.02 also shows that insurance agents selling key employee insurance to other business owners should position their product around different benefits, specifically:

1. Cash to keep the business running; and
2. Assurance to creditors that the business is secure and that therefore, their loans are safe.

Figure 2.02

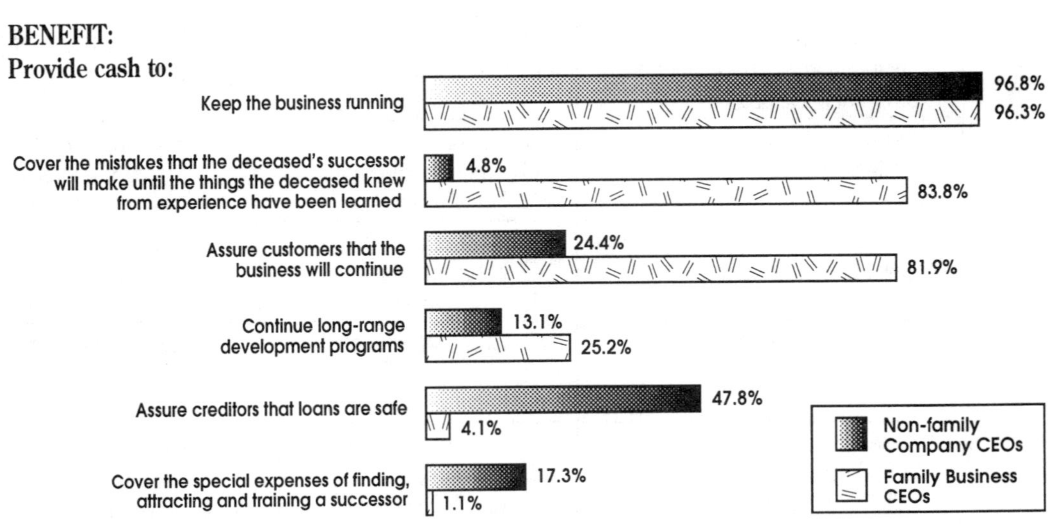

Number of Recent Purchasers of Key-Employee Insurance = 583

Before reading on, take a moment to complete the exercise in Figure 2.03.

Figure 2.03

UNDERSTANDING FAMILY BUSINESS DIFFERENCES EXERCISE #1	
Instructions: For each of the following presentations, identify whether it is being made to a family business or a non-family business. Circle whether it's appropriate for a family or non-family business.	
"I can understand why you're worried about your son taking over. He is still green and there's a chance he can mess things up. That's why it's great that we can create a financial cushion for him."	
FAMILY BUSINESS	NON-FAMILY BUSINESS
"To keep the banks off your back, key employee insurance can let them know that their loans are safe. This way there won't be any problems in getting that line of credit the business needs."	
FAMILY BUSINESS	NON-FAMILY BUSINESS

When insurance is sold, life insurance professionals typically conduct an analysis of a client's needs and then make a proposal which includes a recommended face amount of insurance. Answer the questions in Figure 2.04 before reading on.

Figure 2.04

KEY-EMPLOYEE PROFITABILITY EXERCISE		
Instructions: Identify who will buy more key employee insurance, and how much more they will buy relative to what a life insurance professional would recommend. Check one box.		
% Over Recommendation	***Family Business***	***Non-family Business***
100% more	❑	❑
75-99% more	❑	❑
50-74% more	❑	❑
25-49% more	❑	❑
1-24% more	❑	❑

As illustrated in Figure 2.05, in the case of key employee insurance sold family firms, few CEOs followed the recommendations of their life insurance professionals. Only 15.9% purchased the face amount recommended, as opposed to 77.6% of non-family company CEOs. As Figure 2.06 illustrates, family business CEOs who did not accept the agent's recommendation instead bought a higher face amount — as much as 100% more. No family business owners bought less.

By contrast, most of the non-family business owners accepted the life insurance professional's proposal as given; relatively few opted for a changed amount. If they did change, most bought less than the recommended amount.

Figure 2.05

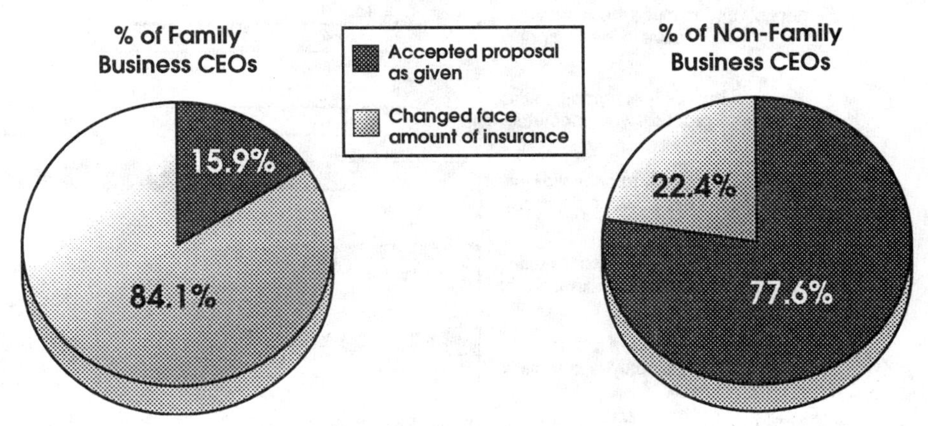

The implication for life insurance professionals is that key employee insurance serves more purposes for family business owners. As a result, they tend to believe that they need more extensive coverage as shown in Figure 2.06. It is significant that relatively few life insurance professionals recognize this and so there is a great opportunity to serve family business accounts more responsively.

Figure 2.06

FINAL FACE AMOUNT OF CUSTOMERS CHANGING KEY EMPLOYEE INSURANCE

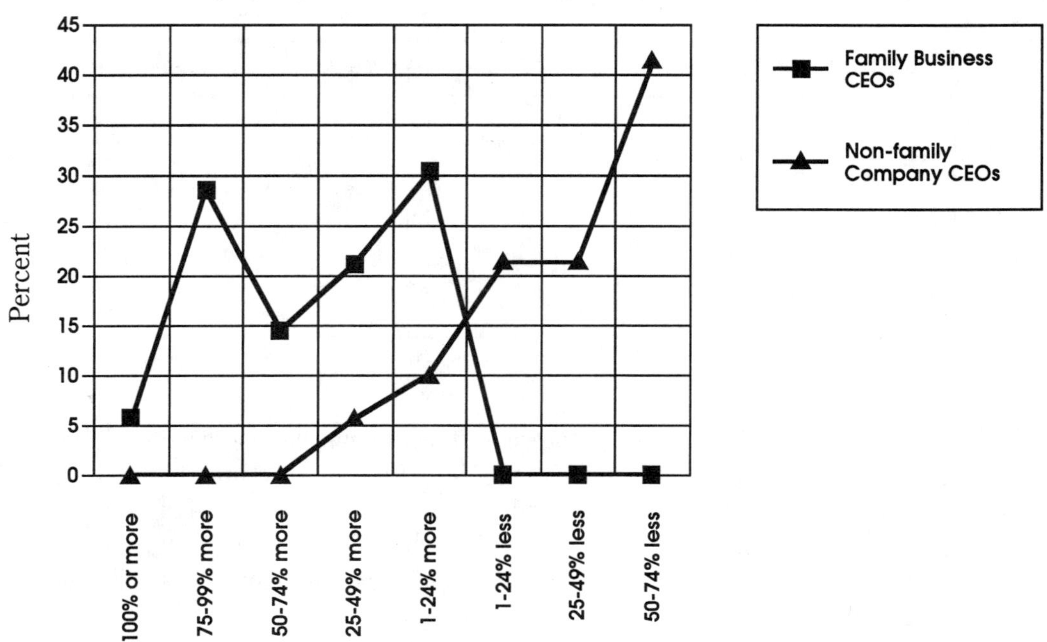

The reason non-family CEOs do not buy the recommended amount is that they are generally price resistant as illustrated in Figure 2.07.

Figure 2.07

VALUE ASSESSMENTS BY FAMILY BUSINESSES AND PUBLICLY HELD COMPANIES

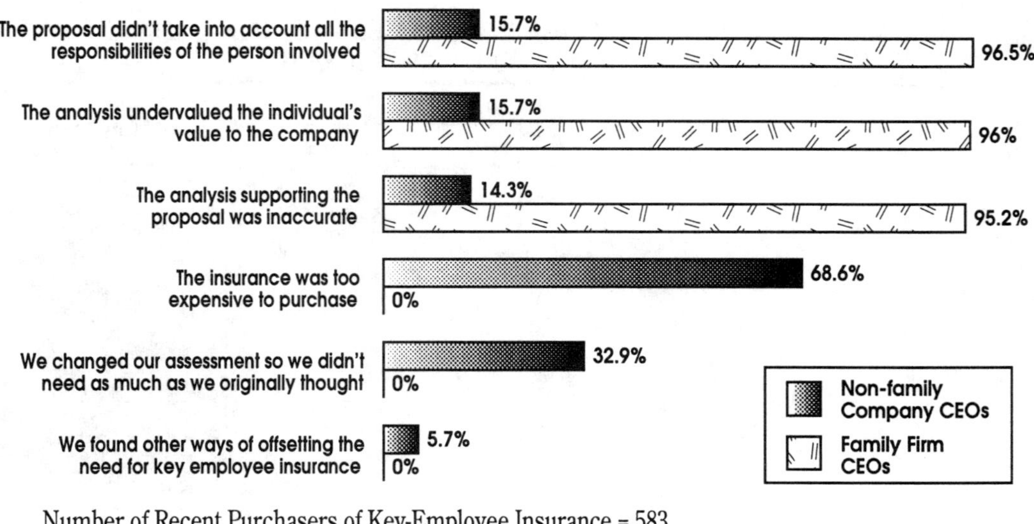

Number of Recent Purchasers of Key-Employee Insurance = 583

It is significant that when life insurance professionals provide too low of a key employee insurance benefit to family business owners, those owners perceive that an error has been made. That is, family business owners tend to believe that the responsibilities of the covered individual were underestimated (96.5%), or that the value of the individual to the business was underestimated (96.%), or that the analysis supporting the proposal was inaccurate (95.2%). These data show that even the analysis supporting the selection of a proposed amount has to be customized for the special needs of family business owners.

In order to confirm the importance of family goals in family businesses, we addressed two additional questions to the family business CEOs. One was, "We make the best decisions for the business and do not take family or personal considerations into account." None of the family businesses in the study agreed with this statement.

On the second statement, "Family matters come first in these types of business decisions," there was widespread agreement among family businesses, as illustrated in Figure 2.08.

Figure 2.08

IMPORTANCE OF FAMILY CONSIDERATIONS FOR FAMILY BUSINESSES

Family matters come first in these types (e.g., key employee insurance) of business decisions	70.7%
We make the best decisions for the business and do not take family or personal considerations into account	0%

Family Goals Come First: The Case of Buy-Sell Agreements

In order to show that key employee insurance is not a exception, but rather the rule for selling insurance to family businesses, we offer a second, shorter example. In this case, we look at insurance purchases attendant to buy-sell agreements. Take a moment to complete the exercise in Figure 2.09.

Again, family and non-family business owners see a world of different benefits in the same product. Family business owners, as shown in Figure 2.10, are much more likely than other business owners to see buy-sell agreements as a way to insure liquidity and pay off estate taxes. They are also seeking ways to insure that family members who will not be involved in the business in the future are financially secure. Of course, the two groups do share some business goals, such as fixing the price of the company for later valuation purposes, providing a market for the stock and also providing funding for the stock purchase. But these are functional goals which do not distinguish the two types of businesses. Life insurance professionals need to pay attention to the relational goals which also drive decisions in family businesses.

Figure 2.09

BUY-SELL BENEFITS EXERCISE		
Instructions: For each of the following benefits, identify whether the benefit is rated high, medium or low by family and non-family business owners.		
Benefits	**Family Businesses**	**Non-family Businesses**
Ensure liquidity (ability to pay estate taxes)	❑ High Importance ❑ Medium Importance ❑ Low Importance	❑ High Importance ❑ Medium Importance ❑ Low Importance
Fix the price of the company for sales valuation	❑ High Importance ❑ Medium Importance ❑ Low Importance	❑ High Importance ❑ Medium Importance ❑ Low Importance
Provide for the funding to purchase the stock	❑ High Importance ❑ Medium Importance ❑ Low Importance	❑ High Importance ❑ Medium Importance ❑ Low Importance
Provide a market for the company's stock at a fixed price	❑ High Importance ❑ Medium Importance ❑ Low Importance	❑ High Importance ❑ Medium Importance ❑ Low Importance
Provide for the financial future of those individuals who will not be involved in the business	❑ High Importance ❑ Medium Importance ❑ Low Importance	❑ High Importance ❑ Medium Importance ❑ Low Importance
Ensure the transfer of the company to selected individuals	❑ High Importance ❑ Medium Importance ❑ Low Importance	❑ High Importance ❑ Medium Importance ❑ Low Importance
Contribute to the orderly transfer of ownership of the business	❑ High Importance ❑ Medium Importance ❑ Low Importance	❑ High Importance ❑ Medium Importance ❑ Low Importance

Figure 2.10

BENEFITS OF BUY-SELL AGREEMENTS AMONG FAMILY BUSINESS AND NON-FAMILY BUSINESS CEOs

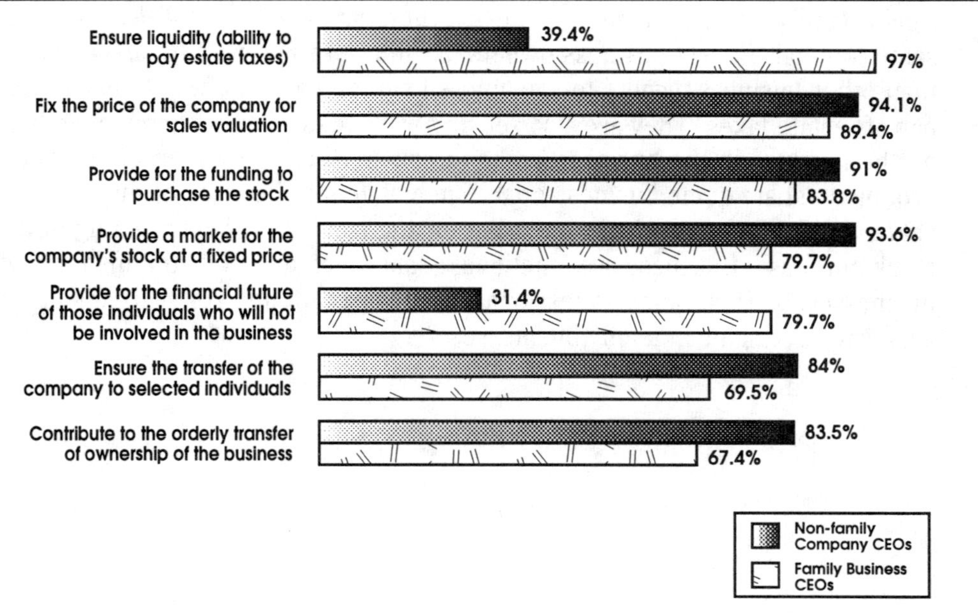

Implications of the Hidden Goals of Family Businesses

As these two cases have shown, family business CEOs seek different benefits in purchasing insurance. They attach a significantly higher value to key employee insurance than do CEOs in other companies. Of importance for life insurance professionals, they display a far greater willingness to pay for that value.

Life insurance professionals should evaluate the extent to which their target customers are family businesses. If a significant proportion are, they should use this framework for assessing the impact of family firm status on their sales tracks.

Life insurance professionals should use the framework presented here to assess the degree to which the family-firm related motivations are triggered by the product they are promoting and whether the organizational buying processes of their customers are affected in the ways indicated here. If family firms constitute a significant portion of sales professionals' customers and if those family firms behave in the patterns described here, then sales people should adapt their sales strategies accordingly.

These findings suggest that distinctive product and product positioning platforms should be created for the goods and services which are bought differently by family businesses. For example, in the case of key employee insurance, assumptions within the analytical software used by insurance carriers to estimate coverage should be adjusted to reflect the different benefits and coverage sought by family business owners.

The Family Business Crisis Point

Because of its unique structure, there are predictable crises in the life of a family business. One of these is the family business crisis point — the succession, or the transition in ownership and management from one generation to another. Succession is the third of four phases of the life cycle of the family firm as shown in Figure 2.11.

During the first phase, business survival and market building are the critical tasks. There is usually little discretionary income left over. These firms are suitable prospects for basic and essential insurance and financial services products, but are not yet ready for asset protection or investment management products. In Phase 2 the family firm becomes a better prospect for the full range of business insurance products as it enters the stage of business maturity and invests in the goods and services it needs to sustain growth and profitability.

Phase 3 is a stage unique to family businesses, the stage of succession from one generation to another. All businesses have a succession of leadership, as when one CEO retires and is replaced by another CEO. However, only in family businesses is there a leadership succession and a transition of corporate ownership and a profound change in the family dynamics happening all at once. The succession phase is when ownership and management of the business is passed between family members, usually from one generation to another.

Succession in family businesses contains all of the system complexities and dynamics of succession in formal business organizations, in addition to being exacerbated by family system dynamics. The situation is complicated further by the commingling of personal and family financial interests and obligations with those of the firm. This is a turbulent stage for family businesses, but a profitable one for life insurance professionals who know how to work with

Figure 2.11

PHASES OF THE FAMILY BUSINESS			
Phase	**Strategic Focus**	**Critical Tasks**	**Key Insurance Services Areas**
Phase 1	Creating the business	Market success and business survival	None Applicable
Phase 2	Growth and development	Investment in business assets	• Retirement planning • Executive benefits • Investment management
Phase 3	Succession to the second generation	Estate planning and the distribution of ownership and assets are major tasks	• Business succession and estate planning • Charitable estate planning • Asset protection planning
Phase 4	Public ownership and professional management	Transitions into professional management and ceases to have the distinctive character of a family firm	• Enhanced Asset Protection Planning

them, for it is the stage when succession, estate planning and retirement planning products and services all come into play.

Phase 4, the transition from a privately held firm to a publicly held one comes when management is professionalized (i.e., position in the company is a result of merit rather than family position) and control passes from the family to public (unrelated) stockholders.

In Phase 3, succession typically intensifies conflict in both the family and the business systems as the following case shows.

Ellen Thomas was working on her charitable estate and succession plan when she began to get recommendations and input from family members. She was looking to retire in a few years and was very concerned about her commitment to social responsibility, the future of the business and the financial well being of her family. Ellen had created what she thought was the ideal transition, estate and charitable plan. Ellen took into account all the financial and interpersonal issues that would ensure the company would run smoothly into the future.

Sadly, Ellen neglected to take into account the hurt feelings of her daughter, Mary. The company was not going to Mary alone. Because Mary was just out of business school, Ellen had designated her as co-president for a number of years. Eventually she would take charge of the entire company. This made Mary very upset. She felt she had worked hard at learning the business and contributing to it. Mary didn't feel she needed other people looking over her shoulder.

Ellen named Robert, her first cousin, the chief financial officer and a participant in the business since it was founded twenty-three years earlier, as the other co-president. Because of his maturity and financial expertise, Robert was also to be Ellen's executor. The fact that he was named executor also upset Mary. She thought that she would be named to that job.

Mary discussed her feelings about the transition plan with her grandparents, Ellen's parents. They then spoke to Ellen about her transition plans for the company. What started off as a casual conversation soon turned into a major screaming match. When all the smoke cleared, Ellen wasn't retiring for a while. Mary was named as executor and would be the sole president when Ellen did retire. Robert was pushed aside even though he was there from the beginning when Ellen founded the company.

These decisions were less than optimal if you consider them from just a business perspective. However, they were best if Ellen wanted to keep peace in the family. And in the end, peace in the family was what Ellen wanted most.

Life insurance professionals looking to work with family businesses must be aware that the best course of action from the vantage point of the business often will not be the selected course of action. This is especially true during the crisis point of succession. During these periods, the usual systems and assumptions in the business and in the family become disrupted with implications for life insurance professionals.

Because of the aging of the generation that started businesses after World War II, it is succession, after all, that opens up most opportunities for life insurance professionals and other services providers. It is estimated that 50% of all family businesses will need some sort of succession or transition planning by the year 2000. Six to ten trillion dollars in wealth will be transferred to the next generation as a result of the natural succession phase of family businesses.

Principle: Succession Drives the Need for Professional Expertise.

The time of succession creates new needs in the family business. Anticipated changes in the administrative and management structure of the firm may precipitate a desire for management consultants. Planning and implementing changes in ownership call for the involvement of accountants and attorneys. Estate planning, which entails anticipating tax obligations for the business-owning individual, creates a need for financial and estate planning expertise. Families entering the succession cycle are favored target market opportunities for financial planners, life insurance professionals, stock brokers, trust departments, management consultants, attorneys, accountants and similar professionals.

Take a moment to complete the exercise in Figure 2.12 before reading on.

Figure 2.12

FAMILY BUSINESS PHASE EVALUATION EXERCISE			
Instructions: Write down ten of your family business clients. Then, write the phase they are in. Note the products you have already sold them. And then identify what products they will be most responsive to.			
Family Business Clients	**Current Phase (Circle One)**	**Products Sold**	**Product Opportunities**
1.	Phase 1 Phase 2 Phase 3 Phase 4		
2.	Phase 1 Phase 2 Phase 3 Phase 4		
3.	Phase 1 Phase 2 Phase 3 Phase 4		
4.	Phase 1 Phase 2 Phase 3 Phase 4		
5.	Phase 1 Phase 2 Phase 3 Phase 4		
6.	Phase 1 Phase 2 Phase 3 Phase 4		
7.	Phase 1 Phase 2 Phase 3 Phase 4		
8.	Phase 1 Phase 2 Phase 3 Phase 4		
9.	Phase 1 Phase 2 Phase 3 Phase 4		
10.	Phase 1 Phase 2 Phase 3 Phase 4		

Why Family Businesses Fail

Why is it that few family businesses survive into the second generation? Many different reasons have been proposed, but until a national study was conducted by the authors, there was no large scale, quantitative national sample of recently-failed family businesses from which to derive data.

In many instances among failed family businesses, the transition and ultimate business collapse was initiated when the founder died or when the founder died unexpectedly, as shown in Figure 2.13. Only in a relatively few instances was business failure an outcome of an orderly transition process between founder and heir or a situation in which the heirs forced the founder to retire.

Figure 2.13

TRIGGER FOR TRANSITION

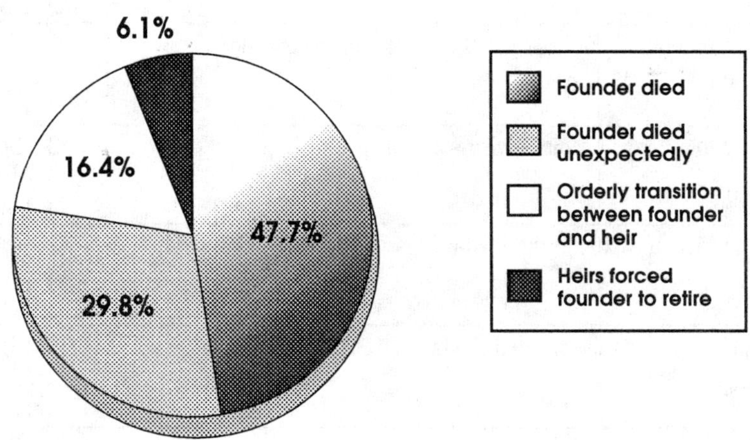

Clearly, the death of the founder precipitates the transition process. But the death of the founder alone wouldn't be enough to cause the successful family business to fail. Without question, other factors are at work. Extensive research in the field has identified broad categories of reasons why successful family businesses fail, as listed in Figure 2.14.

Figure 2.14

WHY FAMILY BUSINESSES FAIL EXERCISE PART I
Instructions: Check the primary category of reasons that successful family businesses fail after transition.
❑ Conflict among family members ❑ Problems in the succession process ❑ Financial planning ❑ Managerial complications ❑ Market competition ❑ Technology and regulatory reasons

The overriding category explaining why successful family businesses fail after transition is less than adequate financial planning. This is almost always associated with conflicts among family members. The other categories of reasons prove not to be as dramatically important. Complete the questions in Figure 2.15 before moving on.

Figure 2.15

WHY FAMILY BUSINESSES FAIL EXERCISE PART II	
Instructions: For each of the following reasons in the financial planning category, check whether it is high, medium, or low in explaining why family businesses fail.	
Financial Planning Reasons	**Ratings**
The founder did not have an adequate estate plan in place	❑ High Importance ❑ Medium Importance ❑ Low Importance
Needed to raise funds to pay estate taxes	❑ High Importance ❑ Medium Importance ❑ Low Importance
The founder did not adequately prepare for the transfer of the business	❑ High Importance ❑ Medium Importance ❑ Low Importance
The founder's financial advisors performed inadequately	❑ High Importance ❑ Medium Importance ❑ Low Importance
Insufficient capital to run the business effectively	❑ High Importance ❑ Medium Importance ❑ Low Importance
An inability to raise needed capital	❑ High Importance ❑ Medium Importance ❑ Low Importance
Their financial advisors performed inadequately	❑ High Importance ❑ Medium Importance ❑ Low Importance

As shown in Figure 2.16, most heirs say that the fundamental cause of business failure was inadequate financial planning. In some cases, poor financial planning resulted in the absence of an adequate estate plan or a lack of adequate preparation for the transfer of the business. Alternatively, a lack of good financial planning resulted in insufficient assets for the payment of estate taxes or insufficient capital for the business to operate.

Regardless of the type of industry, most heirs believe that a root cause of failure is the lack of an adequate estate plan. The percentage of business owners who felt that the lack of an adequate estate plan was the basic reason was in excess of 95%, whether the industry was services, wholesale, retail or manufacturing. Specific failures of the estate plan often caused insurmountable problems for the heir. While it is true that most founders did leave an estate plan in place, it is also true that the heirs viewed these plans as severely flawed, neglecting to provide sufficient resources to transition the business and meet estate tax obligations.

Figure 2.16

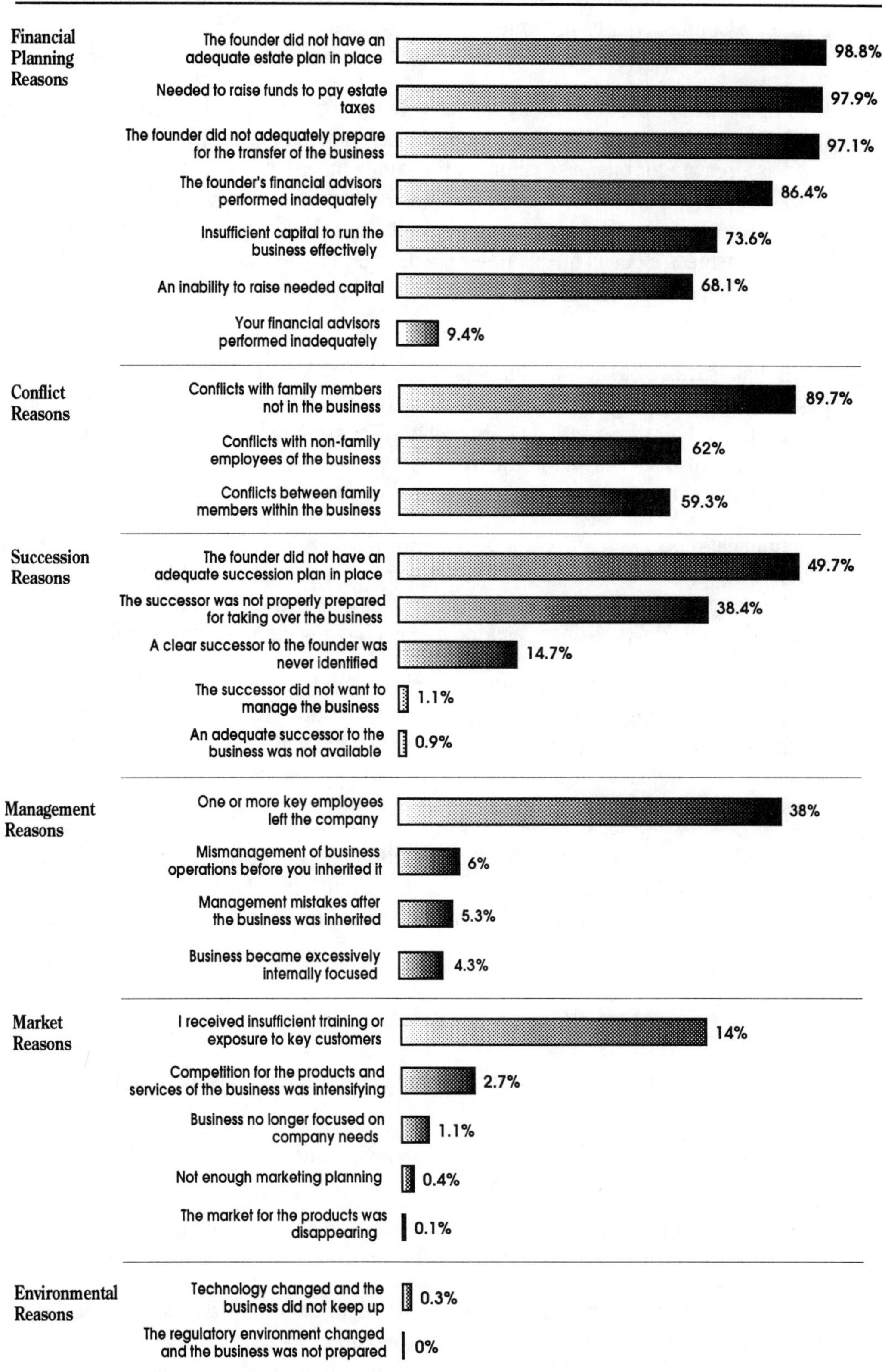

Number of Family Businesses Which Recently Failed = 479

Conflict is associated with business failure but is not the sole reason for failure. As shown in Figure 2.16, many reported conflict between family members within the business, between family members in and out of the business, and conflict with non-family employees of the business. Conflict typifies the time of business transition. This conflict may be a consequence or a cause of the stresses on the system due to an inadequate financial footing.

It's important to note that family business failures are not often the result of management, market or environmental forces. Among family businesses, poor management is not usually cited as a reason for business failure in the family business situation, as shown in Figure 2.16. Marketing forces are also not usually blamed. Most heirs thought they had been exposed to key customers, competition was manageable, that there was adequate marketing planning, that the business focused on customer needs and that the market for their products was ongoing. Changes in the regulatory or technological environment did not account for many family business failures either.

What makes these business failures particularly tragic is that up until the failure of the business, these enterprises were successful employers and valued participants in their local economies. Almost half of recently failed family businesses had over 100 employees. These businesses were also successful. In the five years preceding the transition, 91.3% of these companies had average annual growth rates exceeding 5%.

The implications for current owners of family businesses and their life insurance professional advisors are clear. Steps should be taken to have an estate plan in place which provides for the tax, liquidity and operating needs of the business and the heirs. Such programs should be reviewed on a regular basis to respond to any changes in the business or the family.

Failure to adequately anticipate and manage succession can cause the business to fail. When heirs of failed businesses explain the root causes of the collapse of the enterprise, they point to the death of the prior owner as the principal cause. Only in a few instances was business failure an outcome of an orderly transition process between founder and heir or a coup in which the heirs forced the founder to retire.

The result of the crisis was complete bankruptcy in about half of the cases and piecemeal liquidation of the businesses' assets in about one third. In some cases the business was sold to settle the estate or non-family investors were brought in.

Your Action Items

- You have to be attuned to the differences in the purchasing psychology of family and non-family businesses.
- Be sensitive to the different ways in which family businesses strike a balance between family and business objectives.
- When working with family businesses you need to be attentive to the phase that the family business is in. This will make you more insightful in marketing your services.

Richard Bentley, recognizing the value of working in the family business market, decided to become more strategic in his efforts. Now in every new engagement he is scrupulous about collecting data on the family situation. This includes the phase that the business is in.

CHAPTER 3
How Family Businesses Buy Insurance

Richard Bentley is working with Haley Roberts and seems to be stonewalled. He has created more than a dozen estate planning scenarios. He has been to meeting after meeting with Haley and people he has never seen before — other family members. What surprised Bentley so much was that these other family members weren't even involved with the business.

Bentley understands the need to bring in accountants and attorneys as well as other key advisors. He also recognizes the role of key family members, such as a spouse and children and even key employees of the company. The part that has him confused is the inclusion of the doctor and the academic. They have to know exactly what's going on, and for a while, explaining estate planning to the physician appeared to be an impossible task.

It seemed as if there were so many people who didn't have anything to do with running the family business just sticking their noses in. And each of these people seemed to need at least one more meeting on the topic. Bentley began to wonder if he would ever close the case. He decided he'd better reevaluate whether or not affluent family businesses are worth all the aggravation.

Many financial services providers have targeted affluent family businesses without recognizing some of the challenges they will face. These challenges are unique to family businesses and make marketing to family businesses much more arduous. The whole sales process becomes longer, requires more effort and is more complicated.

If you choose to work in this area, you are going to have a much harder time selling your services and products. Marketing financial services to affluent family businesses is considerably more demanding than marketing financial services to successful, non-family businesses. But, the rewards are significantly greater.

The factors that distinguish the way family businesses buy insurance are:

- The four stages of a family business decision-making process;
- What transforms a family *business* into a *family* business;
- Hidden decision-makers, sometimes called "shadow influencers"; and
- Heart and head buying, which leads to informal decision-making processes.

As a result, selling insurance and financial services to family businesses can be harder and can take longer. But because of their assets and loyalty, it is usually worth the investment of time and effort.

The Four Stages of Buying in a Family Business

Over the past several decades, a number of models of organizational purchasing have been introduced. Although these are useful for understanding non-family businesses, they do not take into account the family dynamics which affect purchasing behavior. Family firms represent significant purchasing power but, more importantly, they exhibit different purchasing behaviors than other firms.

Specifically, family businesses undergo specific stages of purchasing decision-making that other firms do not. These purchasing decision-making stages are unique to family businesses because they provide a framework for family involvement in business decisions. These stages, which are profiled in Figure 3.01, include:

- *Stage 1: Family Involvement Trigger*—The family responds to the decision stimulus by deciding whether or not to become involved.
- *Stage 2: Family Organization for Participation in the Decision*—If the family decides to become involved in the decision, the family must agree which members are to become involved and what the family (as opposed to business) criteria for the decision will be.
- *Stage 3: Family Decision-Making Process* — The family evaluates suppliers and their proposals and reaches a decision. This process mirrors the decision-making dynamics of the family.

Figure 3.01

STAGES OF FAMILY BUSINESS DECISION-MAKING		
Stage	**Critical Task**	**Activities**
Stage 1	Family involvement trigger	Anticipation or recognition of a problem (need) and conceptualization of an initial solution
Stage 2	Family organization for participation in the decision	Determination of decision-making unit membership and decision criteria. Repetitive process.
Stage 3	Family decision-making process	Mirrors family dynamics
Stage 4	Family realignment	Realignment of family members if relative power and emotional relationships have been affected by the decision-making process and its outcome

- *Stage 4: Family Realignment*—The affective (emotional) and power relationships within the business shift as a result of the decision. This realignment does not happen in every instance.

These four stages are affected by other factors in addition to the business dynamic and the family dynamic. Life insurance professionals need to be aware of all these factors.

Stage 1: Family Involvement Trigger

Certain decisions stimulate the family's involvement while others do not. Exactly which products do will be discussed latter in this chapter. Here, however, we wanted to explore the role of other people — including life insurance professionals — in triggering the decision-making process within a family firm.

The person most responsible for triggering a decision about a financial service such as insurance is the chief internal person responsible for financial matters. In very small firms, thus will be the Chief Executive Officer (CEO). As the size of the firm increases, this person will be the Chief Financial Officer (CFO) or vice-president for finance.

As shown in Figure 3.02, the CFO will stimulate the decision-making process in 67.7% of family businesses and 73.4% of non-family businesses. Figure 3.02 also shows that financial advisors and professionals external to the business play an important role. These people include the accountant of the firm and life insurance professionals advising the firm, as well as a banker or a trust officer. Many family businesses and non-family businesses frequently will act on an idea brought in by an external financial services provider. Few say that the ideas and suggestions of colleagues in other businesses or those of other managers are important.

Figure 3.02

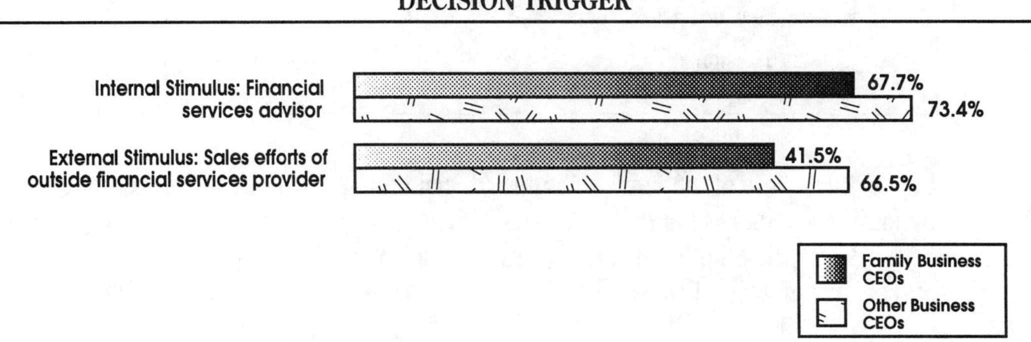

Stage 2: Family Organization for Participation in the Decision

During the second stage, the family organizes around the members who will become involved and the criteria that the family will use in reaching the decision. These are not necessarily orderly processes, as they mirror whatever the family dynamics are. One of these decisions is whether the purchase will be made from a single source or from multiple vendors.

Here we see the first indication of the greater loyalty of family firms. While the differences are not as large here as they are in other portions of the process, a higher number of family firms prefer single source purchasing. As illustrated in Figure 3.03, more family firms prefer to work with a single, well known supplier than do non-family firms. None of the non-family firms prefer single source purchasing.

Figure 3.03

INFORMATION SEARCH		
	Family Business CEOs	**Other Business CEOs**
Routine single source purchasing	13.8%	0.0%
Routine multiple bids	34.7%	31.4%

Stage 3: Family Decision-Making Process

When family businesses make decisions, they are more likely to rely on outside advisors who strongly influence the decisions, as shown in Figure 3.04. Later in this chapter, we will see that they also rely on family members who are not part of the business.

Figure 3.04

EVALUATION OF ALTERNATIVES		
	Family Business CEOs	**Other Business CEOs**
Advisors as new idea gatekeepers	75.4%	90.4%
Advisors as decision influencers	47.5%	13.8%

In the third stage of the family business decision-making process, the actual decision is made by family members in and out of the business who are participating in the process. This process reflects the emotional and power dynamics of the family more than those of the business and can range from dictatorial to democratic, conflict-oriented or consensual.

Stage 4: Family Realignment

Since a decision sometimes affects the relationships between members, a process of family member realignment often follows a decision. For example, business succession and estate planning can solidify the decision about who will become the new head of the business and cause family members to relate to one another differently than before the decision was finalized.

The informality of the decision-making process often continues after the decision is made. Family businesses are less likely to establish periodic review cycles for their business decisions, as shown in Figure 3.05.

Figure 3.05

POST-PURCHASE ACTIVITIES		
	Family Business CEOs	**Other Business CEOs**
Periodic review cycles	62.3%	80.9%

When Is a Family *Business* a *Family* Business?

As we have seen, a specific recommendation from a financial person internal to or advising the business usually triggers the insurance purchasing process in a family business. It might be a sales presentation by a life insurance professional, a recommendation by the accountant, or a conversation between the CFO and the owner. This trigger can occur first within the family or first within the business. The next element is whether or not the family chooses to get involved. If they do not, the purchasing process is limited to members of the business. If the family does get involved, then you need to be aware of this and have strategies to address their concerns.

Since the family and the business tend to exist in a state of overlapping spheres of influence, it is apparent that some purchasing decisions by the business will be influenced by non-employee family members. But the family does not get involved in all decisions, just the ones that concern its interests. The family only gets involved with purchasing decisions which will affect the family's interests in a way that it perceives as material.

We would expect, for example, that the family would become involved when compensation and benefits decisions for the executives are being made or in decisions about benefits for rank-and-file managers and other employees, some of whom may be junior generations of family members or in-laws. The family would also be interested in significant capital procurement decisions, the selection of professional service providers and other types of strategic and far-reaching decisions where outsiders may become involved. Conversely, it would seem less likely that non-employee family members would become involved in more routine procurement activities, such as ordering office supplies or changing telephone equipment.

One feels confident in speculating that the family becomes involved whenever the business contemplates an important decision. This "systemic response" occurs because the family's self interest is so intertwined with the success of the business. Whenever a significant financial, structural, procurement or strategic decision is in process, one or more of the non-employee family members get involved or attempt to exert influence.

It makes sense, therefore, to examine exactly what types of business procurement decisions trigger non-employee family involvement and influence. Such an examination should include decisions ranging from the routine re-order of office supplies and the leasing of cars to capital equipment purchases and the selection of financial and professional services firms.

It is also important to test for family influence in decisions which may also be thought of as perks. This typically includes things which are emblems or badges of acknowledgment, rank, power, or status awarded by the business yet representative of family status. Perks include purchases such as those related to office decor, cellular telephones and car leases. Influence in the business system by leveraging the family system is exemplified by the situation where "Dad" makes the deal to lease the cars and "Son" picks out the color.

Finally, there are two decisions known, at least anecdotally, to be certain triggers to family involvement. One is the decision to hire non-family individuals as senior managers and second is the decision to hire additional family members into the firm. While these are not purchasing or procurement decisions, the available management literature confirms high family involvement.

When family business purchasing decisions are analyzed, four distinct patterns emerge:

1. Important decisions which trigger family involvement. These we call "dual systems involvement" because both the business and the family systems are involved.
2. Important decisions which do not, for whatever reason, trigger family system involvement. These we call routine high involvement decisions because their process is identical to important decisions in non-family firms.
3. Unimportant decisions which trigger family involvement. These we call "limited systems involvement" because both the family and the business systems are involved in the decision but in a more limited manner than with an important decision.
4. Unimportant decisions which do not trigger family involvement. These are routine low involvement decisions and their process is the same as routine decisions in non-family firms.

Being able to predict the particular decision sphere into which a given purchasing decision will fall should enable a marketer of goods or services to better understand which decision system he is dealing with. For example, is it the usual process of business procurement or will the buying decision be complicated by family involvement? Figure 3.06 illustrates the model.

Figure 3.06

THE FAMILY BUSINESS PURCHASING DECISION-MAKING FRAMEWORK		
Importance to the Business	*High*	*Low*
High Influence by the Family System	Extensive Dual Systems Processes	Limited Dual Systems Processes
Low Influence by the Family System	Routine High Involvement	Routine Low Involvement

From the point of view of Richard Bentley and other life insurance professionals, a family business only needs to be handled differently than any other business client if the family becomes involved in insurance decisions. As the model shows, sometimes family members become involved and sometimes they do not. If insurance services are not among the decisions in which the family becomes involved, then family businesses do not represent a special category of clients. But, if families do become involved in insurance decisions, then life insurance professionals need to understand family businesses. Before reading on, take a moment to answer the questions in Figure 3.07.

Figure 3.07

FAMILY BUSINESS TRIGGER EXERCISE		
Instructions: For each of the following products and services, check if the family would likely or not get involved in the decision-making process.		
Products and Services	**Family Involvement**	
Benefits consulting	❑ Yes	❑ No
Director's insurance	❑ Yes	❑ No
Deferred compensation planning	❑ Yes	❑ No
Retirement planning services	❑ Yes	❑ No
Investment and financial services	❑ Yes	❑ No
Key employee insurance	❑ Yes	❑ No
Buy-sell agreements	❑ Yes	❑ No
Property insurance	❑ Yes	❑ No

It turns out that in many family businesses, the family becomes involved in business decision-making. And when the family becomes involved, the selling and relationship management tasks of the life insurance professional become more complicated.

Our recent study of 396 family business owners confirmed that the family becomes involved in many decisions, but particularly insurance decisions. The reason for this is obvious. The purchase of many forms of insurance requires that certain decisions about the allocation of assets and power within the organization be made. Assets and power trigger family involvement in business decisions. For example, the retirement plan of the owner usually includes consideration of when, how, and to whom ownership of the business will be transferred. It is certain that family members will become involved in such issues.

Figure 3.08 shows an array of decisions and classifies them by whether family business CEOs rated them as relatively high or low in importance and family involvement. As Figure 3.08 shows, many insurance decisions are both important to the business and highly likely to trigger family involvement. One group of these decisions includes those concerning current and deferred compensation and benefits of senior (usually family) members. Such decisions include benefits consulting, deferred compensation planning, and retirement planning services.

Another group concerns current strategic financial allocation decisions, including decisions about capital equipment and banking services. Decisions which might affect the direction of the firm trigger family involvement in addition to being important — these decisions include management consulting services and management training services.

Decisions which affect how the public views the family firm trigger family involvement. An example here is advertising agency selection and in the specific services offered by the agency. Two non-procurement decisions included in the study were the hiring of family members and the hiring of top managers. As expected, both are important and are also catalysts to family influence.

Families do not exert influence in all areas which are important or strategic to the firm. Although important to the firm, most CEOs report the family does not exert influence over such decisions as property insurance, accounting services, corporate legal services, software procurement, the selection of computer equipment, local area network evaluation, security services or telephone equipment decisions. A common denominator of important decisions which do not trigger family involvement may be their technical complexity.

There are a few purchasing decisions which CEOs agree are relatively low in importance but which do stimulate the family to become involved. These decisions include corporate philanthropy, key employee insurance, and buy-sell agreements. Like advertising, corporate philanthropy is felt to be an extension of the family's philanthropic philosophy. It is highly visible and reflects on the individuals in the family.

In addition, philanthropy is a way the business makes itself felt within the community and this exposure is important to the status and image needs of the family. Key employee insurance and buy-sell agreements trigger family involvement for a different reason. They are contracts which have real intent, but which also make explicit the relative power and influence of various members (or factions) of the family. They are relatively low in importance to active CEOs because they are infrequently activated. But because they articulate individual family member importance and power, family members exert direct influence on their construction and terms.

Finally, there is a large set of decisions which are both of lesser importance to the business and in which the family chooses not to exert much influence. There are two in this category in which the family exerts some influence, leased cars and office design services. Both of these are perquisites which reflect status and power.

Hidden Decision-Makers

In family firms significant influence over business purchasing decision-making can be wielded by individuals without formal organizational authority. Founders often exhibit highly concentrated authority of a type rarely seen in a stock company. Non-family managers often exhibit considerably less influence than they might in non-family firms because they are not part of the family. These differences in power and status can make it difficult for life insurance professionals to find out who is in the decision-making unit, who is really making the decision, and who is affecting the decision.

Doubt about who is making and influencing the decision represents a two-fold challenge for life insurance professionals. First, the business decision makers (including non-family managers and family executives) may be attempting to achieve a set of unspoken family goals as well as stated business goals. Also, people with whom they rarely come into contact may be wielding great influence over the decision. If the life insurance professional fails to recognize that these forces are present within a family firm, marketing mistakes are not only possible but probable.

The Founder

Founders of family firms tend to concentrate personal power to a very high degree. They tend to distrust other authority figures, to be excessively self-reliant, to reject advice from others, to

Figure 3.08

IMPORTANCE TO THE BUSINESS AND DEGREE OF FAMILY INFLUENCE IN VARIOUS INSURANCE AND OTHER MANAGEMENT DECISIONS		
Matrix: Importance by Family Involvement		
	High Importance	***Lower Importance***
High Family Involvement	• **Benefits consulting** • **Director's insurance** • **Deferred compensation planning** • **Retirement planning services** • **Investment and financial services** • Hiring family members • Capital equipment • Hiring top managers • Management consulting services • Advertising agency services • Management training services • Selecting advertising agency	• **Key employee insurance** • **Buy-sell agreements** • Corporate philanthropy
Low or No Family Involvement	• **Property insurance** • Accounting services • Corporate legal services • Software • Computer equipment • Local area network • Security services • Telephone equipment	• Long distance services • Cleaning services • Office copiers • Printing services • Cellular communications • Office equipment • Office design services • Temporary employee services • Travel agency services • Car leasing services • Office supplies

exercise power arbitrarily and capriciously, to totally control both business and family activities, and to be reluctant to delegate. Because of their concentration of power, they can create and dictate a company philosophy that is followed by everyone. They are often seen as being "larger than life."

As a result, there is a difference in buying behavior between family businesses where the founder is still active and those where the founder has retired or become less active. In companies where the founder is still active, life insurance professionals can expect that the founder will make insurance related decisions.

The Successor Generation

Family members of different generations often vary significantly with respect to their education and training. The younger, successor generation tends to have received more formal business training. As a result, differences in sources of power competence and empowerment (family role, business role and expertise) are more likely to affect and complicate purchasing processes in family firms than in non-family firms.

Founder-led family firms are characterized by a relative lack of training and development for top managers. This leads to feelings of inadequacy and powerlessness among the family members holding those positions. Thus, criteria and processes used in purchasing decision-making in founder-led family businesses are likely to be different from those used by professionally managed firms.

Life insurance professionals need to understand the type of formal business training (or lack thereof) of the decision-makers they are working with and be aware of the biases that may result. Decision-makers with formal business training will rely on skills of quantitative analysis and the like. Decision-makers who have not had formal business training will rely more heavily on common sense and the opinions of trusted advisors and analysts.

Employees

Because of the overlap of business and family systems in the family business, some managers are also family members and some are not. Those who are family members tend to have more power than their titles and positions in the business might indicate. Those managers of the business who are not in the family have comparatively less influence over decisions.

Shadow Influencers

"Shadow influencers" are family members who are not directly involved in the family business yet influence decisions that affect both the family and the business. There are lots of decisions that affect the business. These decisions will not necessarily get the shadow influencers excited. As we have seen, only those decisions that have a strong impact on the family (such as insurance and financial services) result in the involvement of the shadow influencers.

In family businesses, decisions are often influenced by individuals whose formal role in the hierarchy would not cause them to be involved. Someone not involved with day-to-day management may actually be making key decisions or have a great deal of influence. It is not easy for a life insurance professional to determine who in the family is responsible for making decisions about insurance and financial services. Identifying members of the decision-making unit is very difficult in family firms because an organizational chart usually is not available.

As shown in Figure 3.09, 90% of family business CEOs say they discussed the purchase of key employee insurance with one or more family members who are not part of the business. Interestingly enough, the same pattern was true of nearly half of CEOs of publicly held companies. However, consulted family members of family firms play a far more definitive role in the family firm buying center than do family members in other firms.

Figure 3.09

RELIANCE ON SHADOW INFLUENCERS

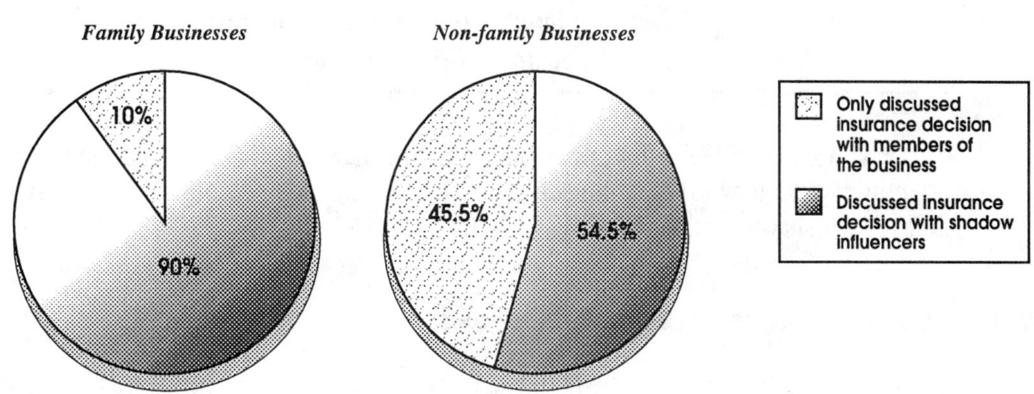

A shadow influencer can be any family member whose position is respected and whose opinion is important. Among these shadow influencers are women who have been singled out for particular study. Purchasing decisions in family firms are more likely to involve women as decision influencers who hold family roles but no formal business role. Often these individuals are wives and mothers.

The way Haley Roberts tends to make decisions illustrates the role of shadow influencers. Roberts talks over major decisions that affect the business with an uncle and two of his cousins. He talks to these family members even though none of them are actively involved in the business. Roberts' uncle, Morris, retired from the company over a decade ago. The two cousins, Shelly, a physician, and David, a college physics professor, are not familiar with the workings of the business. Nevertheless, these are the people Roberts always turns to. Why?

While not involved with the business, all three of them are important in the family. Their input is always requested on major family decisions. They are liked by almost everyone in the family. More importantly, they are respected by almost everyone in the family.

Keep in mind that for most family businesses, the business and the family are intimately connected. Roberts is looking to these family members to make sure the decisions he is making will not cause major problems with the family. And, they won't if he takes the advice of the shadow influencers. Their involvement will make whatever decisions are made palatable to all the people Roberts does not want to offend.

Along the same lines, when Susan Myers was involved in creating her succession plan, she found a number of her family members who weren't in the business making all sorts of recommendations. They were suggesting different ways of looking at "things." These different ways were very much based on family, not business, considerations. These new criteria were then used by Myers as the basis for her creation of a succession plan and an estate plan. Once again, we see that the decision-making process of affluent family business owners can be affected by shadow influencers. In Myers' case their input resulted in new criteria being used in the decision-making process.

Principle: Shadow influencers can dramatically affect the decision-making process because they focus on family-oriented criteria instead of business-oriented criteria.

When you are working with a family business, one of the most crucial tasks in fact-finding is to identify everyone who will influence a decision. This task is complicated in family businesses because of shadow influencers.

Assessing The Influence Of Shadow Influencers

It is often best to be proactive when dealing with shadow influencers. Drawing on the experiences of seasoned financial services providers, we recommend drawing a "map" of the shadow influencers. It is beneficial to keep track of how the shadow influencers in a particular affluent family business are affecting the decision-making process. To make such a "map" complete the exercise in Figure 3.10.

When Shadow Influencers Become Involved

Life insurance professionals encounter the business system every time they seek to establish relationships with prospects among family business owners. However, because certain types of goods and services are trigger items, the family system may become involved as well. The great difficulty is that the family system operates in ways that are unseen, and often undetectable, by marketers. Based on this research, marketers should assume family system, as well as business system, involvement under certain conditions:

- When the stature and standing in the community of the business and individuals associated with it might be affected (as in philanthropic and advertising decisions);
- When the actual or symbolic structure of ownership and control may be affected (as when management consultants are retained, buy-sell agreements are created or key employee life insurance is taken out);
- When the financial operations of the business are impacted (as in capital equipment decisions, benefit consulting and retirement planning, or deferred compensation planning); and
- Perquisites (but to a lesser degree).

When Thomas Kelly was deciding which life insurance professional to use for both personal and company business not a single family member made a comment. His sister, Alice, is exceedingly interested in the business although she is not formally involved. She wasn't concerned at all about which life insurance professional Kelly would select. Alice was confident that Kelly would do an excellent job in picking a professional.

On the other hand, she was in the middle of every decision when the life insurance professional was called on to help in designing Tom's estate plan. She criticized every suggestion that was made. Kelly's estate plan not only dealt with his personal financial situation, it also determined the ownership structure for the family firm.

Figure 3.10

EVALUATING THE IMPORTANCE OF SPECIFIC SHADOW INFLUENCERS	
Instructions: Think of a recent case where you worked with a family business. On the lines below write the names of five or fewer individuals who do not work in the business, yet were influential in deciding which insurance and financial services would be purchased. Then, check the box showing the individual's relative degree of influence.	
Shadow Influencers	***Degree of Influence***
1.	❑ Extreme Degree of Influence ❑ High Degree of Influence ❑ Moderate Degree of Influence ❑ Slight Degree of Influence
2.	❑ Extreme Degree of Influence ❑ High Degree of Influence ❑ Moderate Degree of Influence ❑ Slight Degree of Influence
3.	❑ Extreme Degree of Influence ❑ High Degree of Influence ❑ Moderate Degree of Influence ❑ Slight Degree of Influence
4.	❑ Extreme Degree of Influence ❑ High Degree of Influence ❑ Moderate Degree of Influence ❑ Slight Degree of Influence
5.	❑ Extreme Degree of Influence ❑ High Degree of Influence ❑ Moderate Degree of Influence ❑ Slight Degree of Influence

Moreover, Alice wasn't the only family member not involved in the business who was dissecting each and every possible estate planning scenario. A few of Kelly's children, some of Alice's children, their retired parents, and three cousins were all eager to help in crafting the estate plan. They were happy to help even though their input was not requested.

This is the defining nature of shadow influencers. These family members are not particularly concerned about the selection of a professional services provider. Picking the law firm, the accounting firm, the insurance provider, the trust company, and so forth is not what brings the shadow influencers into the discussions.

The reason for this is straightforward. The professional service providers are not, at this time, doing anything which will directly impact on the financial status of the family. On the other hand, when these professional services providers are called on to do something that will affect the financial status of the family, the shadow influencers become active. The shadow influencers tend to become involved only when the decisions being made have a direct impact on the financial well-being of the family and the business.

Principle: Shadow influencers will become involved when your services and products will impact the financial status of the family.

As a life insurance professional, your services will usually draw the shadow influencers into the decision-making process. What you specialize in are the very services which will not only impact the affluent family business owner but many of the family members.

You have to be aware of what happens when these people become involved. They are critical players, making the marketing of financial services to affluent family businesses much more trying than marketing to successful non-family businesses.

The Adverse Impact Of Shadow Influencers

Shadow influencers will have both a positive and a negative impact on your practice. The bad news is that they will make the process of marketing to affluent family businesses much more arduous. The good news is that once you have been successful with an affluent family business, you are likely to be able to tap the affluent market and leverage that success for quite a while. However, it is the adverse impact of shadow influencers that is most readily apparent.

There are three negative consequences of shadow influencers on your ability to sell your services and products to affluent family business owners. They are:

1. The decision is unlikely to be based purely on business considerations.
2. The decision-making process will usually be more complicated and take longer.
3. A great number of demands will be placed on financial services providers in their attempt to sell their services and products.

Undeniably, these consequences will make it much harder for you. But, at the same time, they will make it much harder for all your competitors. By being forewarned, you are able to mentally prepare yourself for the detrimental effect of shadow influencers.

The Benefits Of Shadow Influencers

Clearly, marketing financial services to affluent family businesses is much harder than marketing financial services to successful non-family businesses. Is it worth the hassles? Why should you bother with affluent family businesses when they are certainly going to make your life more exasperating?

There are two reasons for going through all the hassle brought about by shadow influencers:

1. If you want to gain access to the wealthy, you don't have much of a choice.
2. You will have very loyal clients.

These are the reasons that the financial services industry is targeting affluent family business owners. And, to a large degree, they are a function of the impact of shadow influencers.

Head and Heart Buying

Family businesses are noted for the relatively informal way they make decisions. In family businesses, especially first-generation businesses, decisions are made based more on the intuition of the owner than on the rational logic and analysis characteristic of professional managers.

The information shown in Figure 3.11 confirms the hypothesis of greater informality among family business CEOs. Family business owners are more likely to describe their processes as more informal and as "based on business sense, not numbers." Family business owners are less likely to describe their processes as formal or quantitative and analytical.

Figure 3.11

THE RELATIVE FORMALITY OF THE DECISION-MAKING PROCESS

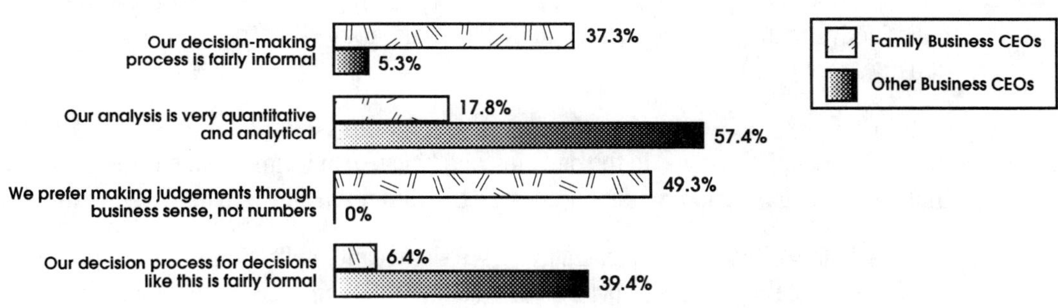

It's Harder and It Takes Longer, But It's Worth It

When James Keith was involved in establishing retirement plans for himself and the senior officers of the company, a number of shadow influencers became involved in the process. Because the retirement program was likely to have a significant effect on the personal finances of many family members, it became a major family issue.

Eventually, nearly everyone in the family became involved. This means that the various retirement programs being considered had to be explained to all the shadow influencers. Keith's Aunt Callie even went so far as to bring in her own consulting actuaries to review the calculations produced by Keith's actuaries.

Once everyone understood what the various retirement programs were all about, the fighting began. As you can imagine, the involvement of all these people slowed the decision-making process considerably.

At the same time, with so many people involved the decision-making process became much more complex. Keith acted as a mediator of family concerns as much or more than as a decision-maker. He saw his role as bringing together all the different perspectives and opinions and molding them into something that worked for both the family and the business.

Principle: It often takes much more time for affluent family business owners to purchase financial services when the family will be affected.

You have to be patient when marketing to affluent family business owners. It is a long sales cycle. With so many people involved in the decision making and complicating the whole process, any expectations of a quick sale are unrealistic.

Because of the longer sales cycle, it is likely that a fair number of financial services providers will give up on the affluent family business market. Since decisions are not made quickly, those financial services providers who need immediate satisfaction will find this market frustrating, to say the least.

Family businesses require demonstrably more effort to sell. Greater numbers of interactions, both in person and by telephone, are required and the extended decision-making cycle itself implies higher costs to sell. Sales professionals targeting the family business market must prepare for longer sales cycles and allocate greater resources to the task.

Sales professionals must also adapt to decision-making processes of different length. Indeed, a distinctive feature of organizational decision-making is that the decision process can span a considerable period of time.

Within family firms, there is evidence that some decisions take longer due to the greater number of people involved in the decision and because of its informal nature. Thus it is thought that purchasing decision-making processes take longer in family firms than in other businesses.

If these dynamics can be confirmed, there are significant implications for sales professionals. The combination of the process informality and longer decision-cycle would imply the expenditure of greater resources to complete the sale — more meetings and telephone calls, for example.

New research is confirming the effect of choice factors on differentiating decision time and much literature has been devoted to the optimization of selling time. More sales effort is required by the inclusion in the buying center of individuals who have no formal role or authority within the business. Their concerns are relatively difficult to address.

Greater Demands Are Placed On Financial Services Providers

Peter Wilson provides life insurance and related services to Andrew Vicks, his family, and the business. Peter almost dreads having to review the family's insurance. He feels that he's going into battle.

Wilson has to really psych himself up for these meetings. Not only will Vicks be there but all manner of family will also be in attendance. While Wilson is exceptional about being patient and explaining the various options that are available, the Vicks are extraordinarily difficult to work with.

Wilson has had to produce more than five times as many proposals for each product being discussed. While most of the proposals were simply discarded, he still had to be able to produce them on demand. He would make them knowing they would not even be looked at.

Principle: When shadow influencers are involved, greater demands are placed on financial services providers.

There is no debate. Selling to affluent family businesses will make your life much more arduous. You must be mentally prepared for all the obstacles that are going to be put in your way.

Decision-making informality and the complexity of non-employee family member involvement in the buying center creates additional burdens for the life insurance professional. Family businesses estimated that they had 7.45 face to face meetings with their insurance agent or broker, on average. This is significantly more than the 6.42 meetings estimated by other business CEOs. Family businesses also required more telephone calls on the average — 6.78 as compared to 6.20. In addition, the decision cycle is significantly longer in family businesses, running almost a year (11.42 months) as compared to an average of 7.11 months for non-family businesses.

Client Loyalty

Jumping through all the hoops will pay off. Not only because you have sold your services and products to an affluent business, but also because you now have a very loyal client.

For example, Thomas Kelly eventually ended up with an estate plan he and his family were quite happy with. The attorneys and the insurance agent who assisted were given a hard time. These professional service providers were all well compensated for their efforts on this project, but that was only the beginning.

These are the professional service providers Kelly goes back to every time. He isn't interested in talking to other service providers. He is comfortable with these people. He is confident that they are high-quality professionals.

At the same time, these professional service providers have won over the shadow influencers. They are comfortable with these people. The shadow influencers are confident that they are high-quality professionals.

It doesn't matter that another lawyer might charge less or that another insurance agent may come along with the latest in financial wizardry. What does matter is that these professionals were helpful, competent, understanding and willing to jump through all the hoops.

Principle: Affluent family business owners are much more loyal clients. Loyalty is the payoff for addressing all the challenges they create.

Affluent family businesses are much more loyal to their financial services providers. Once the affluent family business is comfortable with a supplier, it is unlikely to switch. This is your non-material compensation for all the obstacles they put in your way and for all the illogical behavior that you had to deal with and never quite understood.

That loyalty takes another form as well. Loyal affluent family business owners are much more inclined to recommend you to their associates. Client referrals are your best source of new business. Due to the effect of shadow influencers, you will build a relationship with affluent family business owners that will result in recommendations of your services.

Your Action Items

- Factor in more meetings and more time when you plan the effort it will take to close cases with family businesses. Develop your own set of benchmarks and standards so you will have a better sense of when it makes sense to continue to sell and when it makes sense not to invest more effort.
- Expect to take full advantage of the loyalty of the affluent family business owners. This will lead to more business with them and their associates.
- Decide which products trigger considerable involvement by shadow influencers and which trigger less. Review your cases and interview a select number of your clients.
- Reduce uncertainty among family firm prospects and shorten the decision-making cycle.
- Invest in interactions with family business customers.
    - Set aside appropriate resources for the longer cultivation time family firms require.
    - Participate in on-going training about the needs of family business owners and their firms.
    - Target a higher communications intensity.

Richard Bentley feels like he was really put to the test working with the Roberts. There were a number of times along the way he was seriously considering throwing in the towel. It was just so much work for who knew what return.

They seemed to take forever to make even the simplest decisions. They used criteria that did not lead to good business decisions and they made choices that an astute non-family business president probably wouldn't have made.

Was it worth it? For Bentley the only answer to the question is yes. Bentley is now providing estate planning services to all the wealthy Roberts as well as some senior non-family officers of the firm. In addition, Roberts has recommended that some of his business associates use Bentley's services. It was well worth it.

Section II

Eight Family Business Owner Identities

CHAPTER 4
EIGHT AFFLUENT FAMILY BUSINESS PERSONALITIES

Richard Bentley is an insurance agent who wants to sell insurance and other financial services to affluent family business owners. He has been told that few affluent family business owners have up-to-date estate plans that will ensure that their heirs do not confront onerous estate taxes.

Bentley has carefully written a presentation in which he concentrates on the potential estate tax problems the heirs to the family business may face and the solutions to these problems. To make sure his presentation is well received, Bentley has hired a design professional to produce a flip chart and handout materials for use with prospects.

Bentley was introduced to Peter Quinn, a family business owner, and made his well designed and rehearsed presentation. Quinn told Bentley that his presentation and the handout materials were excellent, but he wasn't interested. Bentley, sensing defeat, asked Quinn if he was confident his family would not have to pay exorbitant estate taxes. Quinn responded, "They might have to, and frankly, I just don't care."

There was no question about the quality of Bentley's presentation or about his ability to sell when his sales pitch is directed at the right prospect. The problem was that he was attempting to sell certain products and services to the wrong person. Quinn isn't concerned about passing on the business to his heirs. Although he is a family business owner, Quinn is more interested in maximizing his personal wealth.

Bentley would be much more successful using his presentation with family business owners who are concerned about succession. We call such family business owners "Loving Parents." In contrast, Quinn falls into a type of family business owners called the "Fortune Hunters." Like you, Bentley has to understand which type of family business owners will respond to his presentation. He has to understand the eight affluent family business personalities.

When people talk about family businesses, they usually discuss them as if they were all the same. Sometimes it seems as though the only unique quality about family businesses is that they are businesses owned by families.

If you have been a life insurance professional for any period of time, you certainly recognize that family businesses are diverse. You have probably observed that some family businesses are more interested in growth than others. Some seem to be running smoothly, while others are engaged in an internal war over how the business will be passed on to a new generation. Use Figure 4.01 to jot down some of the other differences you have personally observed between one family business and another and one family business owner and another.

Figure 4.01

NOTEBOOK: DIFFERENCES BETWEEN FAMILY BUSINESSES AND OWNERS
Instructions: On the lines below, jot down some of the ways you have seen family businesses differ from one another and how family business owners differ from one another.
1.
2.
3.
4.
5.

Among the differences many life insurance professionals often observe are relative emphasis on growth or stability, the extent to which other family members are involved in the day- to-day affairs of the business, the degree of community commitment of the family business, and whether the current owners place more emphasis on taking assets out of the business for personal wealth or keeping assets in the business to secure the future of the family.

Your observations and these reports all lead to the same conclusion. We need a systematic understanding of how family businesses are different from each other. To do so, we will have to determine the major types, or segments, of family businesses.

This is because you, as a life insurance professional, will want to sell your services and products to affluent family business owners. To do so successfully, you need to know how to modify the way you market and sell your offerings to different types of family firms and their owners. In order to help you, we need to segment the affluent family business market so that you can be more effective with them in two ways:

1. Target particular types of affluent family businesses that will be receptive to your services, products, and approach.
2. Modify your approach and how you position your services and products to meet the needs and wants of the affluent family business you are dealing with.

The most successful life insurance professionals do both. You need to be able to identify and target specific types of affluent family business owners who will be attracted to the insurance services you want to promote.

Once you have targeted certain types of family businesses, you want to motivate the affluent owners to buy based on an effectively-prepared presentation. The best presentations are tailored to the precise needs of particular types of family business owners. By knowing the types of family businesses and owners, you can quickly adjust your presentation to the needs and wants of the individual prospect sitting in front of you.

All affluent family business owners need life insurance. They all need retirement programs. They all need estate plans. They all need personal investment management services. However, they need them for different reasons. By matching your products to the reasons motivating family business owners to buy, you can be more successful. By understanding which personality you are dealing with, you can adapt your presentation to motivate him or her to buy.

The Family Business Personality Framework

In order to be effective in marketing financial services to affluent family business owners, you have to understand market segmentation. Market segmentation is a process that divides a market into sub-groups which share similar needs and buying processes. When applied to a large market such as all family business owners, you can expect that segmentation will create sub-groups of family business owners who share unique sets of values and attitudes towards their businesses as well as values and attitudes about the role of insurance and financial services. Simply put, by using segmentation you will gain an unparalleled perspective into the underlying purchasing psychology of affluent family business owners.

The family business personality segmentation framework described here is based on an extensive empirical evaluation of 985 affluent family business owners. In this segmentation, we have identified the significant segments in the family business market. We have focused on what the key decision maker in the family business considers the goals and reasons for the family firm. The results are the eight affluent family business personalities:

- Loving Parents
- Autocrats
- Empire Builders
- Fortune Hunters
- Recruits
- Rebels
- Status Seekers
- Social Benefactors

Principle: An affluent family business personality is a characterization of the needs, wants, and desires that encapsulate the very reason for the existence of the family firm at this point in time.

Figure 4.02 shows the core motivations of each type of family business owner. These motivations range from taking care of the family (Loving Parents) to personal wealth accumulation (Fortune Hunters) to social responsibility (Social Benefactors).

Figure 4.02

PSYCHOGRAPHIC SEGMENTS OF AFFLUENT FAMILY BUSINESS OWNERS	
Segment	**Core Motivations**
Loving Parents	• I get great pleasure having my family involved with me in building the business. • I enjoy working with my family in the business.
Autocrats	• I want to control every aspect of my business. • I am the best person to make sure the business and the family will both be successful.
Empire Builders	• I want to create a business empire. • It is my fondest hope that my family will succeed me in the business.
Fortune Hunters	• My major goal in owning a business is to become wealthy. • I expect to become rich through the business.
Recruits	• I was drafted into the business by my family. • Because of family considerations, I joined the business.
Rebels	• I want to prove to myself and others that I can be a successful businessperson. • People like me have to own our own businesses; we are not good corporate employees.
Status Seekers	• I want recognition for my business success. • I want to be publicly acknowledged as a successful businessperson.
Social Benefactors	• I want to make the world a better place through the success of my business. • I take social and environmental impacts into account every time I make a business decision.

The proportion of family business owners of each type ranges from 34.1% to 4.8%. The largest group is the Loving Parents and the smallest is the Social Benefactors. Figure 4.03 shows the percentage of each family business owner type.

By being able to identify the motivations for the existence of the family business, you can strategically position your insurance and financial services offerings to fit the agenda of the family business key decision makers — the affluent owners.

At the same time, by being aware of the mission of the affluent family business owners you will be able to most effectively market your services and products to them. You will know what they want to accomplish with the family business and this will permit you to insightfully position your offerings.

Of equal importance, you will know what they are not motivated to accomplish. You will be able to recognize when it would be counter-productive to try to sell certain types of services and products.

Figure 4.03

THE EIGHT FAMILY BUSINESS OWNER TYPES

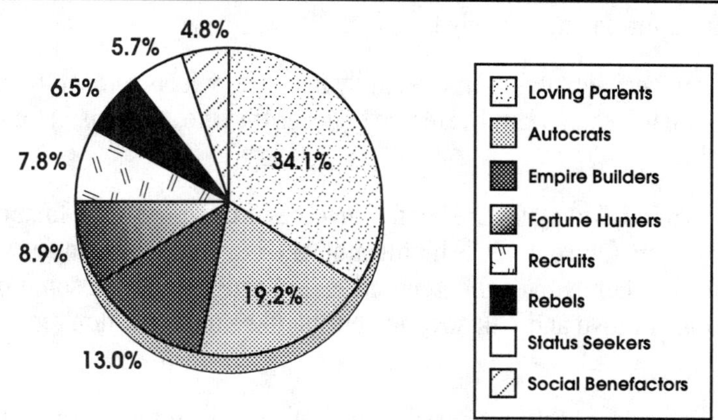

You will also know what they will expect from you both at the time of the sale and on an ongoing basis. Effective relationship management is critical in working with any affluent individual. It is especially important when it comes to affluent family business owners. The insights garnered from this research will enable you to be more effective. Although an increasing number of financial, legal, accounting, and related service providers are targeting the affluent family business market, you will have a distinct competitive advantage by being able to tap into and leverage the motivations described here.

Introducing the Eight Family Business Personalities

Following is a profile of each of the eight affluent family business personalities.

Loving Parents

At 34%, this is the largest segment of family business owners. They are the prototypical family business owners and the type most frequently described in the management literature. Their goal for the business is to care for their families. They get great pleasure from having their families involved with them in building the business. Loving Parents say that they enjoy working with their families in the business.

The Alex Baker Insurance Agency is typical of a Loving Parent family business. The first of several generations involved in the agency founded the firm in 1921, and later generations of children have joined the firm to work with other members of the family. In typical Loving Parent style, the firm evolves to meet the needs of the family members. For example, when Steve Baker indicated an interest in joining the fully-staffed firm in 1971, senior members of the agency (and the family) made the decision to open a second office to accommodate him. A decade later, in the mid-1980s, Wendy Baker joined and was able to pursue her interest by focusing on marketing issues. Most recently, the firm has added Robert Baker who is interested in community relations. Providing jobs for the family has been good for business. It is the largest agency in the state for the carrier it most frequently represents.

Thomas Kelly, age 52, is the CEO of Kelly and Sons, an industrial wholesaling firm employing approximately 350 people. He looks at the business that he is responsible for as an instrument for attending to the needs and wants of his family. For all Loving Parents, this is the number one reason for having a family business.

As the key decision maker in the family firm, Kelly feels himself responsible for doing whatever he can to help his family. He also believes that the sole reason for the business is to "do for the family."

In Kelly's mind, "doing for the family" involves providing for the financial security of his family now and in the future. Kelly is highly motivated to create a business which will provide a good living for the family over the generations. In order to do so, some of Kelly's decisions may seem conservative and risk-adverse, but he likes to say, "I don't gamble with the family's future."

The business also makes it possible for Kelly to spend more time with his family because he likes to have his family work in the business. Kelly sincerely enjoys being with his family. He derives enormous pleasure having his family work side-by-side with him in managing and building the firm.

Of course, there are conflicts and problems having the family so intimately involved in the firm. Family conflicts can seep into the business and business problems can come home in such an arrangement. Nonetheless, Kelly says his family gives him such satisfaction that all the difficulties are worthwhile for the pleasure they bring.

Another aspect of the family business for people like Kelly is that it provides a framework for the family. Since the family is "in it together," the business creates a sense of purpose and provides direction for individuals within the family and the business.

As with all the affluent family business personalities except the Fortune Hunters, the family business is considered a legacy. Kelly wants future generations to remember him and how he served his family. The business was the mechanism of that servitude and so he hopes it will be preserved and passed on from generation to generation of Kellys.

Take a moment to complete Figure 4.04 before moving on to the next affluent family business personality.

Figure 4.04

LOVING PARENT EXERCISE	
Instructions: Write down the names of up to three Loving Parents family business owners you know. Next to each name write down the things they have said or done which make you believe they are Loving Parents.	
Name	**Things They Have Done or Said**
1.	
2.	
3.	

Autocrats

These family business owners have a high need for personal control which translates into a preference to control every element of their business. Autocrats are personally convinced that they are the best individuals to make sure the business and the family will both be successful. Autocrats are a large segment, comprising 19.1% of family businesses. This type can provide the entrepreneurial force necessary to create and grow successful businesses. However, the autocratic style can also cause businesses to fail.

John Lavallo may be an example of a business owner expressing autocratic objectives. He was the founder and driving force behind the family's business which included the landmark Italian Restorante Lavallo and a small chain of Apulia pizzerias. However, his insistence on an over-ambitious expansion plan caused the business to lose money. Within a short period of time, the family was forced to close the restaurant and to sell off the pizzeria chain.

Michael Black, CEO of Star Enterprises, is another example of an Autocrat. He owns a cable manufacturing company with 233 employees and takes a very hands-on approach to the management of the firm. He is 64 and nearing retirement, but still firmly in charge. Black has the last say on any major decision. He believes he is the only one who truly understands all the nuances of the business and is therefore obligated to take a very active — if not total — approach to managing the firm.

Nevertheless, he derives considerable enjoyment from having his family work with him. He wants his heirs to one day take over the reins of the family business. However, that day is not yet here — and his heirs sometimes wonder if it will ever come.

Black says he will delegate more when he is confident that he can trust the decision-making skills of others. For the time being, he just can't. The business is too important, not only to him personally, but to the well being of the family. He cannot afford the disasters that even a few wrong decisions will produce.

Black feels that he is the one in the family who is best suited to provide for the well being of his family. Providing for the security of his family is a major concern of his and he recognizes that he can do this only if the business continues to be successful. He considers it an obligation to serve his family. Black does so in a way that he feels best accomplishes this goal. He must continue to be highly involved in each and every decision to lead his family firm to success. Most importantly, Black considers himself the only person who can guarantee the success of both the business and the family.

Figure 4.05

AUTOCRATS EXERCISE

Instructions: Write down the names of up to three Autocrat family business owners you know. Next to each name write down the things they have said or done which make you believe they are Autocrats.

Name	Things They Have Done or Said
1.	
2.	
3.	

Black feels the business sets a course that the family can follow. It is a direction that will not only benefit the business, but the family as well. The family business is Black's legacy. It is a sign of his commitment to his family and the accomplishment of his responsibilities. As such, he hopes that the business will exist far into the future. He actively seeks to properly train his heirs to manage the family business.

Take a moment to complete Figure 4.05 before moving on to the next affluent family business personality.

Empire Builders

These individuals exhibit dynastic behaviors and seek to create a business that is large enough and successful enough to extend across multiple generations. They account for 13.1% of family business owners. They articulate the goal of creating a business empire and the intention for other family members to follow them in the business.

Empire Builders are not only a first generation phenomenon. Charles H. Jackson III expresses Empire Builder goals in his approach to running his family's 109 year old regional food wholesale and distribution company. He shifted the company's focus to higher volume sales with the US government and established a foothold in the more lucrative national and international food distribution markets. James' goal is to grow the company rapidly. Company sales now average 38% annual increases and an ambitious 18 month timetable is in place.

It has always been the dream of Aaron Velton to build a business that would stand the test of time. He founded Velton Industries, a diversified manufacturing company, nearly 35 years ago when he was 21. Velton Industries has prospered and now employs more than 400 people. Velton is committed to more growth.

Velton's goal is to create a large business. Through growth, the business will become so substantial it will last. Velton, like all Empire Builders, will quickly admit to his dreams of building a business empire. He wants to build an empire he can pass on to the next generation who will do the same thing again.

The family business as an empire is not just a monument to the managerial expertise of Aaron Velton. It is important for the family that the business always be there to provide security. Velton feels responsible for the well being of his family. Only by creating a business empire does he feel that they can always be properly taken care of. In addition, Velton gets a great deal of satisfaction working with his family in building his business empire. In order to create the empire he craves, he needs to grow the firm and looks to his family for help in the process.

Empire Builders want other members of the family to share in the triumphs and failures of the business. Velton feels that by being a part of the business in good times and bad, his family will truly appreciate their joint accomplishments. Having the family highly involved in the business and focused on growing the firm, Velton recognizes that the needs and successes of the business furnish a sense of direction for the family.

On a personal level, Velton is not a traditional corporate player nor could he be. Psychologically, Velton needs the family business because he can't quite fit in as a corporate employee. He is a leader at heart and he needs to be a leader in practice. Velton also considers that the success of the family business is due, in large part, to his ability to stay the course when confronting difficult situations. He looks at adverse situations as challenges to be overcome.

Further, Velton finds his business success gives him power within his community. His desire to be influential within his community is satisfied because of the increasing success of the family firm.

Take a moment to complete Figure 4.06 before moving on to the next affluent family business personality.

Figure 4.06

EMPIRE BUILDER EXERCISE	
Instructions: Write down the names of up to three Empire Builder family business owners you know. Next to each name write down the things they have said or done which make you believe they are Empire Builders.	
Name	**Things They Have Done or Said**
1.	
2.	
3.	

Fortune Hunters

These individuals seek extensive personal wealth in order to support their lifestyles. Fortune Hunters say their major goal in owning a business is to become wealthy and that they intend to become rich through the business. Fortune Hunters do not share the willingness of other family business owner segments to sacrifice current income in order to build a long standing enterprise capable of offering employment opportunities to multiple generations of family members. Fortune Hunters are a relatively small segment. Only 8.9% of family business owners are in this category.

Fortune-Hunter-type goals on the part of any member can cause deep conflicts within a family that owns a business. That is what has happened in the $105 million Patterson family business. Granddaughters of founder Anthony Patterson have sued two current top executives, both sons-in-law, to strip them of their ownership interests. The lawsuit attacks a recapitalization of the business implemented a decade ago which was allegedly undertaken to further the financial interests of the executives over those of other family members.

Having an equity stake in a successful family business is the most likely way to become personally wealthy. Daniel Foster validates this principle. His primary objective is to become personally wealthy. He says he wants to become "filthy rich" and makes no excuses for this. Foster, now 41, founded The Electronic Connection about 18 years ago. It is a chain of retail stores selling all types of electronic products including computers and software. In his stores he has 127 employees.

Fortune Hunters readily acknowledge that becoming wealthy is their principal reason for owning and managing a family firm. Fortune Hunters are singularly focused on making money. All the other motivations for the existence of a family business that are apparent in the other personalities are conspicuously absent in this personality.

For example, for Foster the security of the family is not a major concern. Fortune Hunters do not think of the family business as a way to care for the long-term financial well being of the family. The pleasure that other personalities get in working with their families is also not a factor. Creating a legacy or a desire to one day transfer the business to the next generation is not important.

Fortune Hunters have the least complicated agenda for owning and managing a family business. They just want to be rich. This is why, in the example at the beginning of the chapter, Bentley, the insurance agent, could not even get Quinn's attention by talking about the need for insurance to transfer the business to the next generation. However, if he had talked about the ways insurance can be used to enhance Quinn's personal wealth, he might have made better headway with this "Fortune Hunter."

Take a moment to complete Figure 4.07 before moving on to the next affluent family business personality.

Figure 4.07

FORTUNE HUNTER EXERCISE	
Instructions: Write down the names of up to three Fortune Hunter family business owners you know. Next to each name write down the things they have said or done which make you believe they are Fortune Hunters.	
Name	**Things They Have Done or Said**
1.	
2.	
3.	

Recruits

This segment is comprised of second or third generation sons and daughters who were enlisted by the family to be involved in the business. Originally, they had no intention of participating in or taking over the business, but did so out of a sense of family obligation. Recruits represent 7.7% of family business owners.

Norma Wilson is an example of a Recruit. She was recruited into the family business by her father, the founder of the business, after she expressed ambivalence about her future. Since taking over Louisville, she has transformed the business from a small tooling shop to a world leader in heating manufacturing equipment.

Robert Haley, age 49, is the president of Consolidated Construction Services, a company that operates in three states and employs more than 400 people. Before joining the family business, he had been rising through the ranks of a corporation. He was recruited by other family members to join and run the family business when his father died and there was no one else to run the family business.

Haley grew up in a world where the family and the company were one. The annual family picnic was a gathering of the senior mangers of the firm. The annual business picnic brought the family together with the non-family employees and their families. Haley's entire family always knew he would one day run the company just as they always knew he would one day get married and have a family. Even though for years he expressed a desire to make his own independent career, the family always expected he would come around.

Haley resisted until the time of his father's death. He feels that he was drafted into the family business and had very little choice but to take on the responsibility.

Having accepted the responsibility, one of Haley's greatest fears is not being able to maintain the success of the business and the security of the family. He feels this obligation as a great weight pressing down upon his shoulders.

With this perspective in mind, Haley understands why he is president — a post he never wanted. It is to preserve the family to which he is completely loyal. This translates into a striving to ensure the future of the business for the future of the family. Like nearly all the personalities, he wants to guarantee the family business is transferred to the capable hands of future Haleys.

Take a moment to complete Figure 4.08 before moving on to the next affluent family business personality.

Figure 4.08

RECRUITS EXERCISE	
Instructions: Write down the names of up to three Recruit family business owners you know. Next to each name write down the things they have said or done which make you believe they are Recruits.	
Name	**Things They Have Done or Said**
1.	
2.	
3.	

Rebels

Rebels are 6.6% of family business owners. From a psychological standpoint, Rebels are an interesting group. All share the need to prove to themselves and to others that they can be successful. They also feel that they do not make good corporate employees. It has also been suggested that Rebels create or join family firms because operations and management in such firms is not as demanding or as technical as it is in corporations. This appears to often be the case in the distribution industry which is dominated by family businesses.

Susan Myers is an example of a Rebel. She has always been a creative and innovative sort. She has always had the ability to see better ways of doing things. After college, though, this ability got her in trouble with the companies she was working for. Myers tended to rub people the wrong way when she talked about her ideas. She could seem critical rather than helpful.

For her part, Myers felt out of place and unappreciated. Because many of her ideas were not accepted, she felt as though she was always swimming upstream. When her grandmother died and left her a little money, Myers decided to take the plunge into her own business where she would be the boss and no one would get in the way of implementing her ideas.

Now, at the age of 48 Myers is President and CEO of Distribution Unlimited. It is a wholesale firm supplying jewelry to department stores throughout the Southeast. Distribution Unlimited employs approximately 250 people.

By establishing her own firm, Myers has the freedom to pursue her dreams. She also sees her own business as allowing her to move quickly as circumstances and conditions change. This was something she found nearly impossible in corporate bureaucracies.

Now that she has established her own business, Myers wants to grow it. For her the business represents her legacy to her teen-aged children and vindicates her belief in her ideas and in herself.

Take a moment to complete Figure 4.09 before moving on to the next affluent family business personality.

Figure 4.09

REBEL EXERCISE	
Instructions: Write down the names of up to three Rebel family business owners you know. Next to each name write down the things they have said or done which make you believe they are Rebels.	
Name	**Things They Have Done or Said**
1.	
2.	
3.	

Status Seekers

Business success can translate into social recognition. Some affluent family business owners actively cultivate opportunities to achieve respect, attention and honors. For some, the family business is the means of obtaining the desired status and attention. For this segment, the chief goal and reward of family business ownership is the amount of public acknowledgment, fame and power it brings. Status Seekers represent 5.8% of family business owners. Status Seekers want public recognition for their business success.

Marta Johnson may exemplify the status-seeking family business owner. She left the family jewelry business to go out on her own. Under the Marta line, she has been attracting affluent customers with hand-crafted designs and aggressive public relations. She achieves additional recognition through public appearances.

Frank James is also a Status Seeker business owner. James, age 55, uses the successes of his family business, a chain of grocery stores employing 200 people, as a springboard to obtain the personal prestige he wants. To continue to garner honor and recognition, James wants to grow the business.

For James, a key goal of having a family business is to enable him to be acknowledged as a successful businessperson. He craves the formal recognition of his business acumen. It is important to James that both he and his business are well known and respected. Even though James wants fame and seeks to achieve it by capitalizing on the success of the family business and his position as its leader, he views the family firm as a way to care for the family. The financial security of the family falls to him. It is his responsibility to make certain everyone is properly cared for.

Most of the time, he even enjoys having the family work together to grow the business. He likes for his family to share in the prosperity of the business and in the attention it produces.

James also sees the ability of the family firm to survive through several generations as a way of conferring status on the family and (posthumously) to him. He is concerned about making sure that the next generation will receive the family business unencumbered by financial complications. Thus, he sees the family business as a legacy to his talents.

Take a moment to complete Figure 4.10 before moving on to the next affluent family business personality.

Figure 4.10

STATUS SEEKERS EXERCISE	
Instructions: Write down the names of up to three Status Seeker family business owners you know. Next to each name write down the things they have said or done which make you believe they are Status Seekers.	
Name	**Things They Have Done or Said**
1.	
2.	
3.	

Social Benefactors

This is the smallest segment of family business owners, making up only 5.8% of the group. Social Benefactors exhibit an awareness of community, social and family improvement through the business. Social Benefactors are candid about their goal of making the world a better place and they do so, in part, by taking social and environmental considerations into account in making business decisions.

Bill Mackey and his daughters Maggie and Lisa exemplify the Social Benefactor orientation through their gas and convenience store chain. They offer assistance programs for college students, put on holiday giveaways and are active sponsors of fund-raisers such as car washes. On the business side, they look for abandoned properties in economically depressed areas and turn them into profit centers. Because many locations are in minority communities, community leaders have singled out the Mackey family for awards to recognize their efforts to help the local economy.

Ellen Tomley, age 49, is another Social Benefactor. She now owns an employment agency that employs nearly 100 people in two western states. Tomley grew up as the daughter of a high school principal and a nonprofit administrator who emphasized to her from an early age that making money is not nearly as important as "doing good."

To Tomley, it feels as though many people are out there tearing people down. It seems as though few are trying to build people up. She feels business should be about building people up not tearing them down.

Tomley sees her family business as an the opportunity to help others and to better society. By supporting businesses seeking to hire people and being kind to people looking for jobs, she feels she can make the world a better place through the success of her business.

Moreover, Tomley wants to be a positive influence in her community. There isn't any question that Tomley is extremely socially conscious. She firmly believes in the adage, "Do well by doing good." Tomley carefully incorporates the potential social and environmental impacts of her business decisions in every situation.

Before starting her own firm, Tomley worked for others and her socially conscious perspective put her into conflict with her superiors. Tomley is not a good corporate employee. Thus, establishing a family business gave Tomley the authority to live by her convictions.

Further, by owning and managing the business Tomley is able to quickly respond to changes in both the social and competitive environments her company inhabits. This was never possible when she worked for others. In effect, she can be a better businessperson and this is reflected in the success of her firm.

Tomley's socially beneficial orientation in no way takes away from her concern for her family. Her family ranks number one on her list of concerns. Tomley perceives the business as the primary way to provide for the security of the family. She considers it her responsibility to ensure the financial, personal, and educational future of her family.

Further, she feels that having the family work together is very important. Not only does she readily enjoy spending the time working with her family, she sees the process as a means to communicate what is important in life. By working together, her values are taught by example. Thus, the business provides direction for the family by teaching the best way to grow a successful business.

Tomley sees her family business as a legacy. However, for Social Benefactors the nature of that legacy is different than for the other personalities. Where the other personality types are concerned with being immortalized because of their business skills and acumen, Tomley wants her legacy to reflect her contributions to making the world a better place. She wants people to recognize that because of her the life of other people has been improved. While she would like her business to be passed on to her heirs, Tomley recognizes this might not happen. Nevertheless, if her values are passed on to her children she will have created a worthwhile legacy.

Take a moment to complete Figure 4.11 before reading on.

Figure 4.11

SOCIAL BENEFACTOR EXERCISE	
Instructions: Write down the names of up to three Social Benefactor family business owners you know. Next to each name write down the things they have said or done which make you believe they are Social Benefactors.	
Name	**Things They Have Done or Said**
1.	
2.	
3.	

Types of Family Business Owners And Insurance Purchasing

Market segmentation is only useful if the segments differ from one another. Later chapters of this book present a detailed analysis of different ways that the various segments buy insurance products. Here we will take a preliminary look at how the segments differ in order to prove that looking at this market in terms of the eight family business types is useful.

This was tested in the research by providing family business CEOs with a list of factors which could be important in optimizing the business or reflect a concern about the family. The different family business owner types rate different factors as important in making purchasing decisions which include insurance products.

For example, as shown in Figure 4.12, purchasing products which place the business on a better financial footing for the long term is very important to 77.5% of all businesses. Examples of such products include key employee insurance and buy-sell agreements. It is also possible

Figure 4.12

THE PURCHASE WOULD HELP PUT THE BUSINESS ON A BETTER FINANCIAL FOOTING FOR THE LONGER TERM

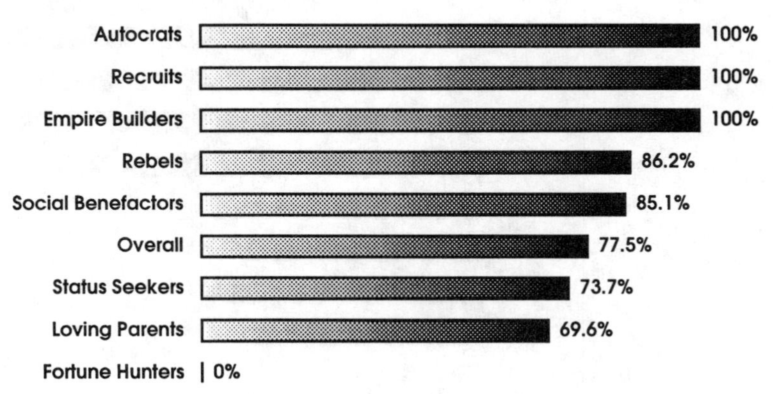

Number of Family Business Owners = 397

to position other products, such as an asset protection plan, as contributing to this goal. However, the significance of this benefit varies across the segments. For example, all Autocrats, Recruits and Empire Builders rate this factor as very important in purchasing. A majority of Social Benefactors, Loving Parents, Status Seekers and Rebels agree, but none of the Fortune Hunters do. This is, of course, because Fortune Hunters are relatively unconcerned about the long term future of the firm and far more interested in amassing personal wealth immediately.

A different pattern emerges when considering the importance of any given purchase helping to determine the direction of the business in future years, as shown in Figure 4.13. Such purchases include a business succession and retirement plan, for example, or some types of executive benefit plans. Although all Autocrats and Empire Builders agree such purchases are very important to themselves, no Fortune Hunters or Rebels do. Rebels and Fortune Hunters

Figure 4.13

THE PURCHASE WOULD DETERMINE THE DIRECTION OF THE BUSINESS IN FUTURE YEARS

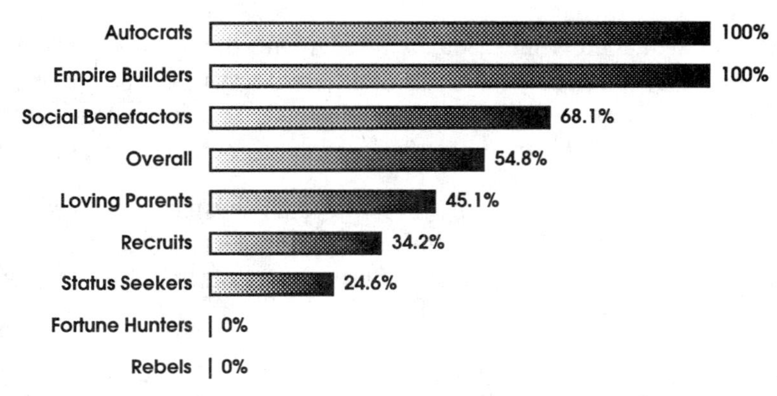

Number of Family Business Owners = 397

Figure 4.14

THE PRODUCT HELPS TO GROW THE BUSINESS

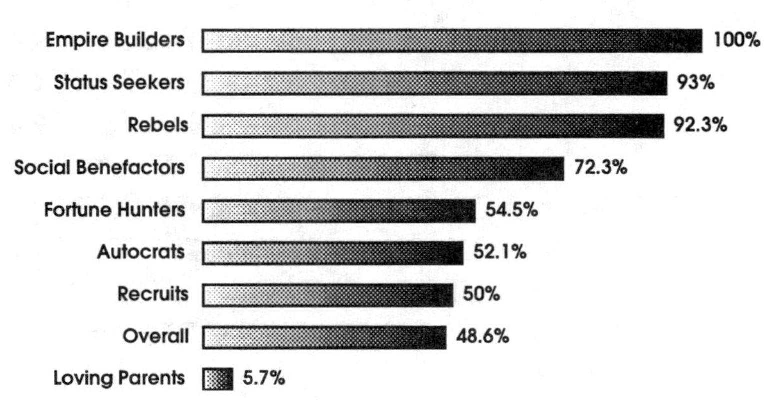

Number of Family Business Owners = 397

prefer flexibility of action as much as the other two types value control, focus and direction. The other segments have mixed opinions. Fewer than half of the Loving Parents, Recruits and Status Seekers think this factor is very important, while more than half of Social Benefactors do. The overall rating of this purchasing criterion is in the mid-range at 54.8%.

Growth is sometimes considered a universal value of businesses but this is not true for all family business owners, as shown in Figure 4.14. Positioning a product as conducive to growing the business has low to moderate salience for Autocrats, Recruits, and Fortune Hunters. Considering a procurement as instrumental to growth is extremely important to Empire Builders, Status Seekers and Rebels and of some importance for Social Benefactors. On the other hand, very few Loving Parents (the largest of these segments) are interested in growth.

Figure 4.15

THE PRODUCT RESULTS IN REAL ASSET GROWTH

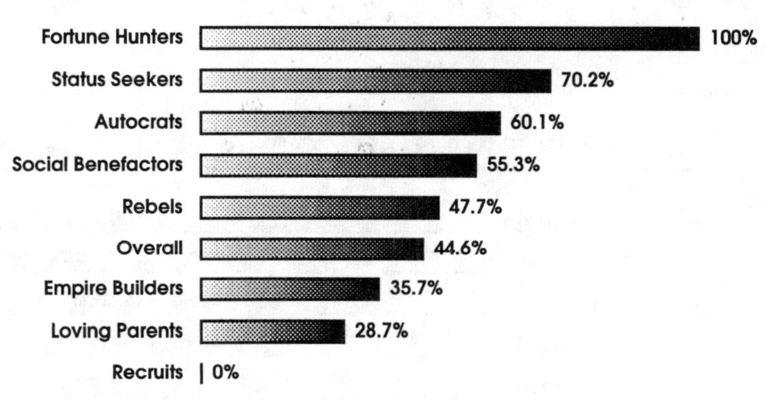

Number of Family Business Owners = 397

As Figure 4.15 illustrates, Fortune Hunters, Status Seekers, and, to a somewhat lesser degree, Autocrats and Social Benefactors are interested in whether the product purchased results in real asset growth. Real asset growth as a product benefit is less compelling to Rebels, Empire Builders, and Loving Parents. Recruits are not interested at all.

Figure 4.16

THE PURCHASE INCREASES MY ABILITY TO CONTROL THE BUSINESS

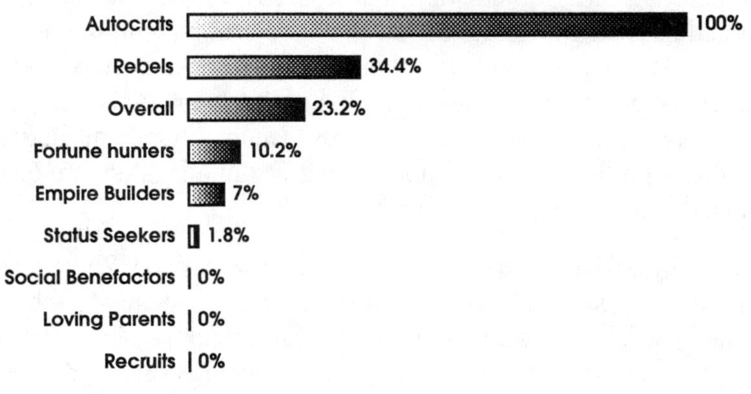

Number of Family Business Owners = 397

The usefulness of a product in extending the control of a family business owner is also more appealing to some segments than to others, as shown in Figure 4.16. Trusts and buy-sell agreements are examples of arrangements which enable the owner to exert control. All Autocrats find products which increase their control to be very appealing. A third or less of the other segments find control a compelling reason to buy.

Because family businesses also seek to achieve family goals through the business the effect of procurement policies on family goals was also explored. Family business owners rated several items describing benefits to the family in terms of their importance in purchasing decision making.

As might be expected, many family business owners value aspects of products which help to knit the family together. Overall agreement on this item was 74.8%, as Figure 4.17 shows. It would be possible to promote key employee insurance in such a manner as well as retirement planning services, for example. However, even this factor is not important to all family business owners. While it is of great importance to Social Benefactors, Status Seekers, Loving

Figure 4.17

THE PURCHASE WOULD HELP KNIT THE FAMILY TOGETHER MORE

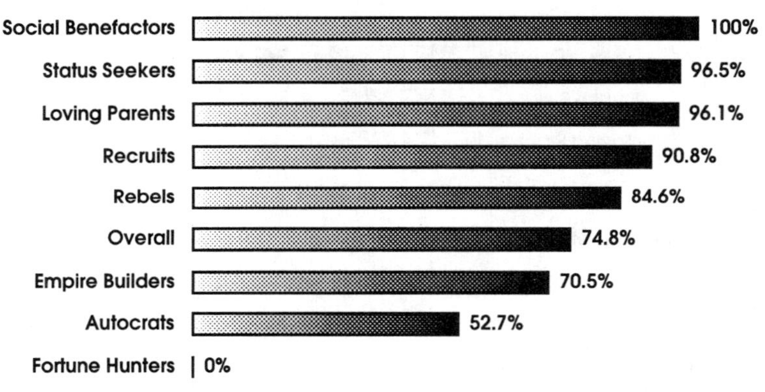

Number of Family Business Owners = 397

Parents, Recruits and Rebels, it is of lesser importance to Empire Builders and Autocrats and of no relevance to Fortune Hunters.

Many family business owners want their families involved in the business, but many do not, as illustrated in Figure 14.18. Recruits (who were brought into the business by their families) and Loving Parents (who want to be with their children in the business) are especially in favor of products which will integrate the family. Charitable estate planning is one very effective way insurance products can encourage collective family action in making nonprofit support decisions. As might be expected, Autocrats and Fortune Hunters are disinterested in products positioned to help a family stay together.

Not all family business owners are interested in succession. While many are, there are some who have other goals. Thus, when an insurance arrangement such as business succession planning is positioned as a way to insure a successful transition of ownership, not all family business owners are interested. Loving Parents and Recruits — the two most family oriented of the segments — do respond favorably to such a positioning, at 80.6% and 76.3% respectively.

Figure 4.18

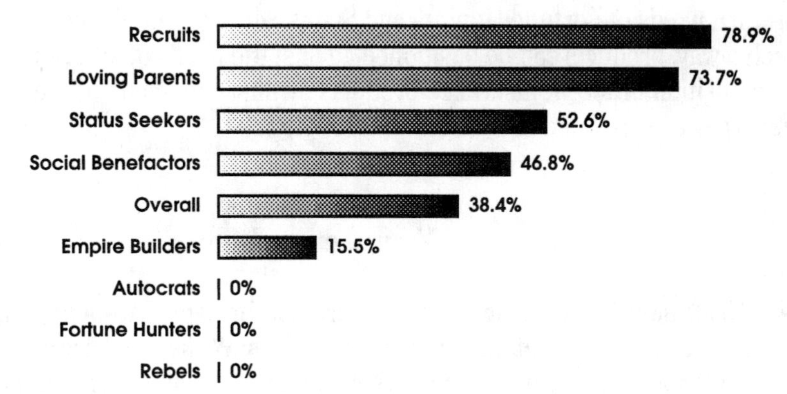

Number of Family Business Owners = 397

Figure 4.19

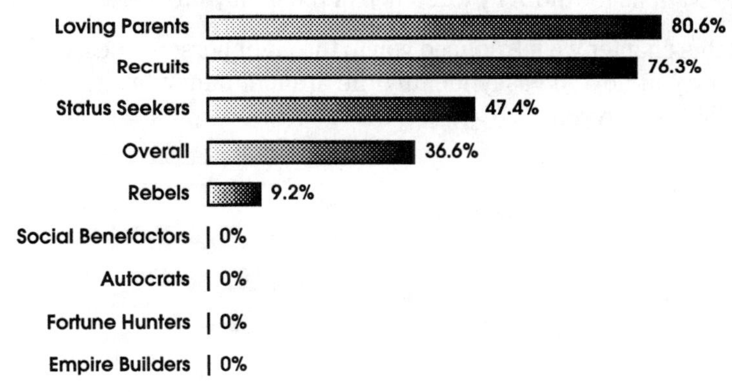

Number of Family Business Owners = 397

However, there are four segments which do not find much relevance in this positioning. They are Social Benefactors, Autocrats, Fortune Hunters and Empire Builders, as shown in Figure 4.19.

As we have seen, family business owners can be segmented into groups sharing similar motivations for their businesses. Theses segments are recognized by people who have had significant dealings with family business owners. They were created using the expertise of life insurance and other professionals as well as the motivations drawn from the family business literature. These segments were created using rigorous research methodology which is described in Appendix B. As this chapter has shown, the framework is useful when applied to case studies of family businesses, as well as to surveys of purchasing criteria.

Micro-segmentation approaches, like the psychographic segmentation described here, are especially suitable for one-on-one selling. Life insurance professionals targeting the family business market should work out ways to identify the different types of family business owners. Chapter 5 describes several ways to do this.

Life insurance professionals should also become adept at positioning products differently for different segments. For example, a life insurance professional specializing in retirement benefits products should position these products effectively for different family business types. For example, they should relate their product to the legacy values of Loving Parents, the financial return needs of Fortune Hunters and Status Seekers, and the control needs of Autocrats. In such a way, products can be positioned against the needs of different segments. Details on how to position different insurance products against the needs of the eight family business owner types are provided in Chapters 6 through 11.

Your Action Items

- All affluent family business owners are not the same. Affluent family business owners can be divided into eight unique personalities. While there are similarities, you must be skilled at working with each personality to most effectively market financial services and products.
- The starting point in being able to adroitly sell to affluent family business owners is to understand them. We are not talking about a peripheral understanding. On the contrary, we are talking about an in-depth awareness of their needs and wants and the motivations for the very existence of the family business.
- In this chapter we introduced you to the eight personalities. In the next chapter, we will show you how to easily identify the affluent family business personality that may be sitting before you.

CHAPTER 5
THE AFFLUENT FAMILY BUSINESS OWNER PERSONALITY ASSESSMENT TOOL

Richard Bentley doesn't want to repeat the mistakes he made with Peter Quinn. He wants to be able to adapt his sales approach to the personality of the affluent family business owner he is seeing. This way he not only saves time but is most likely to get the business.

In order for him to adapt his sales approach he has to be able to identify which of the eight affluent family business owner types he is talking to. Initially Richard saw the answer in the person who referred him to the prospect. Since Richard knows his clients well and can determine which of the eight personalities they are, he mistakenly assumed that if an Autocrat made the referral it was to another Autocrat. This strategy proved to be a mistake. Richard approached Susan Myers, a Rebel, on the recommendation of Arron Velton, an Empire Builder. He quickly focused on the things that are important to an Empire Builder. Once again, his sales pitch was flawless save for the fact that he was giving it to the wrong person.

Richard learned that he has to approach each and every affluent family business owner without any pre-conceived notions about his or her affluent family business personality. Still, he wants to be more effective and this means he has to gear his presentations to his prospect's personality. What should he do?

The answer is quite simple. All Richard needs to do is use the affluent family business owner personality assessment tool or P.A.T. (personality assessment tool) for short.

An intellectual knowledge of affluent family business personalities is only sufficient if you are an academic studying the field. On the other hand, if you're interested in marketing financial services and products to wealthy family business owners, you have to move from a theoretical understanding to pragmatic applications.

Selling financial services to affluent family business owners requires an ability to determine which of the eight personalities you are speaking with. This is not a difficult task since each of the eight affluent family business personalities is distinctive.

Remembering the Names

The first task is to find a way to remember the eight names of the eight family business types. There are many ways to remember concepts and you no doubt have your favorite. If you do, you may skip this section. If, on the other hand, you would like an explanation of the method we use in training different groups in the application of psychographic segmentation, read on.

The first thing is to be confident that you can master this technique. There is a considerable body of literature on learning that confirms that the human mind finds it easiest to learn up to nine concepts. The eight family business owner types fit easily within this limit.

Your challenge is to commit these names to memory:

- Loving Parents
- Social Benefactors
- Autocrats
- Rebels
- Recruits
- Empire Builders
- Fortune Hunters
- Status Seekers

We typically present a number of different ways to allow people to find one they are comfortable with. One idea is to rearrange these letters to make a word or two. Try this in Figure 5.01.

Figure 5.01

LSARREFS
Instructions: Rearrange the letters to create a word or short phrase.

There are many solutions. One we like is FARR LESS as in, "Learning the names of the eight family business owner segments is far(r) less difficult that I thought it would be."

Another approach is to create a sentence with the initials of the family business owner types as the first letter of each word. Try this approach in Figure 5.02.

Figure 5.02

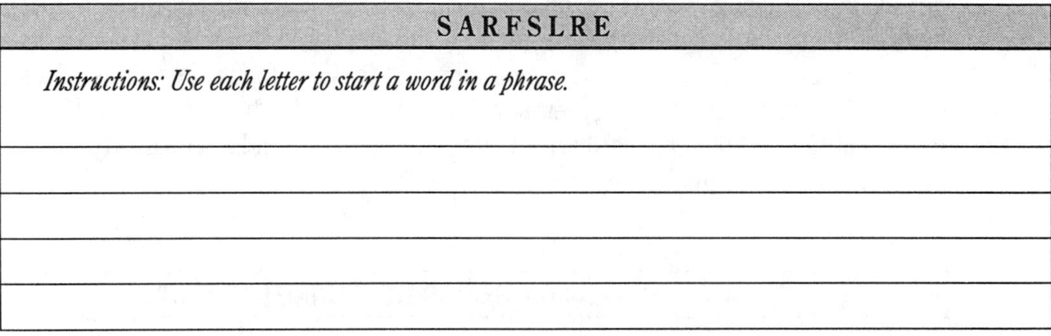

It is always easier to remember things you have made up yourself. If you would like to see ours, it is:

All Families Love Swimming, Racing, Socializing and Eating at Reunions

All = Autocrats

Families = Fortune Hunters

Love = Loving Parents

Swimming = Status Seekers

Racing = Rebels

Socializing = Social Benefactors

Eating = Empire Builders

Reunions = Recruits

Classifying Family Business Owners Using the Personality Assessment Technique

Once you have memorized the names themselves, the next step is to practice classifying business owners you know into each of the types.

Identifying family business owners by their types can be challenging, given the variety of human personalities. However, we have found that successful identification can be made if you inquire into several areas of a family business owner's background and current interests. Family business owners, like most people, like to talk and generally appreciate good listeners.

We call the process of classifying family business owners the Personality Assessment Technique (P.A.T.). The three dimensions you need to be aware of are:

- Use of wealth generated by the business
- Opportunities created by the business
- Internal (family) or external (community, world) orientation

When these three dimensions are crossed, the framework emerges as shown in Figure 5.03. For example, Loving Parents are distinguished by their main objective which is helping their families. This is both a use of wealth (helping the family) and an internal — family — orientation. Another group has a internal orientation, but they are focused on themselves (and their personal wealth) rather than on their families. In this way, Fortune Hunters differ from Loving Parents although both groups share an internal orientation and are focused on using the business for some other goal.

Figure 5.03

PERSONALITY ASSESSMENT TECHNIQUE (P.A.T.)		
Leverage of the Business	**Internal (family) Orientation**	**External (community, world) Orientation**
Use of wealth generated by the business	• Help family *(Loving Parents)*	• Help others *(Social Benefactor)*
	• Help self *(Fortune Hunter)*	• Help the business *(Empire Builder)*
Opportunities created by the business	• Power over family *(Autocrat)*	• Status *(Status Seeker)*
	• Duty to family *(Recruit)*	• Prove managerial skills *(Rebel)*

Two other groups are most interested in the wealth generated by the business but they have an external orientation. Social Benefactors are interested in using the business wealth to create a better world and express their social responsibilities. Empire Builders are interested in the wealth created by the business because they can use it to expand their businesses.

Four business types are primarily interested in the opportunities created by the business rather than in the wealth generated by the business. When the opportunity of the business is internally oriented it can become the basis for power over family members, as Autocrats like to have, or it can become duty to family, as expressed by Recruits. When the orientation is external, the objective can be to demonstrate one's competence as a manager, as Rebels are motivated to do, or to achieve status in the outside world as Status Seekers want to do.

Once you understand the framework, the next phase of the P.A.T. process is to become comfortable talking to family business owners about these topics because it is only when you know the responses to these topics that you will be able to accurately classify family business owners into one of the eight personalities. Complete the exercise in Figure 5.04 to begin learning this process.

Figure 5.04

P.A.T. BUSINESS GOALS SALES TRACK EXERCISE
Instructions: Create at least three ways you could ask questions designed to let you understand where a family business owner stands on each of the three dimensions.
Dimension 1: Use of wealth generated by the business.
Dimension 2: Opportunities created by the business.
Dimension 3: Internal or external focus.

Now let us provide you with some answers given by actual family business owners. At the end of each section in Figure 5.05, you will be asked to name the family business owner type.

Now that you have been introduced to each of the eight family business owner types, it's time to relate this framework to your clients and your practice. For this exercise, select a family business owner you know well. Take a moment to review what you know about this business owner. Then complete the questions in Figure 5.06.

On the basis of this information, you may be able to classify this family business owner into the family business owner framework. What is your best judgment about which of the family business owner types this family business owner is? Indicate your answer in Figure 5.07 and then move on to answer the questions in Figure 5.08.

Figure 5.05

CLASSIFYING FAMILY BUSINESS OWNERS EXERCISE
Instructions: Read each selection. At the end of each selection, apply the Personality Assessment Technique and name the type of family business owner.
A. "Glad you asked what I'm trying to get out of the business. Not many people ask, and I figure they don't want to get to know me. But you seem interested. Well, the family is the largest manufacturing company left in the city. There used to be more, but they all relocated to where wages are cheaper. So we're left. I've got Bill and Dorothy in the business with me and Bill will probably take over. The business has taken good care of the family since the 1890's, and I hope it will take care of another generation or two." ________
B. "I don't know how to answer your question. There are a lot of things I want to do with the business. I guess I'd have to say that I came from a large corporation, and I learned a lot about how big business is done. I want to run a small business in a big way, and I want to make it a big business someday." ________
C. "I think the most important thing in business is to be respected. You can either build things up or you can tear them down. I build them up. I think the community we have is the most important thing, and I want the business to be part of building the community. My company is respected, and I think I am too." ________
D. "I'm different from other family business owners you know. I have no particular interest in someone else running the business. If they do, fine, and if they don't, fine too. The business has been good to me. Because of the business, I have been able to have the life-style I want." ________
E. "My main problem with the business is getting anyone else up to speed. I have to make every decision. I have all kinds of family members wanting into the business, and I'm glad to have them up to a point, but it boils down to having to manage them, and everyone else, like a hawk. I need to be involved in every decision to be sure it's right." ________
F. "I think business should make the world a little better. We take ethics very seriously here. It's important to make good products, to treat employees well and to add a little it back to the community." ________
G. "Some of us are not cut out to work in a corporation. We're too independent-minded. But I'm professional. Sometimes, when I talk to other small business owners, I think I'll go crazy, they're so unsophisticated." ________
H. "I was off doing something completely different when my uncle came to me and asked me to come run the business. It's not anything I would have even done, but I'm glad I did it. I am closer to my family than before, sometimes too close. But when your family calls on you to help, what can you do. There was no one else." ________

Figure 5.05 (Continued)

Answers

A. Loving Parents

B. Empire Builder. If you thought it might be a Rebel, you could ask a few more questions to separate Empire Builders from Rebels.

C. Probably a Status Seeker, but might be a Social Benefactor

D. Fortune Hunter

E. Autocrat

F. Social Benefactor

G. Rebel

H. Recruit

Figure 5.06

CLASSIFYING YOUR PROSPECTS AND CLIENTS EXERCISE	
Family Business Owner: ______	
What is his attitude toward the business? Is it a means towards personal wealth or community status? Taking care of children or doing good in the world?	
How did the owner come into the business? Did he have a corporate career? Was he recruited into the business?	
What is the history of the business? Did this owner start it or has it been around for a while?	
Are there heirs to the business? Sons or daughters or other relatives? What is the owner's attitude towards succession?	

Figure 5.07

Check one

_____ Autocrat
_____ Empire Builder
_____ Fortune Hunter
_____ Loving Parent
_____ Recruit
_____ Rebel
_____ Status Seeker
_____ Social Benefactor

Figure 5.08

YOUR FAMILY BUSINESS OWNER

Instructions: Think for a moment how you would describe this family business owner to others and then list below the three principal attributes that convince you this family business owner is the type you selected.

1. ______________________________

2. ______________________________

3. ______________________________

Creating Family Business Owner Portraits

Learning, especially learning that involves long-term memory, is enhanced when symbols and images are used with words. In using images and symbols to further our understanding of the eight family business owner types, we will improve your ability to recall the types and to label the family business owners you see. Please complete Figure 5.09.

Typing Your Major Family Business Owners

Once you feel confident with classifying individual family business owners according to the framework, it is important to extend your mastery of the approach. In Figure 5.10, you should try to list as many as ten affluent family business owners you know by their type. In the first column, list the family business owners who come to mind. In the second column, write their types. Use the third column to make notes to yourself, including notes about what other information you may need about the family business owner in order to feel more confident about your choice of type.

As you start this exercise, please keep a few points in mind. First, because this way of thinking about family business owners is new, you may not have all the information you need. That's fine. It is a good learning outcome. Second, you may find that your family business owners do not include all of the types. This may reveal something about your professional style or your practice.

By using the tools in this chapter, Bentley is able to easily identify the affluent family business personality he is dealing with. In the beginning, using the tool was a bit cumbersome. However, Bentley became quite proficient with the personality assessment tool after studying the material and putting it to use.

Aside from formal training, experience is the best means of learning how to identify the eight affluent family business personalities. Bentley had to use the personality assessment tool and other techniques from this chapter, including the feedback component of the process, repeatedly in order to become capable at quickly and accurately identifying the personalities of affluent family business owners.

Figure 5.09

CREATING PORTRAITS	
Instructions: The specific process we will use is imaging. For each family owner type, draw one or more images of this family business owner in the spaces provided. Pay attention to accessories which symbolize aspects of this family business owner's archetype. For example, cars can symbolize the type of owner in some cases. Be sure to draw the background (add a house, etc.). Surround the family business owner with images which tell his unique story.	
Autocrat	**Fortune Hunter**
Recruit	**Empire Builder**
Loving Parent	**Rebel**
Status Seeker	**Social Benefactor**

Figure 5.10

YOUR FAMILY BUSINESS OWNERS		
Family Business Owner	*Owner Type*	*Notes*
1.		
2.		
3.		
4.		
5.		
6.		
7.		
8.		
9.		
10.		

Your Action Items

- Classify all your major current prospects into one of the eight family business owner types using the Personality Assessment Technique.
- If there are some you are not certain about, use the other tools from this chapter to make a classification. It may take more information than you have on hand.
- Keep these active prospects in mind as you go through the next chapters about the various insurance products.

Section III

Power Positioning Products

CHAPTER 6
EXECUTIVE BENEFITS

Richard Bentley has just met Tom and Nancy Smith, owners of a small chain of organic food stores. Because of the kind of business they are in, he thought they might be Social Benefactor types. After talking with them for a while during a back-to-school night, he decided he was right. Bentley knew that health and disability insurance products are particularly tough issues for small retailers but he thought that people as socially oriented as the Smiths might be interested, particularly in disability. He worked out several ways to link disability coverage to social responsibility and created a few anecdotes from cases in his files. Then Bentley dropped by the food store where he knew the Smiths spent much of their time.

Executive benefits are part of the responsibilities and the rewards of being family business owners. The business can be a platform for providing family members and employees with health and disability insurance, life insurance and medical expense reimbursement plans. There are ways life insurance professionals can insure that family members are particularly well covered in such plans. Rewards of business ownership include such executive benefits as company cars and restricted stock or stock option plans. Family business owners vary in the extent to which these executive benefits are meaningful to them and in their awareness of how much they can do with executive benefits.

The Importance of Executive Benefits

Executive benefits include a range of indirect forms of compensation and reward for employees and management. Life, health and disability are well known executive benefits, but also available are medical reimbursement programs and various stock programs such as stock options and restricted stock plans. Common executive benefit programs are rounded out by severance pay plans and corporate car programs.

Prevalence of Executive Benefits

Family business owners, as a group, tend to agree that some executive benefits programs are more important than others and they have a greater interest in buying these plans. Check your knowledge of the executive benefits market among family business owners in Figure 6.01.

Figure 6.01

EXECUTIVE BENEFITS EXERCISE			
Instructions: Check whether family business owners as a group feel that each of these executive benefits is very important, somewhat important or less important.			
Executive Benefit	**Very Important**	**Somewhat Important**	**Less Important**
Health insurance	❑	❑	❑
Life Insurance	❑	❑	❑
Disability insurance	❑	❑	❑
Corporate car	❑	❑	❑
Restricted stock or stock options	❑	❑	❑
Severance pay plan	❑	❑	❑
Medical expense reimbursement plans	❑	❑	❑

More than half of all family business owners agree than health, life and disability insurance are important elements of an executive benefits plan, as shown in Figure 6.02. These products are the most widely sold of all executive benefits.

Fewer family business owners are interested in the other executive benefits. For example, only about 28% feel that corporate cars are an important executive benefit and just about 27% agree that restricted stock or stock options are important executive benefits. Similarly, about 26% think severance pay plans are important executive benefits while only about 17% agree that medical expense reimbursement plans are important. Significant opportunities exist among family business owners for life insurance professionals who can develop these markets by emphasizing the benefits of such programs.

Figure 6.02

IMPORTANCE OF EXECUTIVE BENEFITS

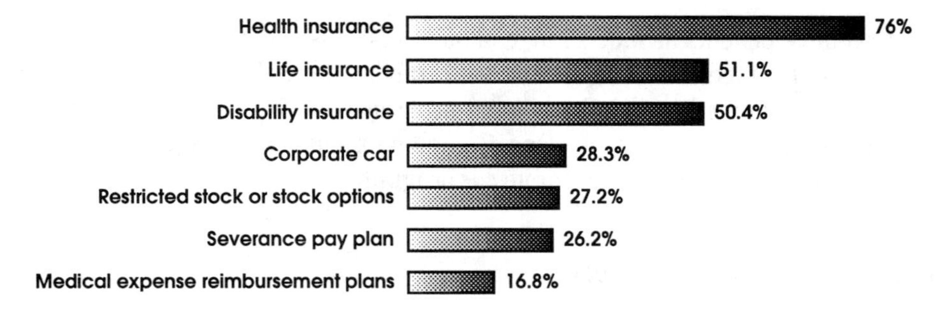

Number of Family Business Owners Who Recently Purchased Executive Benefits = 1,074

As Bentley suspected, health insurance is especially important to the Social Benefactor segment. All Social Benefactors agree that health benefits are an important executive benefit to provide, as illustrated in Figure 6.03. Five other groups also emphasize the importance of health insurance in their businesses: Loving Parents, Status Seekers, Empire Builders, Rebels and Recruits. Only about half of Autocrats and Fortune Hunters believe health benefits are important.

Figure 6.03

IMPORTANCE OF HEALTH INSURANCE

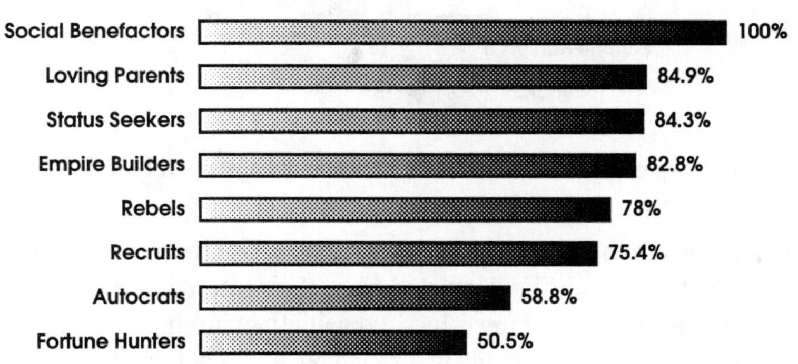

Number of Family Business Owners Who Recently Purchased Executive Benefits = 1,074

There is even more variation in the extent to which the various segments of family business owners perceive the value of life insurance. As Figure 6.04 details, those who think that life insurance is an important executive benefit range from 95% of Social Benefactors to only 15% of Autocrats. Judging from the degree of importance they attach to life insurance four groups seem to be excellent prospects for life insurance as an executive benefit. They are Social Benefactors, Status Seekers, Recruits, and Rebels.

Social Benefactors provide these benefits because they believe it is the right thing to do while Status Seekers believe that providing such benefits is a prerequisite to social standing in the business community. Recruits and Rebels provide life insurance because they have longer history as corporate employees where life insurance is a common component of benefits packages.

Significantly, Loving Parents are less likely to think life insurance is important and this may be linked to the often observed aversion business founders have to considering their own death. Fortune Hunters do not typically value life insurance because they are focused on maximizing current assets rather than on asset protection while Autocrats do not associate life insurance with a means of controlling the behavior of members of the firm.

Figure 6.04

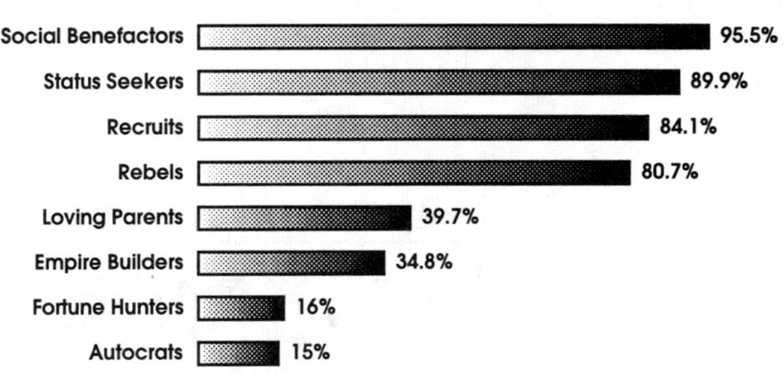

Number of Family Business Owners Who Recently Purchased Executive Benefits = 1,074

When it comes to the use of disability insurance, the results are equally diverse as illustrated in Figure 6.05. As might be predicted from their interest in health and life insurance, Social Benefactors are the most interested in disability insurance. Loving Parents find disability insurance more appealing than life insurance because such insurance can be directly associated with taking care of family members now and in the future. In other groups, interest is mixed. About half of Rebels, Empire Builders, and Recruits agree that disability insurance is important. In contrast, Autocrats are relatively less interested in disability insurance as are Status Seekers.

Figure 6.05

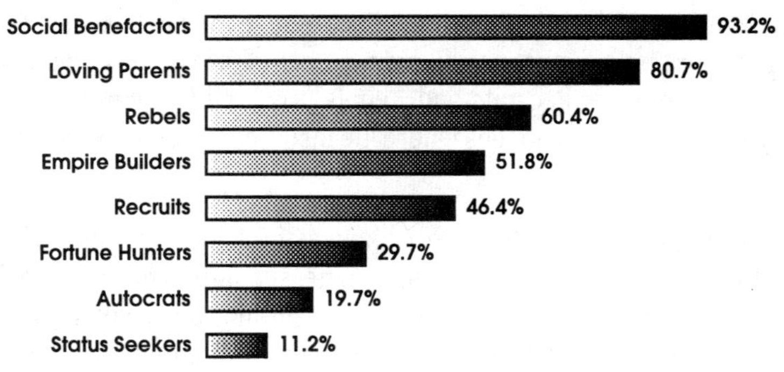

Number of Family Business Owners Who Recently Purchased Executive Benefits = 1,074

Status Seekers are far and away the group with the greatest interest in a corporate car, as shown in Figure 6.06. Almost all Status Seekers think a car provided by the company is a very important component of executive benefits. For all other groups, interest in corporate cars is substantially lower. Around half of Fortune Hunters and Autocrats think corporate cars are important executive benefits, while even fewer Loving Parents, Rebels, Recruits, Empire Builders, and Social Benefactors do.

Figure 6.06

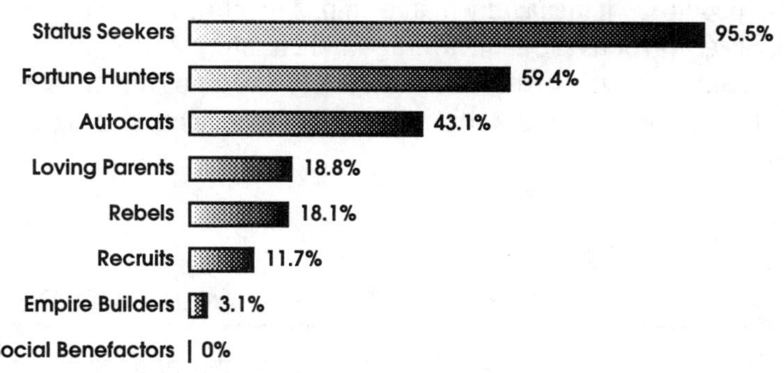

Number of Family Business Owners Who Recently Purchased Executive Benefits = 1,074

Although various forms of stock benefits could be applicable to many family businesses, relatively few value them as executive benefits or appear to be making use of them. Of all the groups, only Loving Parents seem to be making any substantial use of restricted stock or stock options, as illustrated in Figure 6.07. There is some use of stock programs among Empire Builders, Recruits, Status Seekers, and Rebels. Consistent with their psychological types, Social Benefactors, Autocrats and Fortune Hunters are relatively uninterested in stock plans.

Figure 6.07

IMPORTANCE OF RESTRICTED STOCK OR STOCK OPTIONS

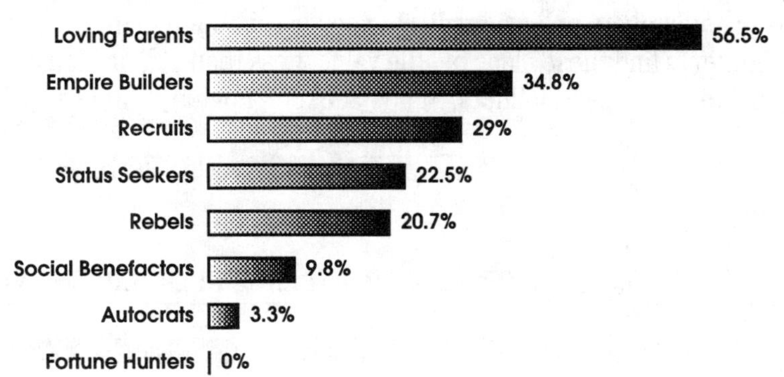

Number of Family Business Owners Who Recently Purchased Executive Benefits = 1,074

Severance pay plans have the interest of only about a quarter of family business owners overall. As shown in Figure 6.08, only Autocrats are significantly more likely than other segments to value severance plans, perhaps because they want the greatest degree of flexibility in removing people from management and employment while still being able to effectively recruit talent. Several groups are about average in their interest. They are Social Benefactors), Loving Parents, Status Seekers, Rebels, and Recruits. Fortune Hunters and Empire Builders are significantly below average in their interest in severance pay programs as a part of executive benefits.

Figure 6.08

IMPORTANCE OF SEVERANCE PAY PLANS

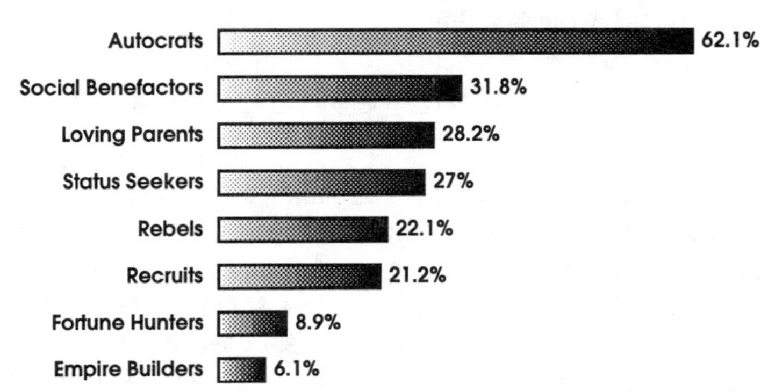

Number of Family Business Owners Who Recently Purchased Executive Benefits = 1,074

Medical expense reimbursement plans were the least valued of all the executive benefits evaluated in this research as shown in Figure 6.09. Medical expense reimbursement plans do not appear to have a large presence in family businesses. As might be predicted, Social Benefactors are most likely to believe medical expense reimbursement plans are important while all other segments find these plans of little value. Less than 10% of each of four segments is interested, including Empire Builders, Status Seekers, Fortune Hunters and Autocrats.

Figure 6.09

IMPORTANCE OF MEDICAL EXPENSE REIMBURSEMENT PLANS

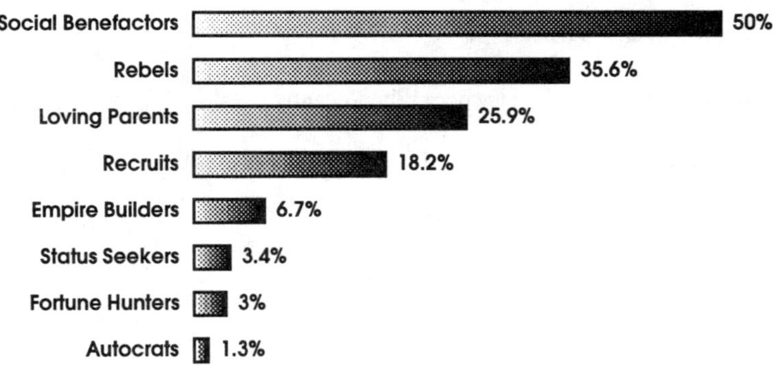

Number of Family Business Owners Who Recently Purchased Executive Benefits = 1,074

Key Market Segments for Executive Benefits Plans

Just three family business types make up over half of the total executive benefits market, as illustrated in Figure 6.10. They are Loving Parents (22.2%), Empire Builders (15.2%) and Autocrats (14.2%). Life insurance professionals seeking to increase executive benefits sales should concentrate on these three segments. Fortune Hunters, Status Seekers and Social Benefactors each account for less than 10% of the market.

Some segments are slightly over represented as executive benefits customers and could be targeted on this basis. Comparing the second and third columns of Figure 6.10 shows that Empire Builders, Rebels, Recruits, Fortune Hunters and Status Seekers are slightly more likely to be among those who buy executive benefits than they are normally represented among family businesses as a whole. For example, 15.2% of Empire Builders were among recent purchasers of executive benefits but Empire Builders make up only 13% of the overall population of family business owners.

Figure 6.10

DISTRIBUTION OF FAMILY BUSINESS SEGMENTS: *BUYERS OF EXECUTIVE BENEFITS PLAN PRODUCTS AND NATIONALLY*		
Family Business Segment	**Recent Purchasers of Executive Benefits**	**National Distribution of Segments**
Loving Parents	22.2%	34.1%
Empire Builders	15.2%	13.0%
Autocrats	14.2%	19.2%
Rebels	13.9%	6.5%
Recruits	12.8%	7.8%
Fortune Hunters	9.4%	8.9%
Status Seekers	8.3%	5.7%
Social Benefactors	4.1%	4.8%
Number of Family Business Owners Who Recently Purchased Executive Benefits = 1,074		

Looking at Figure 6.10 another way, you should note that over a third of the market for executive benefits is made up of Empire Builders and Loving Parents alone. This implies that you should be strongly positioning executive benefits toward these two segments.

Positioning Your Practice

As we will see here and in the other chapters of this section, each type of family business owner sees insurance and related financial products differently. That is, each perceives a different need or want and, thus, sees a different benefit. Clearly, emphasizing a benefit that is especially appealing and relevant to a family business owner will be more likely to be successful than one which is not relevant to that segment. Knowing exactly which benefits appeal to each segment is critical to successful life insurance sales.

Figure 6.11

POSITIONING EXECUTIVE BENEFITS EXERCISE	
Instructions: Write out a phrase which describes executive benefits in words especially meaningful to each family business owner segment.	
Loving Parents	
Empire Builders	
Autocrats	
Rebels	
Recruits	
Fortune Hunters	
Status Seekers	
Social Benefactors	

These differences are true in executive benefits. It is crucial that you position executive benefits properly with each family business segment. You can begin with the executive benefits plan positioning exercise in Figure 6.11.

In the sections below you will be able to compare your positioning statements against those we created and tested with over a thousand family business owners.

Loving Parents

For example, we created the positioning statement, "An executive benefits plan enables you to take very good care of your family." Next, we asked all the family business owners in the study how important this reason was in obtaining the coverage that they did.

As Figure 6.12 shows, this reason is extremely important to almost all Loving Parents because they are most interested in taking care of their families now and in the future. Loving Parents, you will recall, manage the business as a living legacy for their families and are most interested in maintaining the economic security of the family. As Figure 6.12 also shows, this reason is of minor or no importance to the other segments. You can see the advantages of positioning executive benefits in this way to this segment. At the same time, it is obvious that positioning executive benefits in this way to any other segment would be a waste of time.

Of all executive benefits, Loving Parents are most interested in health and disability insurance. Many are also interested in restricted stock and stock options, as shown in Figure 6.13. On the other hand, promoting corporate cars to Loving Parents would meet with less success than offering an executive benefits program.

Figure 6.12

POSITIONING STATEMENT: *AN EXECUTIVE BENEFITS PLAN ENABLES YOU TO TAKE VERY GOOD CARE OF YOUR FAMILY*

(Percent of family business owners with an executive benefits plan who say this positioning statement is very important for them.)

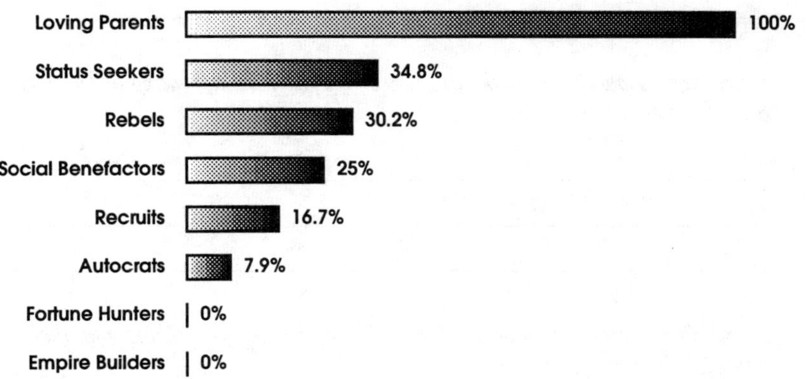

Number of Family Business Owners Who Recently Purchased Executive Benefits = 1,074

Figure 6.13

EXECUTIVE BENEFITS IMPORTANT TO LOVING PARENTS

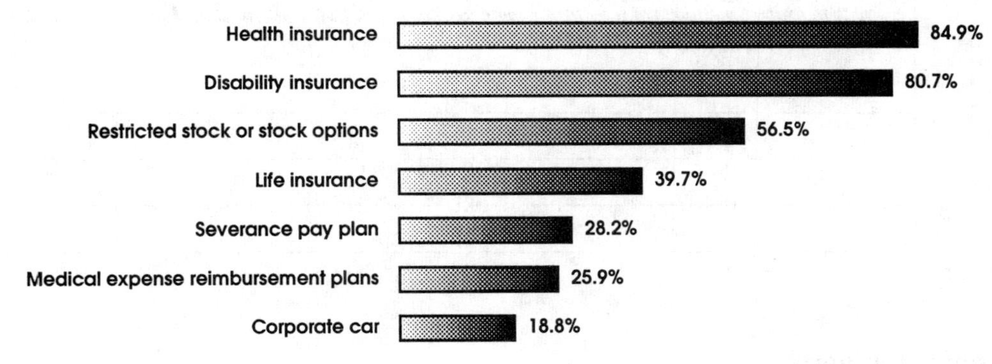

Number of Loving Parents = 238

Based on the information so far, you should be able to create effective sales presentations of executive benefits to the Loving Parent type of family business owner. The exercise in Figure 6.14 will enable you to do so easily by bringing together the information in this section and creating your own sales track.

Figure 6.14

LOVING PARENT/EXECUTIVE BENEFITS SALES TRACK EXERCISE
Instructions: Write the name of a Loving Parent type of family business owner below. If you can't think of a specific person, create a mental picture of a Loving Parent and focus on that image for this exercise.
Instructions: Now list below the insurance products most appealing to Loving Parents. (Refer to Figure 6.13 if you need to.)
Instructions: Next, write down the benefit Loving Parents are seeking from their insurance. (Refer to Figure 6.12 if you need to.)
Instructions: Finally, write out some statements linking the specific features of the executive benefits products Loving Parents are most interested in with the benefit they seek to achieve. For example: "Because disability insurance provides for a continuing income if someone becomes too sick to work, it is an excellent way to protect members of your family who are employed in the business and to take care of their families in times of great difficulty."

Empire Builders

The second most important segment for executive benefits is Empire Builders. Empire Builders seek to create a large, sustainable enterprise from their family business. In other words, they want to build a big business. Accordingly, for this segment we created the positioning statement, "An executive benefits plan helps you keep people focused and committed to building the business." For Empire Builders, the key benefit of all products is how effectively they contribute to the goal of business growth.

Since it is possible to see executive benefits as a way to increase motivation among the members of the business's management team, we tested this approach. As Figure 6.15 shows, it is an extremely effective approach for Empire Builders. All Empire Builders who have recently purchased executive benefits said that this statement is a very important reflection of their reason for doing so. Note, also, that this reason is not particularly relevant for any other segment.

Figure 6.15

POSITIONING STATEMENT: *AN EXECUTIVE BENEFITS PLAN HELPS YOU KEEP PEOPLE FOCUSED AND COMMITTED TO BUILDING THE BUSINESS*

(Percent of family business owners with an executive benefits plan who say this positioning statement is very important for them.)

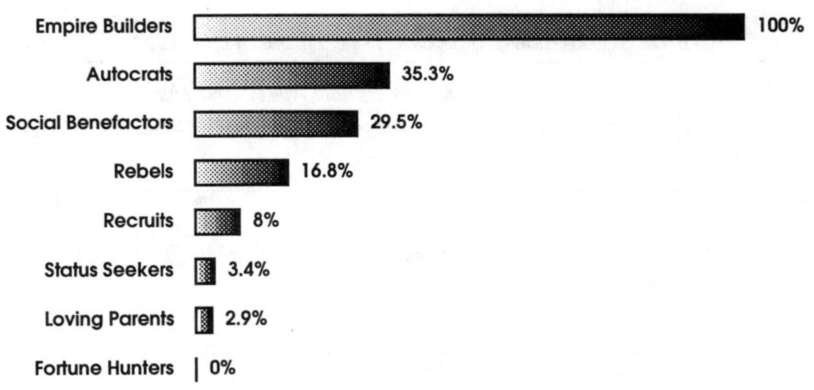

Number of Family Business Owners Who Recently Purchased Executive Benefits = 1,074

Among all executive benefits, it is health and disability insurance which most interest Empire Builders. Some are also interested in life insurance and restricted stock and stock options, as Figure 6.16 shows. Promoting medical expense reimbursement plans, severance pay plans and corporate cars to Empire Builders would not be a successful undertaking.

Figure 6.16

EXECUTIVE BENEFITS IMPORTANT TO EMPIRE BUILDERS

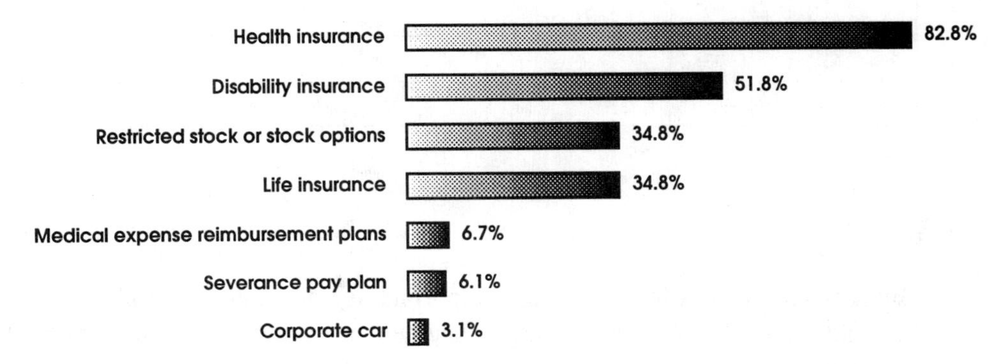

Number of Empire Builders = 163

Based on the information presented so far, you should be able to create effective sales presentations of executive benefits to the Empire Builder type of family business owner. The exercise in Figure 6.17 will enable you to do so easily by bringing together the information in this section and creating your own sales track.

Figure 6.17

EMPIRE BUILDER/EXECUTIVE BENEFITS SALES TRACK EXERCISE
Instructions: Write the name of an Empire Builder type of family business owner below. If you can't think of a specific person, create a mental picture of an Empire Builder and focus on that image for this exercise.
Instructions: Now list below the insurance products most appealing to Empire Builders. (Refer to Figure 6.16 if you need to.)
Instructions: Next, write down the benefit Empire Builders are seeking from their insurance. (Refer to Figure 6.15 if you need to.)
Instructions: Finally, write out some statements linking the specific features of the executive benefits products Empire Builders are most interested in with the benefit they seek to achieve. For example: "Disability insurance can be a valuable benefit to attract and retain the kinds of managers and family members who can best help you grow the business."

Autocrats

Autocrats are one of the three most important segments in the family business market for executive benefits. While not as large a segment as Loving Parents and Empire Builders, it is still important.

Autocrats can be appealed to on the aspect of control. The positioning statement that we created and tested with over a thousand recent executive benefits purchasers was, "An executive benefits program helps you keep employees motivated in the right direction." As shown in Figure 6.18, this positioning statement was extremely appealing to Autocrats because they are oriented towards control. Take note that this positioning statement was somewhat appealing to Empire Builders who also have a need to keep employees and family members goal-oriented. Smaller proportions of the other segments responded favorably to this positioning statement.

Figure 6.18

POSITIONING STATEMENT: *AN EXECUTIVE BENEFITS PROGRAM HELPS YOU KEEP EMPLOYEES MOTIVATED IN THE RIGHT DIRECTION*

(Percent of family business owners with an executive benefits plan who say this positioning statement is very important for them.)

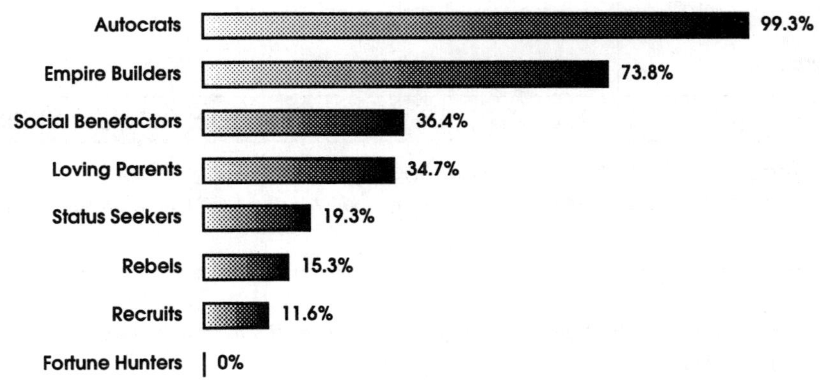

Number of Family Business Owners Who Recently Purchased Executive Benefits = 1,074

Autocrats have a different pattern of preferences in executive benefits. They are most interested in severance pay plans and health insurance with some interest in corporate cars, as illustrated in Figure 6.19. Few Autocrats are interested in disability insurance, life insurance, restricted stock or stock option plans or medical expense reimbursement plans.

Based on the information presented so far, you should be able to create effective sales presentations of executive benefits to the Autocrat type of family business owner. The exercise in Figure 6.20 will enable you to do so easily by bringing together the information in this section and creating your own sales track.

Figure 6.19

EXECUTIVE BENEFITS IMPORTANT TO AUTOCRATS

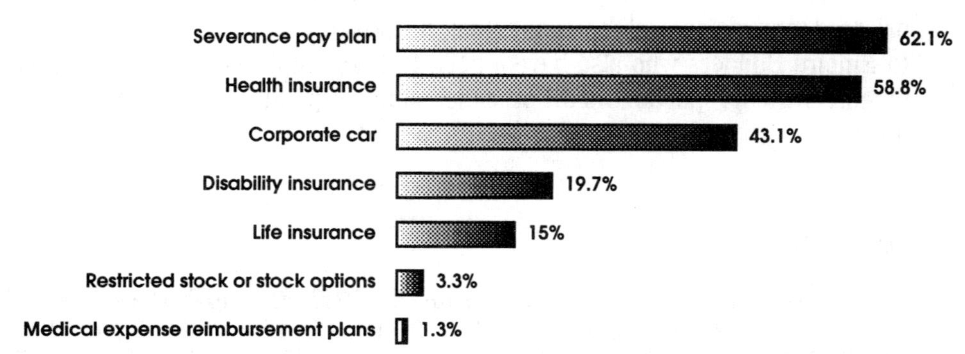

Number of Autocrats = 153

Figure 6.20

AUTOCRAT/EXECUTIVE BENEFITS SALES TRACK EXERCISE
Instructions: Write the name of an Autocrat type of family business owner below. If you can't think of a specific person, create a mental picture of an Autocrat and focus on that image for this exercise.
Instructions: Now list below the insurance products most appealing to Autocrats. (Refer to Figure 6.19 if you need to.)
Instructions: Next, write down the benefit Autocrats are seeking from their insurance. (Refer to Figure 6.18 if you need to.)
Instructions: Finally, write out some statements linking the specific features of the executive benefits products Autocrats are most interested in with the benefit they seek to achieve. For example: "Having the appropriate severance pay plans in place can help you move quickly when you need to replace managers, especially if they happen to be family members."

Rebels

Rebels need to create the impression for themselves and others that they are competent managers. Like the other family business owner segments, Rebels seek to achieve these benefits when they consider and purchase insurance products. In the case of executive benefits, they respond most favorably to an explanation of how an insurance purchase can enhance their image as quality managers. The positioning statement we created and tested was, "A well thought through executive benefits plan allows you to be seen as a high-quality manager." Almost all Rebels said this was the most important reason that they purchased executive benefits, as Figure 6.21 shows. This positioning statement has some appeal to the other segment concerned with its image, the Status Seekers, but note that it is not appealing to any other segment.

Rebels have a distinctive pattern of preferences in executive benefits. While Rebels are a relatively small segment of all family business owners, they are a particularly good market for executive benefits, as illustrated in Figure 6.22. Because Rebels want to be seen as effective managers and because many have prior corporate experience, they associate a comprehensive menu of executive benefits with good managerial ability. Most Rebels believe the core program of life insurance, health insurance and disability insurance (a relatively rich benefits menu for smaller businesses) is important.

This information should enable you to create effective sales presentations of executive benefits to the Rebel type of family business owner. The exercise in Figure 6.23 will enable you to do so easily by bringing together the information in this section and creating your own sales track.

Figure 6.21

POSITIONING STATEMENT: *A WELL THOUGHT THROUGH EXECUTIVE BENEFITS PLAN ALLOWS YOU TO BE SEEN AS A HIGH-QUALITY MANAGER*

(Percent of family business owners with an executive benefits plan who say this positioning statement is very important for them.)

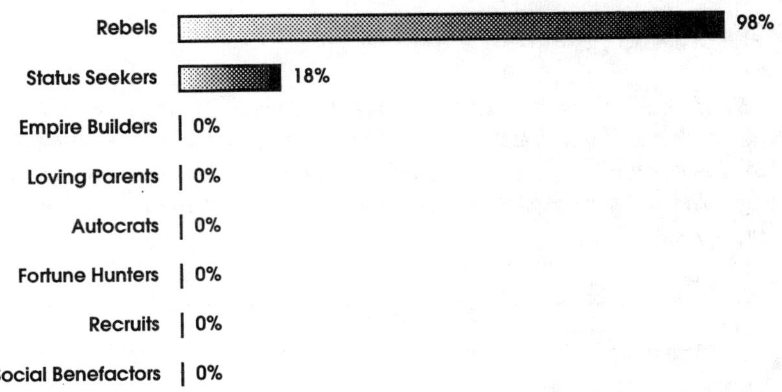

Number of Family Business Owners Who Recently Purchased Executive Benefits = 1,074

Figure 6.22

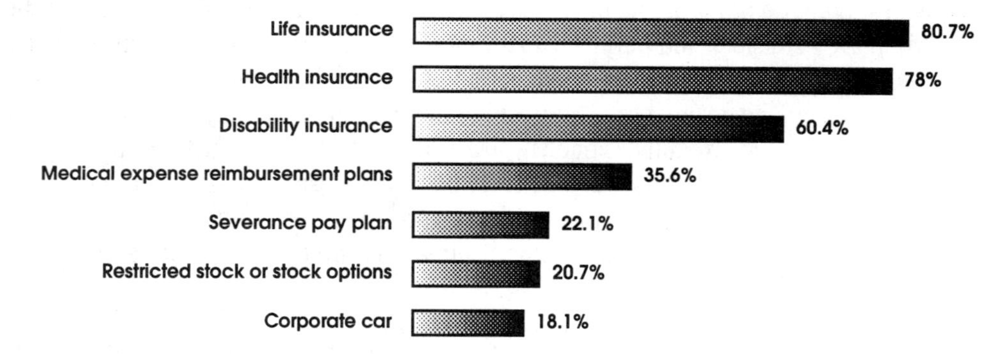

Number of Rebels = 149

Figure 6.23

REBEL/EXECUTIVE BENEFITS SALES TRACK EXERCISE
Instructions: Write the name of a Rebel type of family business owner below. If you can't think of a specific person, create a mental picture of a Rebel and focus on that image for this exercise.
Instructions: Now list below the insurance products most appealing to Rebels. (Refer to Figure 6.22 if you need to.)
Instructions: Next, write down the benefit Rebels are seeking from their insurance. (Refer to Figure 6.21 if you need to.)
Instructions: Finally, write out some statements linking the specific features of the executive benefits products Rebels are most interested in with the benefit they seek to achieve. For example: "A comprehensive executive benefits plan is the sign of good management. Well-run businesses are successful businesses, and a sign of a well-run business is a well-thought-out benefits plan. And life insurance is one piece of a top-flight benefits plan."

Recruits

Recruits are family business owners brought into the business by the family. Recruits have often had other careers or corporate positions before joining the family business. By personality, they respond to feelings of duty and obligation which their families communicate. The positioning statement we tested with over a thousand recent purchasers of executive benefits was, "There are certain kinds of benefits that family members expect." Recruits responded very positively to this positioning statement, with 94.2% agreeing strongly that it was the most important rationale for purchasing executive benefits. This positioning statement had some appeal to Rebels, but few members of other segments agreed, as shown in Figure 6.24. This means that insurance professionals selling to Recruits need to connect their products to family expectations.

Figure 6.24

POSITIONING STATEMENT: *THERE ARE CERTAIN KINDS OF BENEFITS THAT FAMILY MEMBERS EXPECT*

(Percent of family business owners with an executive benefits plan who say this positioning statement is very important for them.)

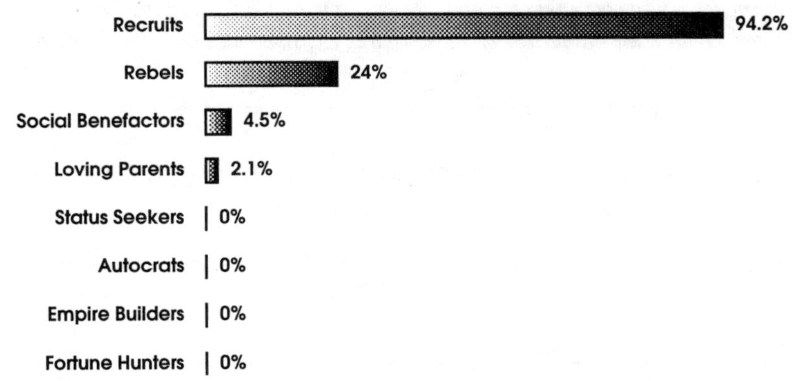

Number of Family Business Owners Who Recently Purchased Executive Benefits = 1,074

Recruits are a good market for executive benefits. Although they are a relatively small family business owner segment, Recruits are particularly good prospects for life insurance and health insurance benefits, as illustrated in Figure 6.25. Because Recruits are sensitive to the expectations of other family business members, they are inclined to obtain more benefits for family member managers in the business.

This information should enable you to create effective sales presentations of executive benefits to the Recruit type of family business owner. The exercise in Figure 6.26 will enable you to do so easily by bringing together the information in this section and creating your own sales track.

Figure 6.25

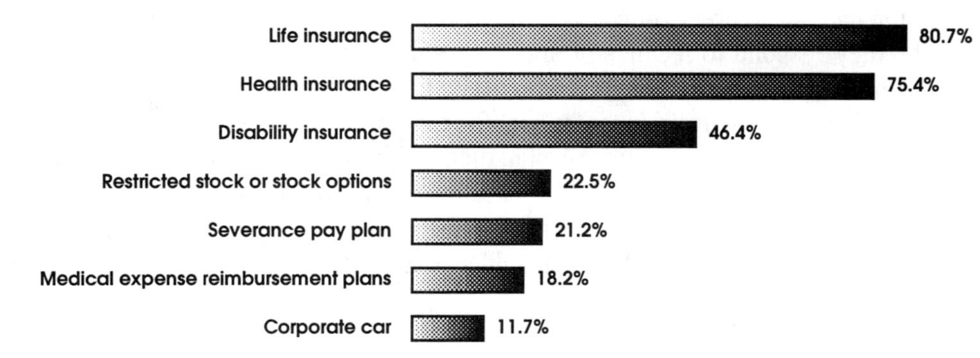

Number of Recruits = 137

Figure 6.26

RECRUIT/EXECUTIVE BENEFITS SALES TRACK EXERCISE
Instructions: Write the name of a Recruit type of family business owner below. If you can't think of a specific person, create a mental picture of a Recruit and focus on that image for this exercise.
Instructions: Now list below the insurance products most appealing to Recruits. (Refer to Figure 6.25 if you need to.)
Instructions: Next, write down the benefit Recruits are seeking from their insurance. (Refer to Figure 6.24 if you need to.)
Instructions: Finally, write out some statements linking the specific features of the executive benefits products Recruits are most interested in with the benefit they seek to achieve. For example: "Many family business owners have to be especially sensitive to the needs and expectations of other members of the family. Executive benefits, especially life and health insurance benefits, can be an effective way of responding to family expectations."

Fortune Hunters

Fortune Hunters are business owners who are motivated to increase their personal wealth. Compared to other business owners, they are less interested in taking care of or providing for other family members. They seek products and services which will enable them to amass personal wealth. Accordingly, the positioning statement we tested for this group was, "Executive benefits allow you to maximize your wealth through the business." As expected, Fortune Hunters responded very favorably to this positioning statement. As shown in Figure 6.27, nearly all Fortune Hunters agreed that this was the most important reason they recently purchased executive benefits products. A few Status Seekers concurred, but an exclusive focus on personal wealth is not particularly relevant for the other family business owner segments.

Figure 6.27

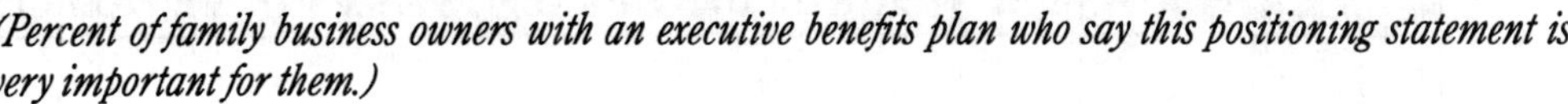

(Percent of family business owners with an executive benefits plan who say this positioning statement is very important for them.)

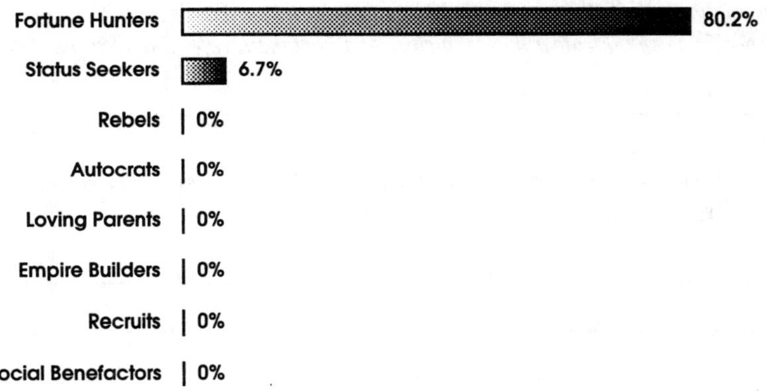

Number of Family Business Owners Who Recently Purchased Executive Benefits = 1,074

Fortune Hunters are less attractive as a market for executive benefits than some of the other segments. As Figure 6.28 illustrates, about half are interested in corporate cars and health insurance, but they are less interested in executive benefits which divert assets to indirect compensation of managers in the business. Because Fortune Hunters are interested in personal wealth, they are relatively disinterested in executive benefits.

This information should enable you to create effective sales presentations of executive benefits to the Fortune Hunter type of family business owner. The exercise in Figure 6.29 will enable you to do so easily by bringing together the information in this section and creating your own sales track.

Figure 6.28

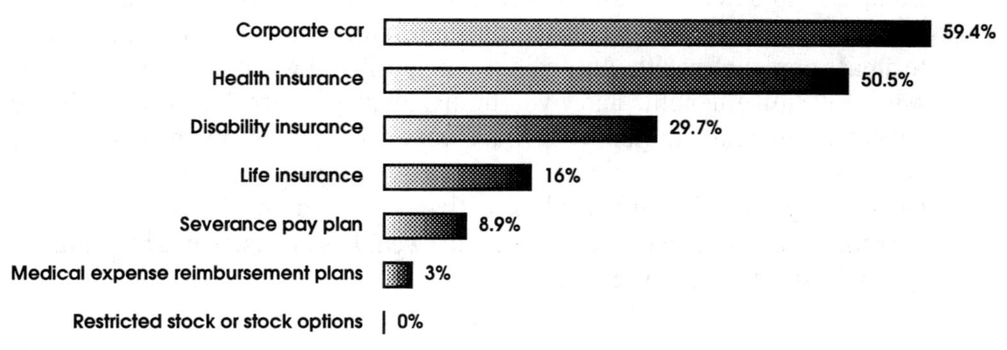

Number of Fortune Hunters = 101

Figure 6.29

FORTUNE HUNTER/EXECUTIVE BENEFITS SALES TRACK EXERCISE
Instructions: Write the name of a Fortune Hunter type of family business owner below. If you can't think of a specific person, create a mental picture of a Fortune Hunter and focus on that image for this exercise.
Instructions: Now list below the insurance products most appealing to Fortune Hunters. (Refer to Figure 6.28 if you need to.)
Instructions: Next, write down the benefit Fortune Hunters are seeking from their insurance. (Refer to Figure 6.27 if you need to.)
Instructions: Finally, write out some statements linking the specific features of the executive benefits products Fortune Hunters are most interested in with the benefit they seek to achieve. For example: "Getting health insurance through the business is a very good way to ensure your future and your ability to make money."

Status Seekers

Status Seekers are interested in social recognition and the respect of others in their various communities. The positioning statement created for them was designed to appeal to this sense, "Executive benefits allow you to reward yourself and be recognized." As expected, the Status Seeker segment responded well to this positioning statement for executive benefits. As shown in Figure 6.30, almost all agreed that this was the most important reason for their recent decision to buy executive benefits. Status Seeking motivations are not important to any of the other family business owner segments.

Figure 6.30

POSITIONING STATEMENT: *EXECUTIVE BENEFITS ALLOW YOU TO REWARD YOURSELF AND BE RECOGNIZED*

(Percent of family business owners with an executive benefits plan who say this positioning statement is very important for them.)

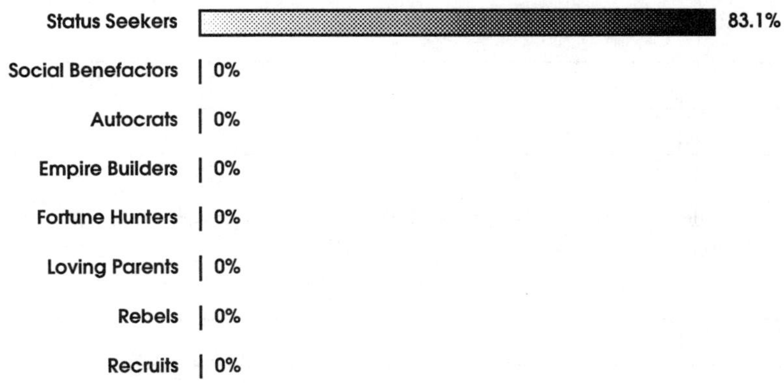

Number of Family Business Owners Who Recently Purchased Executive Benefits = 1,074

Although Status Seekers are a small segment, they are an attractive one for many executive benefits programs, especially those which reflect positively on their status in their businesses and communities. For example, they are extremely interested in corporate cars as executive benefits as shown in Figure 6.31. The "standard" benefits of life and health insurance are also seen as important because a business not providing these benefits will not be viewed well by others.

Figure 6.31

EXECUTIVE BENEFITS IMPORTANT TO STATUS SEEKERS

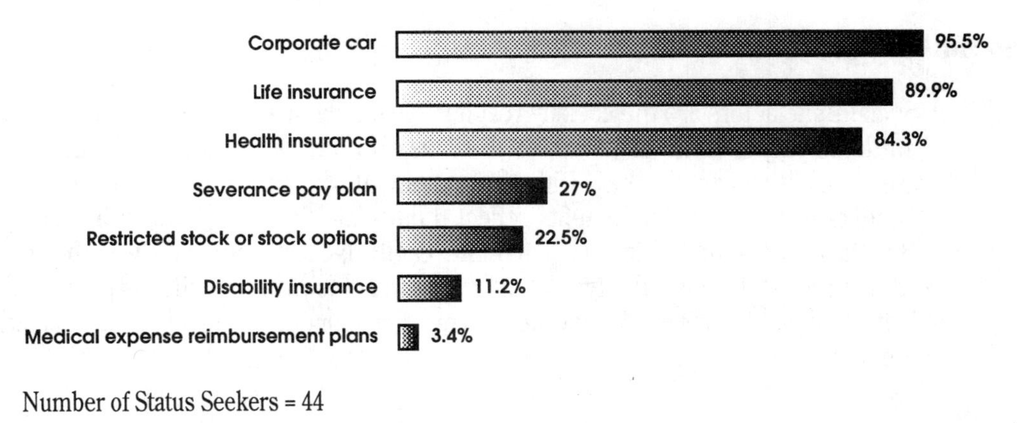

Number of Status Seekers = 44

This information should enable you to create effective sales presentations of executive benefits to the Status Seeker type of family business owner. The exercise in Figure 6.32 will enable you to do so easily by bringing together the information in this section and creating your own sales track.

Figure 6.32

STATUS SEEKER/EXECUTIVE BENEFITS SALES TRACK EXERCISE
Instructions: Write the name of a Status Seeker type of family business owner below. If you can't think of a specific person, create a mental picture of a Status Seeker and focus on that image for this exercise.
Instructions: Now list below the insurance products most appealing to Status Seekers. (Refer to Figure 6.31 if you need to.)
Instructions: Next, write down the benefit Status Seekers are seeking from their insurance. (Refer to Figure 6.30 if you need to.)
Instructions: Finally, write out some statements linking the specific features of the executive benefits products Status Seekers are most interested in with the benefit they seek to achieve. For example: "Many of my clients provide life and health insurance benefits. It puts them up there with other top business owners they know."

Social Benefactors

Social Benefactors are the socially responsible family business owners. They have a concern for the impact of their businesses on the lives of others and on the communities of which they are a part. Accordingly, the positioning statement written for them with respect to executive benefits was, "Executive benefits reflect the social responsibility of every company." Social Benefactors responded to this statement readily. Nearly 98% said it was the most important reason for establishing the type of executive benefits plan they did, as shown in Figure 6.33. Note that no members of any other segment responded positively to this positioning statement.

Figure 6.33

POSITIONING STATEMENT: *EXECUTIVE BENEFITS REFLECT THE SOCIAL RESPONSIBILITY OF EVERY COMPANY*

(Percent of family business owners with an executive benefits plan who say this positioning statement is very important for them.)

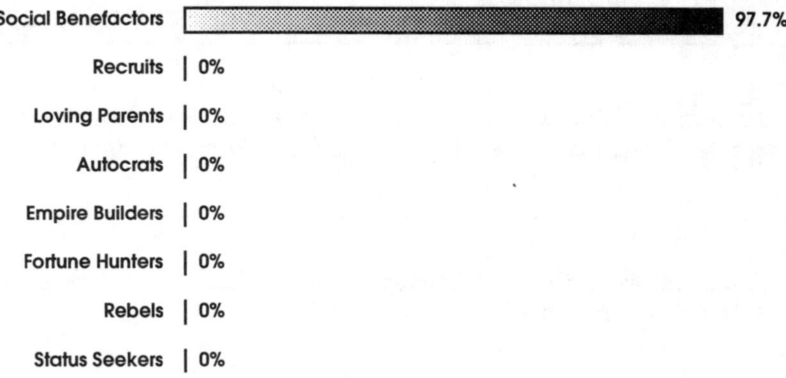

Number of Family Business Owners Who Recently Purchased Executive Benefits = 1,074

Although Social Benefactors are the smallest segment, they are an important one for executive benefits programs which enable them to express their feelings of social responsibility. For example, a higher percentage of Social Benefactors than any other segment was interested in health, life and disability insurance and in medical expense reimbursement plans. No Social Benefactors are interested in corporate car plans, as shown in Figure 6.34.

Figure 6.34

EXECUTIVE BENEFITS IMPORTANT TO SOCIAL BENEFACTORS

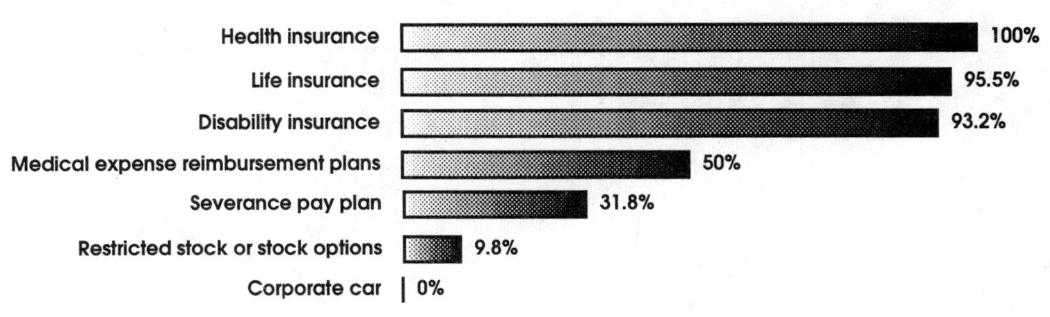

Number of Social Benefactors = 44

This information should enable you to create effective sales presentations of executive benefits to the Social Benefactor type of family business owner. The exercise in Figure 6.35 will enable you to do so easily by bringing together the information in this section and creating your own sales track.

Figure 6.35

SOCIAL BENEFACTOR/EXECUTIVE BENEFITS SALES TRACK EXERCISE
Instructions: Write the name of a Social Benefactor type of family business owner below. If you can't think of a specific person, create a mental picture of a Social Benefactor and focus on that image for this exercise.
Instructions: Now list below the insurance products most appealing to Social Benefactors. (Refer to Figure 6.34 if you need to.)
Instructions: Next, write down the benefit Social Benefactors are seeking from their insurance. (Refer to Figure 6.33 if you need to.)
Instructions: Finally, write out some statements linking the specific features of the executive benefits products Social Benefactors are most interested in with the benefit they seek to achieve. For example: "It's sad that many business owners do not consider life and health insurance to be essential. To my mind, it's just being ethical or socially responsible to provide these as minimum benefits in any executive benefits program."

Your Action Plan

- Identify three current family business owner prospects for your services. Write their names in Figure 6.36.
- Specify which of the eight types of family business owner they are.
- Write down how you would position your services.
- Designate which products you would present to each client.

Figure 6.36

Family Business Owner	Family Business Owner Psychological Type	How I will position my services	Products I will emphasize
1.			
2.			
3.			

CHAPTER 7
RETIREMENT PLANNING

Richard Bentley reviewed the two profit sharing proposals for the final time, then slipped them into his briefcase and set out.

His first visit was the tool and die plant of William Barrister. Bentley has determined that Barrister is an Autocrat. He is commanding and dictatorial with the people in this firm. He is somewhat contentious and demanding to do business with. Bentley started off the discussion of the retirement plan by explaining that profit sharing "is the best way to motivate employees to work hard and focus on the business. If they do produce profits, their retirement plan gets funded, if they don't, it doesn't."

That same afternoon Bentley kept his appointment with Veronica Lister, the owner of Get Away Travel. Bentley had concluded that Lister is a Social Benefactor type. She is very interested in taking care of other members of the family and her employees in a caring, socially responsible way. For Lister, Bentley explained that the profit sharing plan was an "excellent way to be responsible and caring for your people. The travel business is uncertain with all the economic ups and downs but with this plan you can assure everyone that if the business does well, everyone will do well. And if it doesn't, then you will all share in the risks, too. It's a very ethical plan."

That evening, Bentley reflected, "There is something to this personality type thing. I took the same retirement plan to two business owners. The plans even had many of the same features, but because I talked about them in two different ways, it looks like I will close on them both."

Retirement plans are a core part of the benefit structure of many small businesses. Although they can be expensive, they are often demanded by family members who are employees and they are necessary if a business is to attract managers as it begins to grow.

There are many variations in configuring retirement plans which affect the calculation of employer contributions as well as the calculation of the benefit payout to employees. These retirement plan features are typically evaluated on the basis of the financial characteristics and prospects of the business and the values and preferences of the owner.

It is this latter set of factors that makes the segmentation approach meaningful in retirement planning. The values and motivations owners express for their businesses, which we generally have been discussing, extend into the values by which owners make decisions about the scale and type of retirement plan to install in their businesses. As illustrated in the example above, the same retirement plan can appeal to business owners of different psychological types for very different reasons.

Family businesses are a platform for providing family members and employees with retirement plans. There are various ways life insurance professionals can insure that family members and employees participate in such plans. Family business owners vary in the extent to which retirement planning is meaningful to them and in their awareness of what they can achieve with retirement planning.

The Importance of Retirement Planning

Retirement planning presents a range of future forms of reward for employees and management, both direct and indirect. A retirement plan can be a defined contribution or a defined benefit type of plan. It can include various forms of deferred compensation plans and can be skewed to reward certain subgroups in the covered population (e.g., senior employees). The richness of a retirement plan can be linked to the financial performance of the firm.

Prevalence of Retirement Planning

Family business owners as a group tend to agree that some retirement planning programs are more appealing, more important, and more relevant to their circumstances than others. As might be expected, it is these plans that they have a greater interest in buying. Check your knowledge of the retirement planning market among family business owners in Figure 7.01.

Figure 7.01

RETIREMENT PLANNING EXERCISE

Instructions: Check whether family business owners as a group feel that each of these retirement plan structures is very important, somewhat important or less important.

Retirement Plan Provision	Very Important	Somewhat Important	Less Important
Employees share in gains and losses	❑	❑	❑
Flexible contributions	❑	❑	❑
Salary deferrals for employees	❑	❑	❑
Large benefits for older employees	❑	❑	❑
Predictable retirement benefits	❑	❑	❑
Fixed contributions	❑	❑	❑

As shown in Figure 7.02, about three quarters of all family business owners believe that having employees share in gains and losses is an important way to structure a retirement plan. Over half think that some form of flexible contributions is important. Both of these groups of business owners find that their business results are variable and are reluctant to be tied to a fixed contribution obligation for company retirement plans. This is also revealed by the very small proportion (only 1.8%) who feel that fixed contribution plans are important.

Deferred compensation plans, as a part of retirement planning, are important to about a third of all businesses owners. About a quarter want to insure some predictability over what retirement plans will pay out, either in the form of assuring larger benefits for older employees or planning for predictable retirement benefits.

Figure 7.02

IMPORTANCE OF RETIREMENT PLANNING

Employees share in gains and losses	73%
Flexible contributions	60.7%
Salary deferrals for employees	34.5%
Large benefits for older employees	25.4%
Predictable retirement benefits	22.6%
Fixed contributions	1.8%

Number of Family Business Owners Who Recently Purchased Retirement Planning = 1,121

Figure 7.03 illustrates that, as Bentley suspected, profit sharing is important to the Autocrat personality type and the Social Benefactor segment although, as we have seen, for different reasons. Having employees share in company gains and losses is also important to the Recruit segment, the Loving Parent and Empire Builder segments.

Figure 7.03

IMPORTANCE OF HAVING EMPLOYEES SHARE IN GAINS AND LOSSES

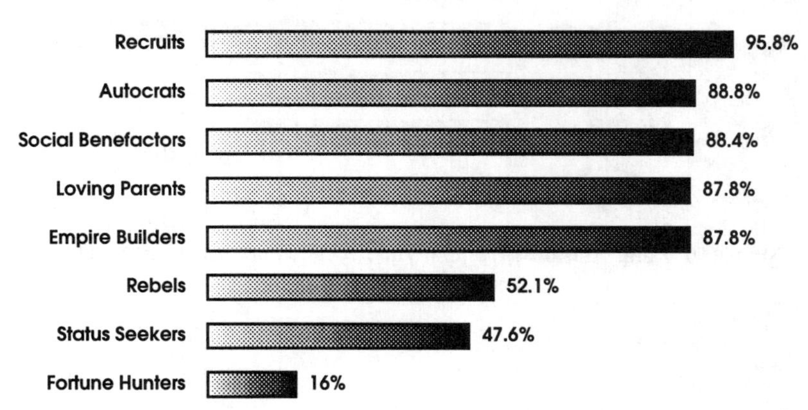

Number of Family Business Owners Who Recently Purchased Retirement Planning = 1,121

Again, the motivation for profit sharing plans is different for the various segments. Recruits, concerned about family opinion and expectations, want a defensible plan. Loving Parents want to keep the family peace and appear equitable and thus find that linking family reward to family effort and performance is appealing. Empire Builders, like Autocrats, want to use benefits to motivate employees to specific business-building behaviors and like variable contribution profit sharing plans because they create a solid bridge between performance and reward.

Rebels and Status Seekers are less drawn to profit sharing plans. These segments think it is important for employees to share in gains and losses by the company. Fortune Hunters are generally disinterested in any retirement plan (except one, as we will see later) since their goal is to amass personal wealth.

As Figure 7.04 shows, the same three groups — Loving Parents, Social Benefactors and Autocrats — think flexible contributions in retirement plans are important. Almost as many Recruits and Empire Builders agree. Fewer Rebels and Status Seekers find flexible contribution plans attractive. And as mentioned before, no Fortune Hunters believe that defined contribution plans are important.

When it comes to the use of salary deferrals for employees, results are spread out as illustrated in Figure 7.05. Loving Parents find deferred compensation a good way to bind children even more tightly to the family enterprise and to help them take care of their own future needs responsibly. Empire Builders also show some interest in salary deferrals because they help motivate employees. Only 32.6% of Social Benefactors, 28.5% of Recruits, 25.6% of Autocrats and 25.2% of Status Seekers say they believe in the importance of salary deferrals for employees. Rebels and Fortune Hunters display little interest.

Figure 7.04

IMPORTANCE OF FLEXIBLE CONTRIBUTIONS

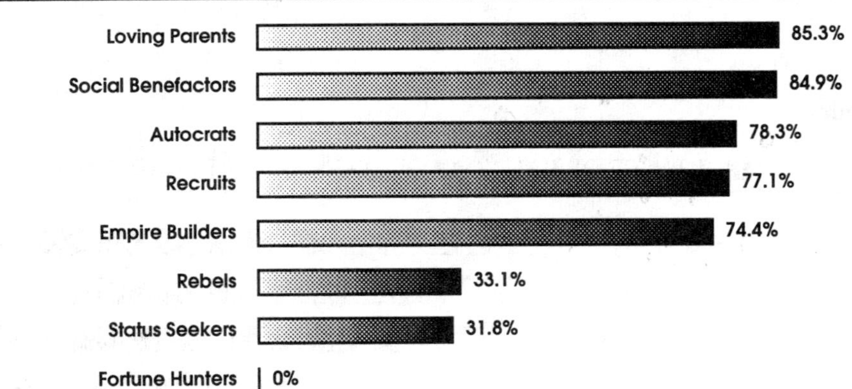

Number of Family Business Owners Who Recently Purchased Retirement Planning = 1,121

Figure 7.05

IMPORTANCE OF SALARY DEFERRALS FOR EMPLOYEES

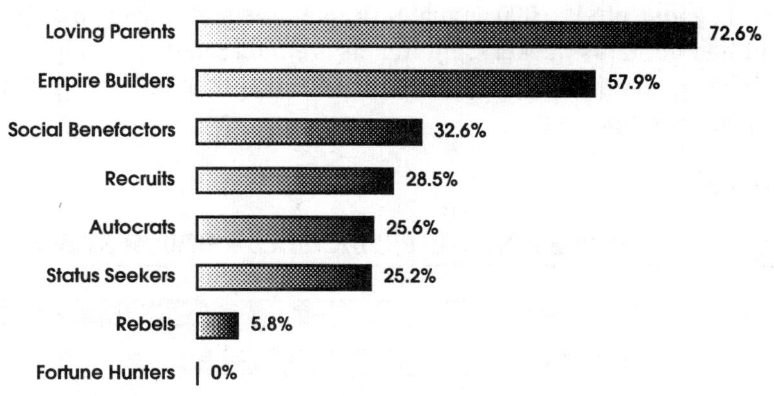

Number of Family Business Owners Who Recently Purchased Retirement Planning = 1,121

Age-weighted plans, where larger benefits are allocated to older employees, appeal to business owners based on their personal situation as well as the factors of company finances and personal values which we discussed before. It is worth noting that Fortune Hunters emerged as the segment most interested in this type of retirement plan, probably because they perceived the possibility that they could emerge with significant personal benefits. Fully 82.7% of Fortune Hunters say such plans are very important to them, as shown in Figure 7.06. About half of Status Seekers and Rebels agree that this type of plan is appealing, as do smaller proportions of the other groups.

Figure 7.06

IMPORTANCE OF LARGE BENEFITS FOR OLDER EMPLOYEES

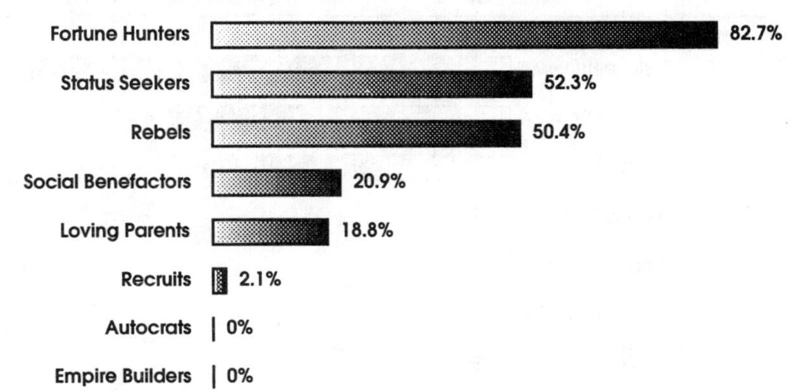

Number of Family Business Owners Who Recently Purchased Retirement Planning = 1,121

Retirement plans with predictable benefits (such as defined benefit plans) are, not surprisingly, especially appealing to Fortune Hunters. They see the possibility for personal gain. As shown in Figure 7.07, 95.5% of Fortune Hunters are very interested in these plans. The idea of $120,000 annual retirement benefit proves to be particularly appealing. About half of Status Seekers and Rebels are interested in such plans because of the "big company status." Less than five percent of each of the other segments think defined benefit plans are important.

Figure 7.07

IMPORTANCE OF PREDICTABLE RETIREMENT BENEFITS

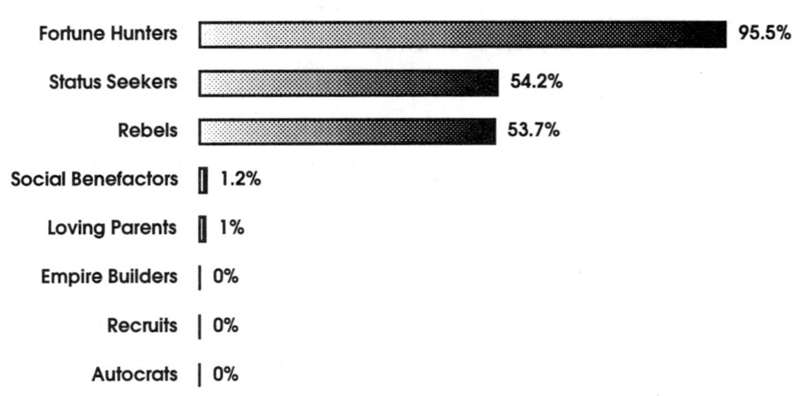

Number of Family Business Owners Who Recently Purchased Retirement Planning = 1,121

Of all retirement plan options, family business owners are least interested in fixed contribution plans. Fewer than 10% of any personality type said they thought fixed contribution plans were a very important part of retirement planning, as Figure 7.08 shows. The reason for this is that most small to medium sized business owners are well aware that revenues can fluctuate significantly. Family business owners also know that family exigencies may also affect the demands on the business. As a result, family business owners try to stay as flexible as possible and generally will not want to commit themselves to any kind of fixed contribution plan.

Figure 7.08

IMPORTANCE OF FIXED CONTRIBUTIONS

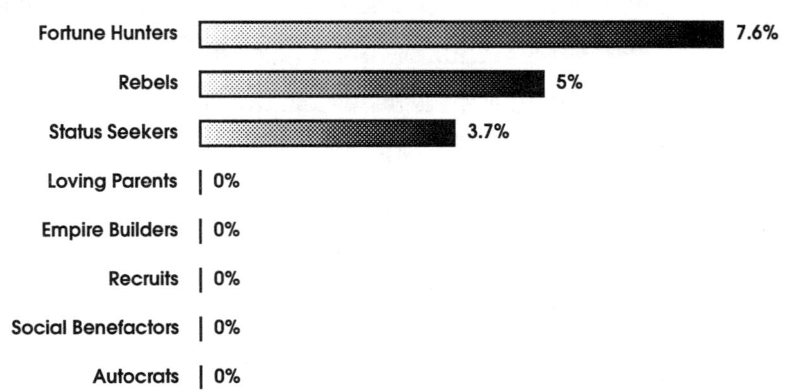

Number of Family Business Owners Who Recently Purchased Retirement Planning = 1,121

Key Market Segments for Retirement Planning

The market for retirement planning spreads across all the personality types. The largest segment, Loving Parents, has less than twenty percent and the smallest, Social Benefactors has less than ten percent, as shown in Figure 7.09. Some segments are more predisposed to retirement planning than their distribution in the population would indicate. Included here are Empire Builders, Recruits, Fortune Hunters, Rebels, Status Seekers, and Social Benefactors. These types are relatively more interested in retirement plans. The interesting exception is Loving Parents.

Figure 7.09

DISTRIBUTION OF FAMILY BUSINESS SEGMENTS: BUYERS OF RETIREMENT PLANNING AND NATIONALLY		
Family Business Segment	**Recent Purchasers of Retirement Planning**	**National Distribution of Segments**
Loving Parents	17.6%	34.1%
Empire Builders	15.3%	13.0%
Autocrats	14.4%	19.2%
Recruits	12.8%	7.8%
Fortune Hunters	11.9%	8.9%
Rebels	10.8%	6.5%
Status Seekers	9.5%	5.7%
Social Benefactors	7.7%	4.8%
Number of Family Business Owners Who Recently Purchased Retirement Planning = 1,121		

Although Loving Parents account for one in three business owners nationally, they make up a smaller proportion of those interested in retirement plans — only 17.6%. Autocrats are also under-represented. This is because the head of the business (and family) of these two groups is highly reluctant to consider retirement. Heads of business owning families in these two groups are attached to the power and role that status gives them within the family. They like control over their children's lives and realize that this control only exists while they remain head of the business as well as head of the family.

Positioning Your Practice

As we have seen with respect to executive benefits in Chapter 6 and with respect to retirement benefits, each type of family business owner sees insurance products differently. That is, each has a unique set of needs and wants, and therefore each personality type sees a different benefit. Clearly, emphasizing a benefit that is especially appealing and relevant to a family business owner will be more likely to succeed than talking up a benefit which is not relevant to the segment. Knowing exactly which benefits appeal to each segment is critical to successful retirement plan sales. It is crucial that you position retirement planning properly with each family business segment. You can begin with the retirement planning positioning exercise in Figure 7.10.

Figure 7.10

POSITIONING RETIREMENT PLANNING EXERCISE	
Instructions: Write out a phrase which describes retirement planning in words especially meaningful to each family business owner segment.	
Loving Parents	
Empire Builders	
Autocrats	
Recruits	
Fortune Hunters	
Rebels	
Status Seekers	
Social Benefactors	

In the sections below you will be able to compare your positioning statements against those we created and tested with eleven hundred family business owners.

Loving Parents

For example, we created the positioning statement, "A retirement plan can be used to take care of future financial needs of family members." All the family business owners in the study were asked to rate how important this reason was for them personally in obtaining the coverage that they did.

As Figure 7.11 shows, this reason is extremely important to almost all Loving Parents because they are most interested in taking care of their families now and in later generations. Because Loving Parents manage the business as a legacy for their families, they respond positively to products positioned to help them maintain the economic security of the family. As Figure 7.11 also illustrates, this reason is of minor or no importance to the other segments. You can see the advantages of positioning retirement planning as a way of taking care of the family to Loving Parents and you can also see that this positioning has little appeal to any other segment. In marketing retirement planning to Loving Parents, however, you should be careful of the anti-retirement feelings of the family head, as discussed earlier.

Figure 7.11

POSITIONING STATEMENT: *A RETIREMENT PLAN CAN BE USED TO TAKE CARE OF FUTURE FINANCIAL NEEDS OF FAMILY MEMBERS*

(Percent of family business owners with a retirement plan who say this positioning statement is very important for them.)

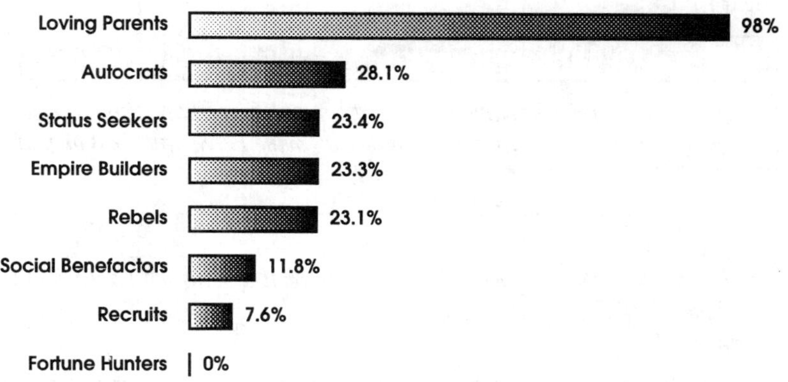

Number of Family Business Owners Who Recently Purchased Retirement Planning = 1,121

Among the different retirement plan structures, Loving Parents are most interested in profit sharing plans, flexible contribution plans, and salary deferrals for employees, as Figure 7.12 shows. The other three types of plans — those providing larger benefits for older employees and predictable retirement benefits and fixed contributions — are less important to Loving Parents.

Figure 7.12

BENEFITS OF RETIREMENT PLANS IMPORTANT TO LOVING PARENTS

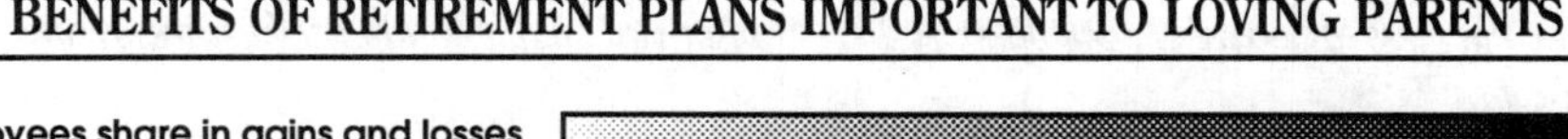

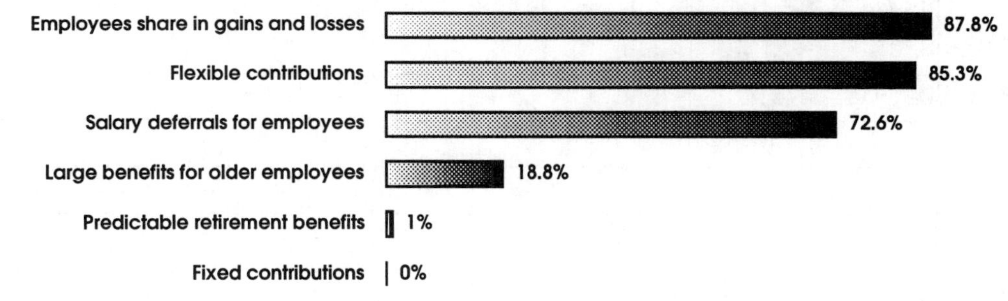

Number of Loving Parents = 197

Based on this information, you should be able to create effective sales presentations positioning retirement planning effectively to Loving Parents. The exercise in Figure 7.13 will enable you to do so easily by pulling together the information in this section and creating your own sales track.

Figure 7.13

LOVING PARENT/RETIREMENT PLANNING SALES TRACK EXERCISE
Instructions: Write the name of a Loving Parent type of family business owner below. If you can't think of a specific person, create a mental picture of a Loving Parent and focus on that image for this exercise.
Instructions: Now list below the types of retirement plans most appealing to Loving Parents. (Refer to Figure 7.12 if you need to.)
Instructions: Next, write down the benefit Loving Parents are seeking from their retirement plans. (Refer to Figure 7.11 if you need to.)
Instructions: Finally, write out some statements linking the specific features of the retirement planning products Loving Parents are most interested in with the benefit they seek to achieve. For example, "I know you may not be personally interested in retiring, but retirement planning is a way other close families in business take care of each other. A 401(k) plan will enable you to use business resources to safeguard your family."

Empire Builders

The second most important segment for retirement planning is the Empire Builders. Empire Builders have a very different goal for their businesses than Loving Parents do. Empire Builders want to create big businesses from small businesses. Only the large scale will do for this ambitious segment. Accordingly, for this segment we created the positioning statement, "A retirement plan is designed to foster maximum growth in the business."

For Empire Builders, the key benefit of all financial and insurance products is how they contribute to the goal of business growth. Since retirement plans can motivate managers and employees in the business, they can be a boon to growth. This is an extremely effective positioning for Empire Builders, as Figure 7.14 shows. Nearly all Empire Builders who have recently purchased retirement plans said that this statement is a very important reflection of their reasons for doing so. Note also that this reason is not particularly relevant for any other segment.

Figure 7.14

POSITIONING STATEMENT: *A RETIREMENT PLAN IS DESIGNED TO FOSTER MAXIMUM GROWTH IN THE BUSINESS*

(Percent of family business owners with a retirement plan who say this positioning statement is very important for them.)

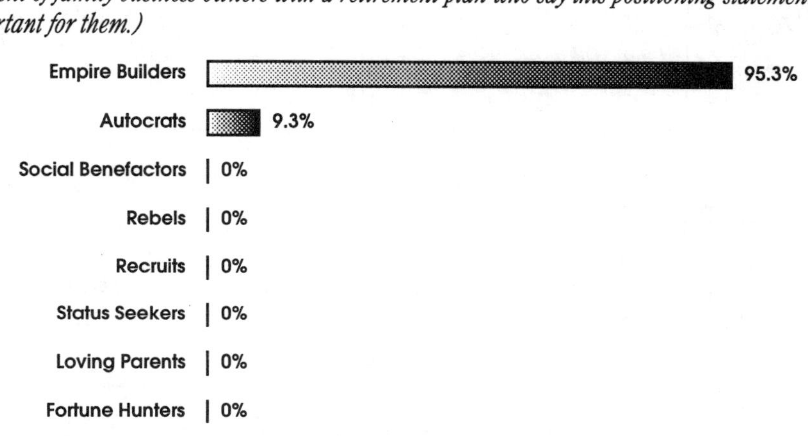

Number of Family Business Owners Who Recently Purchased Retirement Planning = 1,121

Like Loving Parents, Figure 7.15 shows that Empire Builders are only seriously interested in three plan benefits: (1) employees share in the gains and losses; (2) flexible contribution plans; and (3) salary deferrals for employees. This personality type has no interest in the other three benefits of retirement plans.

Figure 7.15

BENEFITS OF RETIREMENT PLANNING IMPORTANT TO EMPIRE BUILDERS

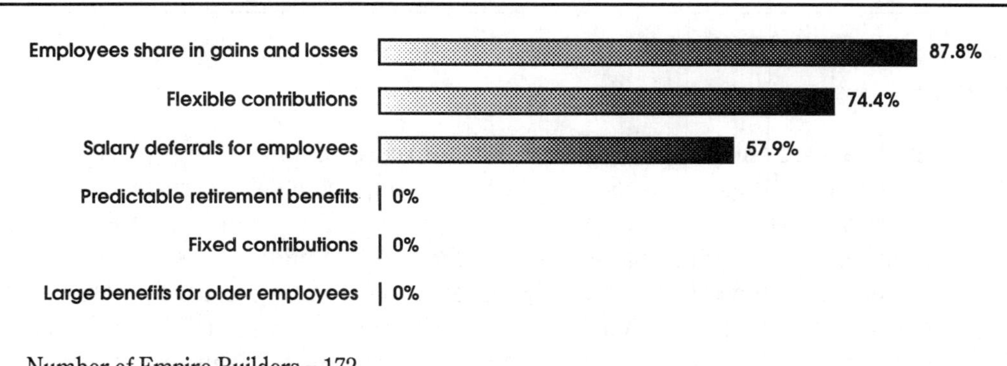

Number of Empire Builders = 172

Based on this information, you should be able to create effective sales presentations positioning retirement planning effectively to Empire Builders. The exercise in Figure 7.16 will enable you to do so easily by pulling together the information in this section and creating your own sales track.

Figure 7.16

EMPIRE BUILDER/RETIREMENT PLANNING SALES TRACK EXERCISE
Instructions: Write the name of an Empire Builder type of family business owner below. If you can't think of a specific person, create a mental picture of an Empire Builder and focus on that image for this exercise.
Instructions: Now list below the types of retirement plans most appealing to Empire Builders. (Refer to Figure 7.15 if you need to.)
Instructions: Next, write down the benefit Empire Builders are seeking from their retirement plans. (Refer to Figure 7.14 if you need to.)
Instructions: Finally, write out some statements linking the specific features of the retirement planning products Empire Builders are most interested in with the benefit they seek to achieve. For example: "Certain kinds of retirement plans have been effective for other business owners I know in motivating managers to grow the business."

Autocrats

Autocrats are one of the larger segments for retirement planning products. They can be appealed to on the aspect of control. The positioning statement we created and tested with over a thousand recent retirement plan purchasers was, "A retirement plan is an effective way of insuring and controlling managerial retention and commitment." As shown in Figure 7.17, this positioning statement was extremely appealing to Autocrats because they are oriented towards control. You should note that this positioning statement was much less appealing to all other segments. If you were to emphasize the use of retirement planning in controlling employee motivation to any other segment they would not be motivated to buy.

Figure 7.17

POSITIONING STATEMENT: *A RETIREMENT PLAN IS AN EFFECTIVE WAY OF INSURING AND CONTROLLING MANAGERIAL RETENTION AND COMMITMENT*

(Percent of family business owners with a retirement plan who say this positioning statement is very important for them.)

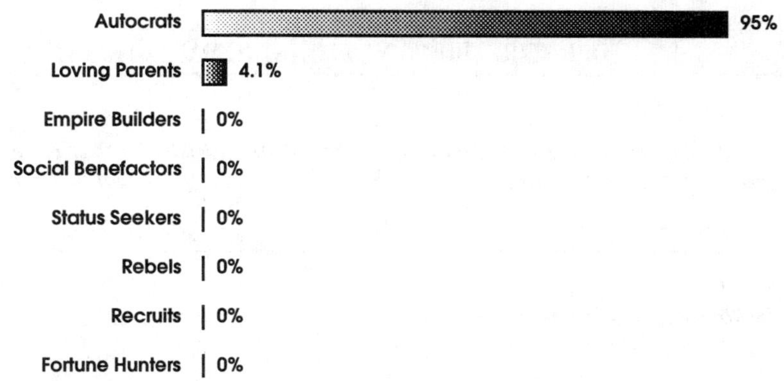

Number of Family Business Owners Who Recently Purchased Retirement Planning = 1,121

Autocrats have a highly restricted set of preferences when it comes to retirement plans. Autocrats are only interested in flexible contributions and salary deferrals for employees — in effect, 401(k) plans. Not a single Autocrat family business owner thought consideration of any of the other plan types was very important, as shown in Figure 7.18.

Figure 7.18

BENEFITS OF RETIREMENT PLANNING IMPORTANT TO AUTOCRATS

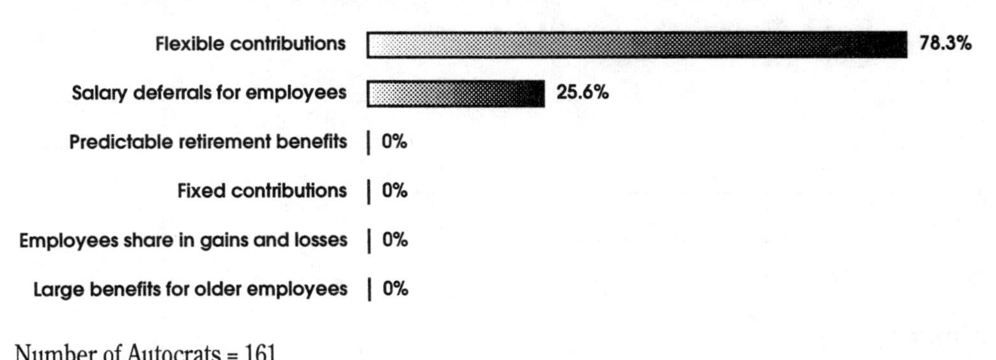

Number of Autocrats = 161

Based on this information, you should be able to create effective sales presentations positioning retirement planning effectively to the Autocrat type of family business owner. The exercise in Figure 7.19 will enable you to do so easily by pulling together the information in this section and creating your own sales track.

Figure 7.19

AUTOCRAT/RETIREMENT PLANNING SALES TRACK EXERCISE
Instructions: Write the name of an Autocrat type of family business owner below. If you can't think of a specific person, create a mental picture of an Autocrat and focus on that image for this exercise.
Instructions: Now list below the types of retirement plans most appealing to Autocrats. (Refer to Figure 7.18 if you need to.)
Instructions: Next, write down the benefit Autocrats are seeking from their retirement plans. (Refer to Figure 7.17 if you need to.)
Instructions: Finally, write out some statements linking the specific features of the retirement planning products Autocrats are most interested in with the benefit they seek to achieve. For example, "Since controlling employees is so critical for success in business today, I would recommend a 401(k) plan for your business. This plan will give you the greatest control."

Recruits

Recruits need to take care of the families that invested them with the responsibility of running their businesses. Thus, the positioning statement we created and tested which was designed to appeal especially to Recruits read, "A retirement plan designed to meet your family's expectations." Almost all Recruits said this was the most important reason they purchased retirement planning, as shown in Figure 7.20. This positioning statement has some appeal to the other segment concerned with meeting the expectations of the family — Loving Parents. But, note that it is not generally appealing to any other segment.

Figure 7.20

POSITIONING STATEMENT: *A RETIREMENT PLAN DESIGNED TO MEET YOUR FAMILY'S EXPECTATIONS*

(Percent of family business owners with a retirement plan who say this positioning statement is very important for them.)

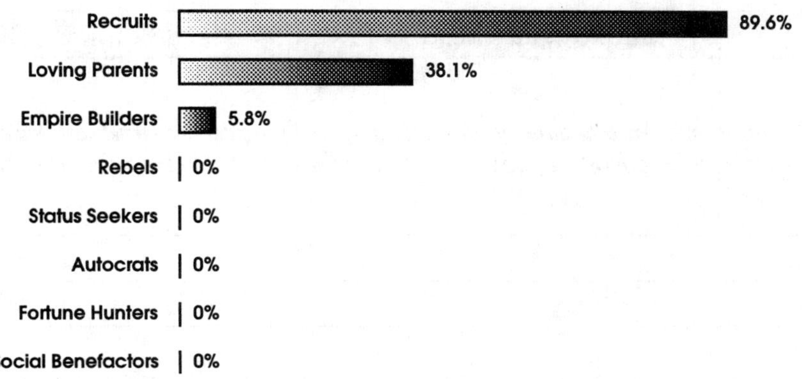

Number of Family Business Owners Who Recently Purchased Retirement Planning = 1,121

As Figure 7.21 illustrates, recruits have at least some interest in several retirement plan benefits. While most favor employees sharing in the gains and losses and flexible contributions, some are interested in predictable retirement benefits and salary deferrals for employees. Only large benefits for older employees and fixed contributions hold little interest for Recruits. In effect, they prefer profit sharing plans.

Figure 7.21

BENEFITS OF RETIREMENT PLANNING IMPORTANT TO RECRUITS

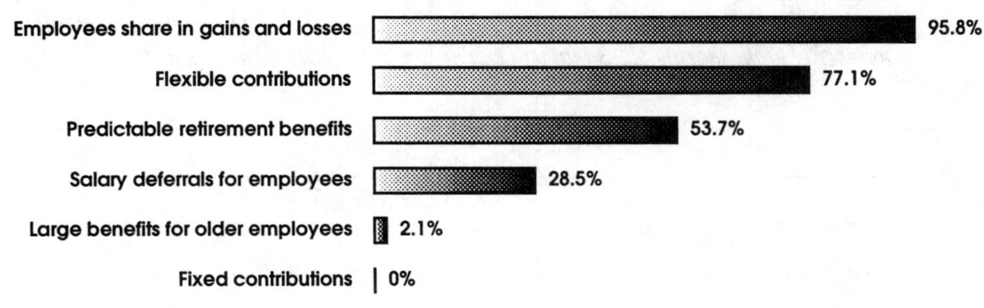

Number of Recruits = 144

Based on this information, you should be able to create effective sales presentations positioning retirement planning effectively to the Recruit type of family business owner. The exercise in Figure 7.22 will enable you to do so easily by pulling together the information in this section and creating your own sales track.

Figure 7.22

RECRUIT/RETIREMENT PLANNING SALES TRACK EXERCISE
Instructions: Write the name of a Recruit type of family business owner below. If you can't think of a specific person, create a mental picture of a Recruit and focus on that image for this exercise.
Instructions: Now list below the types of retirement plans most appealing to Recruits. (Refer to Figure 7.21 if you need to.)
Instructions: Next, write down the benefit Recruits are seeking from their retirement plans. (Refer to Figure 7.20 if you need to.)
Instructions: Finally, write out some statements linking the specific features of the retirement planning products Recruits are most interested in with the benefit they seek to achieve. For example, "There are a number of profit sharing plans that will enable you to comfortably meet your family's expectations."

Fortune Hunters

Fortune Hunters are driven by the need to accumulate personal assets. They are relatively disinterested in the goals of other family business owners such as caring for the family or leaving the business as a family legacy. On the basis of understanding their motivations, the positioning statement we created and tested with over a thousand recent purchasers of retirement planning was, "A retirement plan that will provide a substantial payout to the owners." Fortune Hunters, as expected, responded very positively to this positioning statement. As shown in Figure 7.23, 91.7% agreed strongly that it was the most important rationale in their purchase of retirement insurance. This positioning statement had slight appeal to Rebels and Status Seekers, but none for members of other segments. This means that life insurance professionals selling to Fortune Hunters need to connect their products to wealth accumulation.

Fortune Hunters are a good market for specific types of retirement plans. Figure 7.24 shows that they are very interested in plans which provide predictable retirement benefits and are the only segment to be so interested. They also are interested in plans which provide for a

Figure 7.23

POSITIONING STATEMENT: *A RETIREMENT PLAN THAT WILL PROVIDE A SUBSTANTIAL PAYOUT TO THE OWNERS*

(Percent of family business owners with a retirement plan who say this positioning statement is very important for them.)

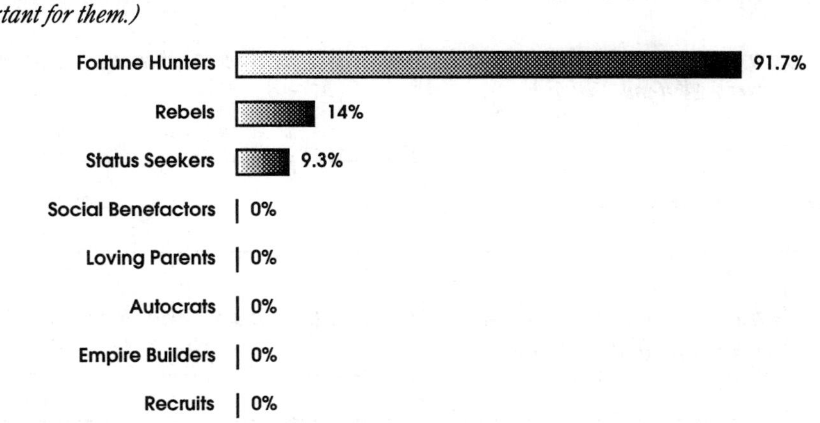

Number of Family Business Owners Who Recently Purchased Retirement Planning = 1,121

Figure 7.24

BENEFITS OF RETIREMENT PLANNING IMPORTANT TO FORTUNE HUNTERS

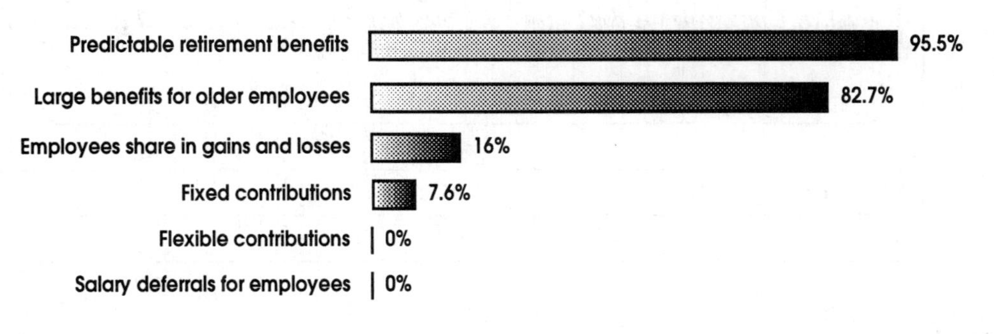

Number of Fortune Hunters = 133

large payout for older employees. Assuming they are among this group, it means they will be able to take advantage of the large benefit amounts. Unlike the other segments, they are not interested in employees sharing in the gains and losses, flexible contributions, or deferred compensation.

Based on this information, you should be able to create effective sales presentations positioning retirement planning effectively to the Fortune Hunter type of family business owner. The exercise in Figure 7.25 will enable you to do so easily by pulling together the information in this section and creating your own sales track.

Figure 7.25

FORTUNE HUNTER/RETIREMENT PLANNING SALES TRACK EXERCISE
Instructions: Write the name of a Fortune Hunter type of family business owner below. If you can't think of a specific person, create a mental picture of a Fortune Hunter and focus on that image for this exercise.
Instructions: Now list below the types of retirement plans most appealing to Fortune Hunters. (Refer to Figure 7.24 if you need to.)
Instructions: Next, write down the benefit Fortune Hunters are seeking from their retirement plans. (Refer to Figure 7.23 if you need to.)
Instructions: Finally, write out some statements linking the specific features of the retirement planning products Fortune Hunters are most interested in with the benefit they seek to achieve. For example: "Considering you don't have a qualified plan yet, a 412(i) plan will provide for a substantial benefit to you, significantly increasing your retirement income."

Rebels

Rebels are typically ex-corporate employees who are striving to prove themselves as competent and independent managers. They tend to use corporations as their reference point when making business decisions including decisions about retirement planning. As a result, the positioning statement we tested for this group was, "A retirement plan that is better than any large company's retirement plan." As expected, Rebels responded very favorably to this positioning statement. As shown in Figure 7.26, almost all Rebels agreed that this was the most important reason they recently purchased the retirement plan they did. A few Fortune Hunters concurred, but no one from any of the other segments shared this viewpoint.

As shown in Figure 7.27, Rebels are one of the few segments interested in predictable retirement benefits such as those provided by defined benefit plans. About as many say they also think the characteristics of a profit sharing plan are important. Age-weighted plans which provide a larger benefit for older employees are of about the same significance.

Figure 7.26

POSITIONING STATEMENT: *A RETIREMENT PLAN THAT IS BETTER THAN ANY LARGE COMPANY'S RETIREMENT PLAN*

(Percent of family business owners with a retirement plan who say this positioning statement is very important for them.)

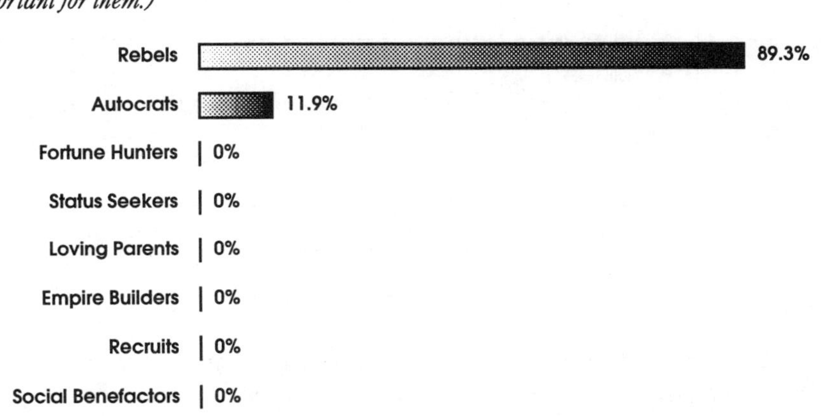

Number of Family Business Owners Who Recently Purchased Retirement Planning = 1,121

Figure 7.27

BENEFITS OF RETIREMENT PLANNING IMPORTANT TO REBELS

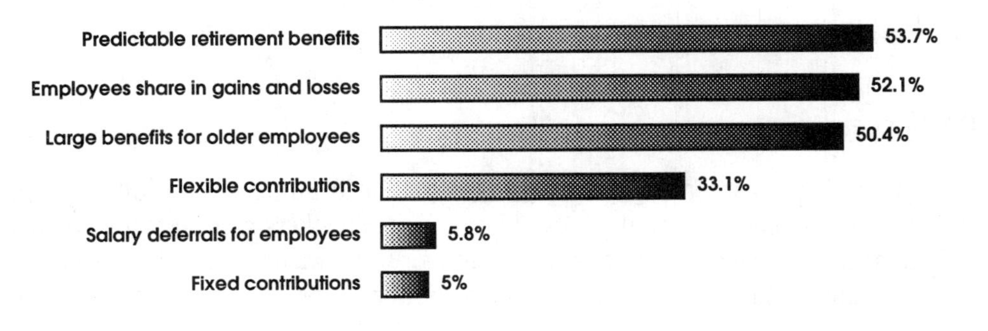

Number of Rebels = 121

Based on this information, you should be able to create effective sales presentations positioning retirement planning effectively to the Rebel type of family business owner. The exercise in Figure 7.28 will enable you to do so easily by pulling together the information in this section and creating your own sales track.

Figure 7.28

REBEL/RETIREMENT PLANNING SALES TRACK EXERCISE
Instructions: Write the name of a Rebel type of family business owner below. If you can't think of a specific person, create a mental picture of a Rebel and focus on that image for this exercise.
Instructions: Now list below the types of retirement plans most appealing to Rebels. (Refer to Figure 7.27 if you need to.)
Instructions: Next, write down the benefit Rebels are seeking from their retirement plans. (Refer to Figure 7.26 if you need to.)
Instructions: Finally, write out some statements linking the specific features of the retirement planning products Rebels are most interested in with the benefit they seek to achieve. For example, "Many professionally run corporations tend to provide defined benefit plans for their employees. Since I know you like to run your business on a professional basis, I've proposed what's called a traditional defined benefit plan."

Status Seekers

Status Seekers are interested in social recognition and the respect of others in the business, in the family and in the community at large. Status Seekers are interested in appearances and image. The positioning statement created for them was designed to appeal to this sense, "A retirement plan enables you to live in the future with the same status you enjoy now." As expected, the Status Seeker segment responded well to this positioning statement for retirement planning. As Figure 7.29 illustrates, almost all agreed that this was the most important reason for their recent decision to buy retirement planning. Status Seeking motivations are not important to any of the other family business owner segments.

Although Status Seekers are a small segment, they can be a good market for some retirement planning programs, especially those which they think would reflect well on their status in the business and in the community. For example, as shown in Figure 7.30, they are interested in defined benefit plans and in plans where employees share in the gains and loses. Providing larger benefits for older employees is also somewhat appealing to this segment. Age-weighted plans are particularly appealing to those who favor profit sharing plans. Some are interested in flexible contribution plans.

Figure 7.29

POSITIONING STATEMENT: *A RETIREMENT PLAN ENABLES YOU TO LIVE IN THE FUTURE WITH THE SAME STATUS YOU ENJOY NOW*

(Percent of family business owners with a retirement plan who say this positioning statement is very important for them.)

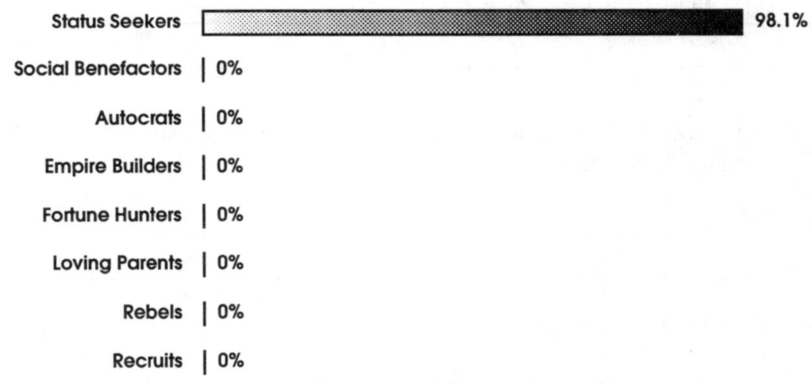

Number of Family Business Owners Who Recently Purchased Retirement Planning = 1,121

Figure 7.30

BENEFITS OF RETIREMENT PLANNING IMPORTANT TO STATUS SEEKERS

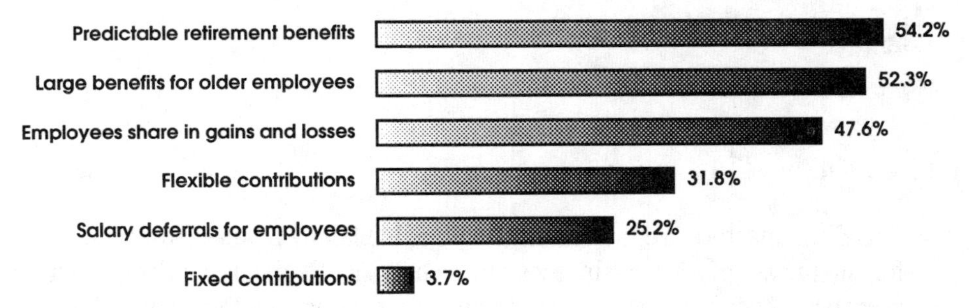

Number of Status Seekers = 107

Based on this information, you should be able to create effective sales presentations positioning retirement planning effectively to the Status Seeker type of family business owner. The exercise in Figure 7.31 will enable you to do so easily by pulling together the information in this section and creating your own sales track.

Figure 7.31

STATUS SEEKER/RETIREMENT PLANNING SALES TRACK EXERCISE
Instructions: Write the name of a Status Seeker type of family business owner below. If you can't think of a specific person, create a mental picture of a Status Seeker and focus on that image for this exercise.
Instructions: Now list below the types of retirement plans most appealing to Status Seekers. (Refer to Figure 7.30 if you need to.)
Instructions: Next, write down the benefit Status Seekers are seeking from their retirement plans. (Refer to Figure 7.29 if you need to.)
Instructions: Finally, write out some statements linking the specific features of the retirement planning products Status Seekers are most interested in with the benefit they seek to achieve. For example, "I've found that business owners who run their businesses most professionally earn the respect of their peers. The most respected business owners I know have implemented the kind of profit sharing plan I'm going to propose to you now."

Social Benefactors

Social Benefactors are the socially responsible family business owners. They have a concern for the impact of their businesses on the lives of others and on the community of which they are a part. Accordingly, the positioning statement written for them with respect to retirement planning was, "A retirement plan reflects your ethical responsibility to your people." Social

Benefactors responded to this statement readily. As shown in Figure 7.32, 93% said it was the most important reason for establishing the type of retirement plan that they did. You should note that only a few Loving Parents also responded positively to this positioning statement.

Although Social Benefactors are the smallest segment, they are an important one for retirement planning programs which enable them to express their feelings of social responsibility and sense of equity. For example, a high percentage of Social Benefactors was interested in profit sharing. Almost as many thought flexible contributions were very important. No Social Benefactors were interested in fixed contribution plans, as shown in Figure 7.33.

Figure 7.32

POSITIONING STATEMENT: *A RETIREMENT PLAN REFLECTS YOUR ETHICAL RESPONSIBILITY TO YOUR PEOPLE*

(Percent of family business owners with a retirement plan who say this positioning statement is very important for them.)

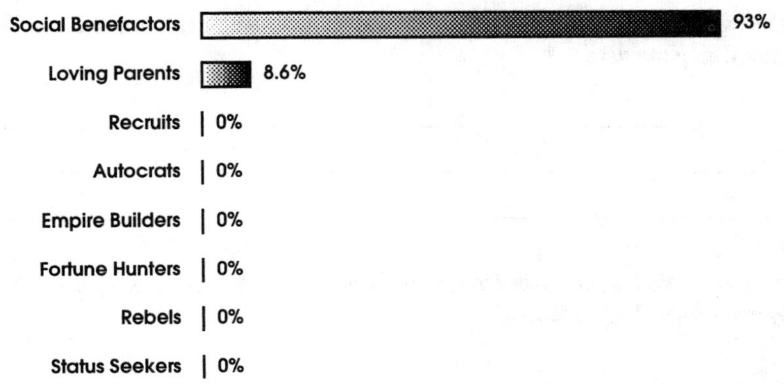

Number of Family Business Owners Who Recently Purchased Retirement Planning = 1,121

Figure 7.33

BENEFITS OF RETIREMENT PLANNING IMPORTANT TO SOCIAL BENEFACTORS

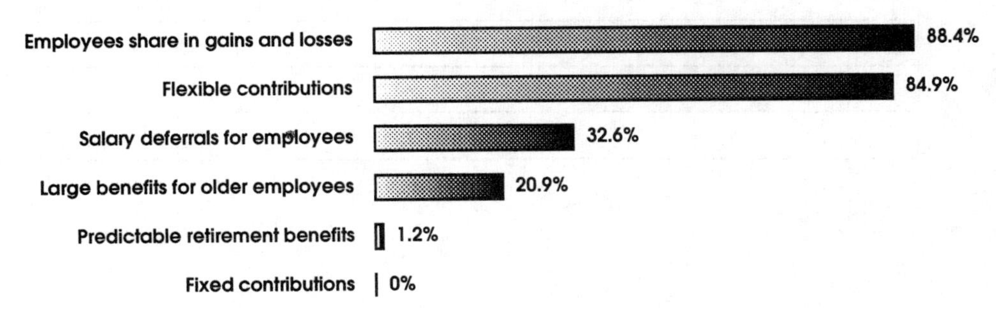

Number of Social Benefactors = 86

Based on this information, you should be able to create effective sales presentations positioning retirement planning effectively to the Social Benefactor type of family business owner. The exercise in Figure 7.34 will enable you to do so easily by pulling together the information in this section and creating your own sales track.

Figure 7.34

SOCIAL BENEFACTOR/RETIREMENT PLANNING SALES TRACK EXERCISE
Instructions: Write the name of a Social Benefactor type of family business owner below. If you can't think of a specific person, create a mental picture of a Social Benefactor and focus on that image for this exercise.
Instructions: Now list below the types of retirement plans most appealing to Social Benefactors. (Refer to Figure 7.33 if you need to.)
Instructions: Next, write down the benefit Social Benefactors are seeking from their retirement plans. (Refer to Figure 7.32 if you need to.)
Instructions: Finally, write out some statements linking the specific features of the retirement planning products Social Benefactors are most interested in with the benefit they seek to achieve. For example, "I agree with you that sharing risks and rewards with your people is a fair and ethical way of doing business. The retirement plan we are about to review is built on a foundation of fairness and sharing."

Your Action Plan

- Identify three current family business owner prospects for your services. Write their names in Figure 7.35.
- Specify which of the eight types of family business owner they are.
- Write down how you would position your services.
- Designate which products you would present to each client.

Figure 7.35

Family Business Owner	Family Business Owner Psychological Type	How I will position my services	Products I will emphasize
1.			
2.			
3.			

CHAPTER 8
BUSINESS SUCCESSION AND ESTATE PLANNING

Richard Bentley knew that Cyrus Wright had most of his assets tied up in his business and approached him several times about business continuation and estate planning. But Wright kept putting him off, "Later, Dick. I'm getting out a major bid," he would say, or "I'm in the middle of year end. This isn't a good time." Bentley thought he figured out the real cause when Wright explained at one point, "My kid is still so screwed up, I'm not sure I can ever leave the business to him. I just can't think about these things now."

Bentley stressed the importance of having a formal, comprehensive succession plan in place until he felt Wright was running out of patience. Then he decided to think about the problem in terms of types of family business owners. As he reviewed what he knew about Cyrus Wright, he exclaimed "That's it! The guy is an Autocrat — he needs control, and the very thought of a succession plan is hateful to him. But if I talk about insurance and trust services in terms of control, not succession, he'd be more likely to hear me out."

Business succession and estate planning are critical to family business owners. Most have built their businesses up and have a high personal stake in seeing the business successfully conveyed to the next generation of family business owners. Others have inherited the business and see it as a form of trusteeship. They feel morally responsible for its safe transition along family lines.

Although family business owners fully agree on the importance of this type of planning, it remains one of the most difficult areas. Normally complex personal estate planning issues become quite complex when the principal asset is a closely-held business. Then, issues of how best to insure business continuity as well as wealth transfer can be muddied by interpersonal issues among family members. The technical and interpersonal skills of the life insurance professional are severely tested in such instances. However, because of the many required products and the scale of the required coverage, these cases are among the most profitable.

The Importance of Business Succession and Estate Planning

Almost all current owners of family businesses believe that it is very important that the business be successfully transferred to the next generation. While most of each type of family business owners agree, it is important to know the differences that exist among family business types, as shown in Figure 8.01. For example, Empire Builders and Loving Parents are extremely focused on the idea of transition, the former because of their vision of the business as a large and enduring entity and the latter because of the vision of the business as a vehicle that can care for their families through the years. On the other hand, one of the groups least interested in transferring the business is the Fortune Hunters. This group is more interested in maximizing personal assets than in conserving assets for the use of other family members. The other group noteworthy for a relative lack of interest in transferring the business is the Social Benefactors who are more interested in addressing the needs of the constituencies they serve than the needs of family members.

Figure 8.01

PERCENT OF EACH FAMILY BUSINESS TYPE WHO THINKS THAT IT IS IMPORTANT TO TRANSFER THE BUSINESS

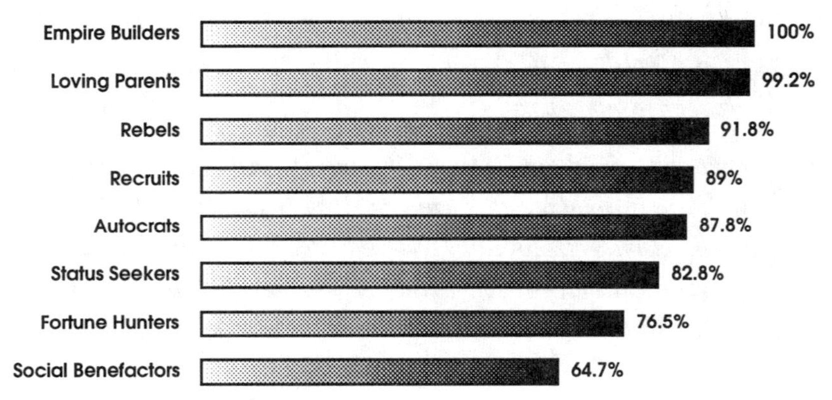

Number of Family Business Owners Who Recently Completed Business Succession or Estate Planning = 1,148

A business succession and estate planning program for the closely-held business takes the form of a number of specific programs, among them a formal (written) succession plan, life insurance to pay estate taxes, buy-sell agreements, trust services and formal training programs for heirs who will run the business. The first and last of these are not insurance services, per se, but are components of a comprehensive business continuity and wealth transfer planning process which may involve the life insurance professional.

Prevalence of Business Succession and Estate Planning Products

Family business owners as a group tend to agree that some of these are more important than others. Check your knowledge of the market in the business succession and estate planning exercise in Figure 8.02.

Figure 8.02

BUSINESS SUCCESSION AND ESTATE PLANNING EXERCISE			
Instructions: Check whether family business owners as a group feel that each of these business succession and estate planning products is very important, somewhat important or less important.			
Business Succession and Estate Planning Program	**Very Important**	**Somewhat Important**	**Less Important**
Formal (written) Succession plan	❑	❑	❑
Life insurance to pay Estate taxes	❑	❑	❑
Buy-sell agreements	❑	❑	❑
Trust services	❑	❑	❑
Formal training program for heirs who will run the business	❑	❑	❑

As Figure 8.03 shows, most family business owners agree that obtaining sufficient life insurance to pay estate taxes due on the value of the business is an important part of business continuity and estate planning.

About two thirds feel the same way about the use of trusts to protect assets during the period of transition. Somewhat fewer feel that buy-sell agreements are important in the succession planning process. These and the low important ratings later may come from a lack of awareness of how these products can benefit the owner, the business and the heirs.

Relatively few of the family business owners feel that a formal, written, succession plan or a formal training program for heirs destined to take over the business are very important. Often, these are family business owners reluctant to give up the business.

Figure 8.03

IMPORTANCE OF BUSINESS SUCCESSION AND ESTATE PLAN COMPONENTS

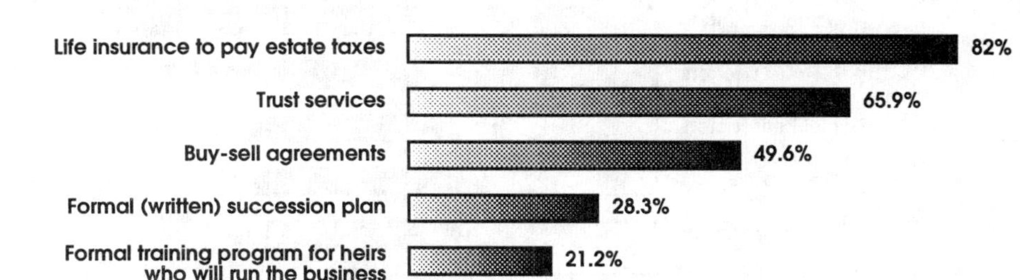

Number of Family Business Owners Who Recently Completed Business Succession or Estate Planning = 1,148

As we have seen, obtaining sufficient life insurance to settle estate taxes is the most important goal of family business owners overall. However, the individual family business owner personalities each have a distinct view of the importance of life insurance in this role. For example, 85% or more of all but two segments think such life insurance is a critical component of any estate and business continuity plan, as Figure 8.04 illustrates. Only Loving Parents and Recruits are less interested because they are more focused on current rather than future family concerns.

Figure 8.04

IMPORTANCE OF LIFE INSURANCE TO PAY ESTATE TAXES

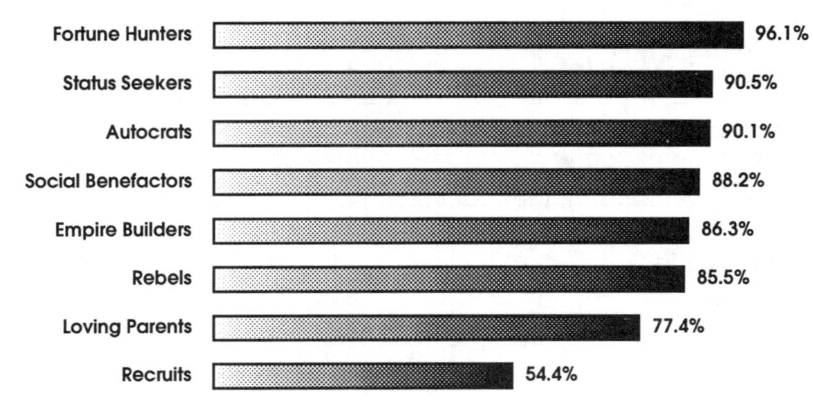

Number of Family Business Owners Who Recently Completed Business Succession or Estate Planning = 1,148

Although trust services are generally thought to be important in connection with estate planning, there is considerable variation across the family business segments, as Figure 8.05 shows. Some segments, such as the Autocrats and the Fortune Hunters are very committed to trusts. They can exert control through the trust instrument, which has particular appeal to these two segments.

Figure 8.05

IMPORTANCE OF TRUST SERVICES

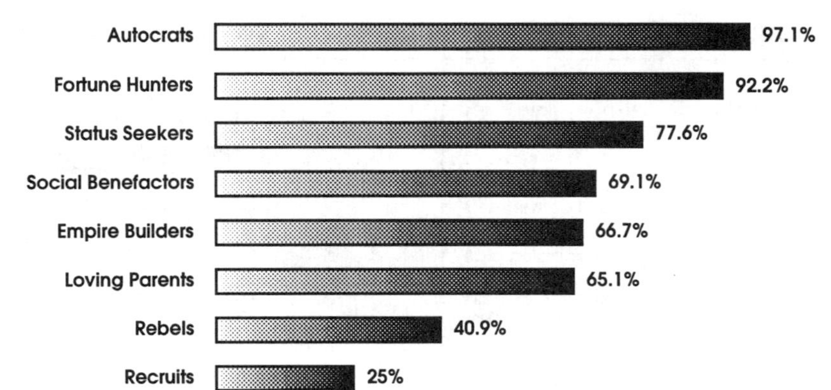

Number of Family Business Owners Who Recently Completed Business Succession or Estate Planning = 1,148

Interests in trusts then drops. Only about two thirds of Social Benefactors, Empire Builders, and Loving Parents agree that trust services are a very important component of business continuation and estate planning. Less than half of the Rebels and Recruits are interested in trust services.

Once again, the product preferences of the various segments reflect their underlying beliefs and motivations. This is best illustrated by the diversity in the segments interested in buy-sell agreements. As could be predicted from their interest in wealth maximization, the Fortune Hunters would be most interested in buy-sell agreements and the advantage of fixing lucrative terms for selling out their interests in the businesses as Figure 8.06 shows. Similarly, since Autocrats wish to control others and not be controlled, they would be the segment least interested in a buy-sell agreement, under which their independence would be constrained. Autocrats are the lowest in terms of thinking buy-sell agreements are important. Other segments vary between 22.8% and 70.1% in how important they believe buy-sell agreements to be.

Figure 8.06

IMPORTANCE OF BUY-SELL AGREEMENTS

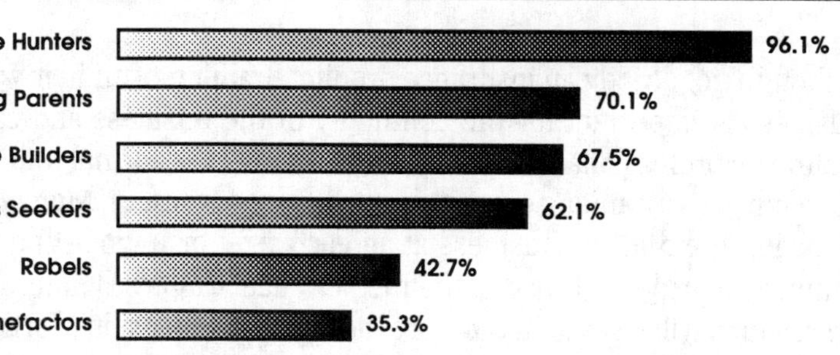

Number of Family Business Owners Who Recently Completed Business Succession or Estate Planning = 1,148

Family firms are not generally in agreement on the importance of a formal succession plan. To have such a plan requires that the family and the owners of the business come to terms with the financial and power implications of a transition. Many business-owning families prefer to put this off because of the emotional issues it can raise. However, the different segments vary in their beliefs about the importance of a formal succession plan.

As illustrated in Figure 8.07, Fortune Hunters are most in favor of such a plan. Since their motivation is often to "cash out," they would be motivated to have such a plan in place. But, a substantial minority of even this group does not have a succession plan. For reasons discussed above, namely their need for control, Autocrats do not believe in succession plans. Status Seekers also do not favor succession plans.

Figure 8.07

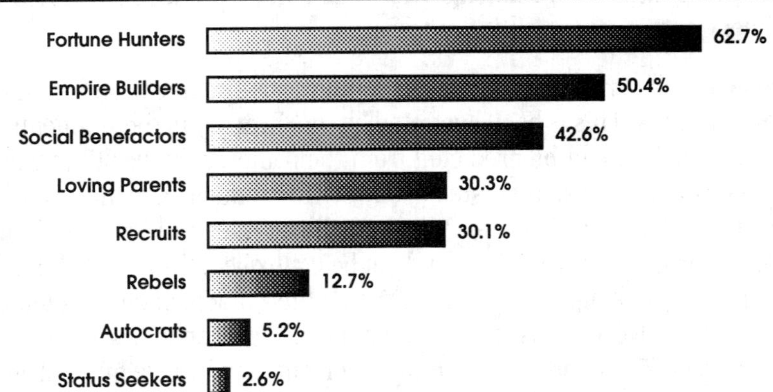

Number of Family Business Owners Who Recently Completed Business Succession or Estate Planning = 1,148

Although not strictly an insurance product, training of an heir who will be responsible for the business is important for the continuity of the business and can be an area in which a life insurance professional becomes involved. However, formal training for the prospective heir is not a top priority among current family business owners. Many train their heirs informally, by involving them in the business at an early age, or by insisting that they work in a different company in order to broaden their experience. Empire Builders, who wish to create an enterprise which will last a long time, are most likely to invest in a formal training program for heirs, as Figure 8.08 shows, but it is still less than a majority. Autocrats who relish control are not likely to value the training of heirs.

Figure 8.08

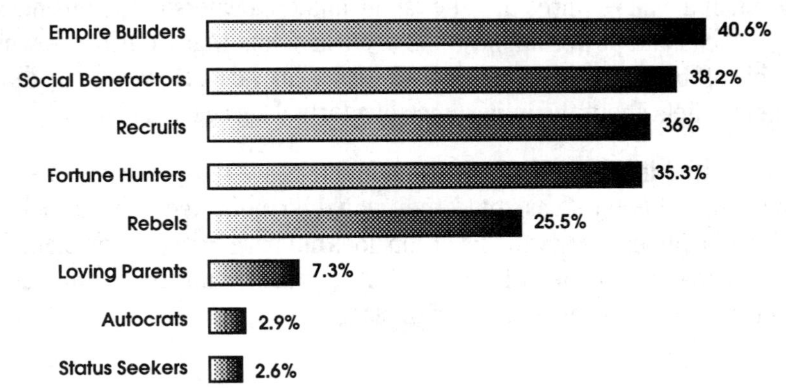

Number of Family Business Owners Who Recently Completed Business Succession or Estate Planning = 1,148

Key Market Segments for Business Succession and Estate Plans

Based on values and attitudes, not all family business segments are vitally interested in business succession and estate plans. This is clearly revealed when a profile of recent buyers is compared to the national distribution of family business owner segments, as shown in Figure 8.09. For example, while Loving Parents make up 22.7% of all buyers of business succession and estate plan programs, they make up 34.1% of family business owners nationwide. Autocrats are also under-represented, at 15.0% of estate planning product purchasers compared to 19.2% of family business owners nationally. These segments are under-represented because they are reluctant to address succession issues in the family and the business.

On the other hand, Empire Builders are over-represented in this group (20.4% of all buyers of estate programs but 13.0% of all family business owners) because they are highly responsive to programs which will help them perpetuate their businesses. Many of the other, smaller, segments are slightly over-represented.

Figure 8.09

DISTRIBUTION OF FAMILY BUSINESS SEGMENTS: BUYERS OF BUSINESS SUCCESSION AND ESTATE PLANNING AND NATIONALLY		
Family Business Segment	**Recent Purchasers of Business Succession and Estate Planning**	**National Distribution of Segments**
Loving Parents	22.7%	34.1%
Empire Builders	20.4%	13.0%
Autocrats	15.0%	19.2%
Recruits	11.8%	7.8%
Status Seekers	10.1%	5.7%
Rebels	9.6%	6.5%
Social Benefactors	5.9%	4.8%
Fortune Hunters	4.4%	8.9%
Number of Family Business Owners Who Recently Completed Business Succession or Estate Planning = 1,148		

Another perspective on Figure 8.09 is that almost half of the market is comprised of Loving Parents and Empire Builders alone. These are the two segments with the strongest stake in the future. This finding suggests that you should be strongly positioning business succession and estate planning programs against these two segments.

Positioning Your Practice

As we have seen over and over again, each type of family business owner sees insurance products differently. This is equally true with business succession and estate planning. It is crucial that you position business succession and estate planning properly with each family business segment. You can begin with the business succession and estate plan positioning exercise in Figure 8.10.

Figure 8.10

POSITIONING BUSINESS SUCCESSION AND ESTATE PLANNING EXERCISE	
Instructions: Write out a phrase which describes key benefits of business succession and estate planning in words especially meaningful to each family business owner segment.	
Loving Parents	
Empire Builders	
Autocrats	
Recruits	
Status Seekers	
Rebels	
Social Benefactors	
Fortune Hunters	

In the sections below you will be able to compare your positioning statements against those we created and tested with hundreds of family business owners.

Loving Parents

The most important segment for business succession and estate planning is Loving Parents. For this segment, we created the positioning statement: "Your business succession insures the health of the business and therefore the health of the family." For Loving Parents, the key benefit of all insurance products is care and protection of the family. Since business succession and estate planning can easily be tied to this goal, we tested this positioning statement and found that it was extremely effective with Loving Parents, as Figure 8.11 shows. Almost all of the Loving Parents who have recently purchased business succession and estate planning said this statement is a very important reflection of their reasons for doing so. Note also, that this reason is not at all relevant for any other segment.

Loving Parents are very concerned that the business survive any transition. As a result, Loving Parents generally think obtaining sufficient life insurance to pay estate taxes is extremely important and that creating all necessary buy-sell agreements in advance is also important to assuring a smooth transition, as shown in Figure 8.12. Trust services are also important to Loving Parents because they can be used to care for family members. Written succession plans are thought to be extremely important by only about a third of the Loving Parents. Loving Parents tend to train family members by moving them through various positions in the business. Thus, they do not generally rely on formal training programs for heirs.

Figure 8.11

POSITIONING STATEMENT: *YOUR BUSINESS SUCCESSION INSURES THE HEALTH OF THE BUSINESS AND THEREFORE THE HEALTH OF THE FAMILY*

(Percent of family business owners with a business succession and estate plan who say this positioning statement is very important.)

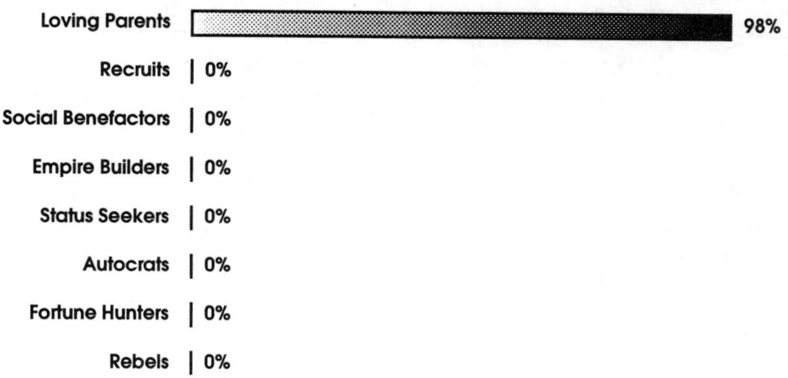

Number of Family Business Owners Who Recently Completed Business Succession or Estate Planning = 1,148

Figure 8.12

BUSINESS SUCCESSION AND ESTATE PLANNING PROGRAMS IMPORTANT TO LOVING PARENTS

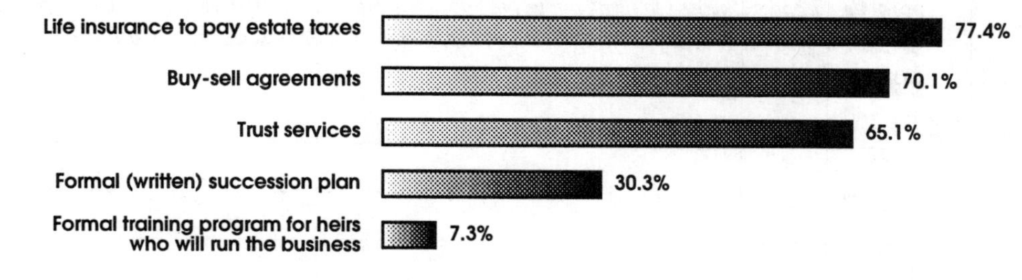

Number of Loving Parents = 261

Based on the response of Loving Parents to the positioning statement and knowledge of the programs which most interest this segment, you are in a position to create your own sales track in Figure 8.13.

Figure 8.13

LOVING PARENT/BUSINESS SUCCESSION AND ESTATE PLANNING SALES TRACK EXERCISE
Instructions: Write the name of a Loving Parent type of family business owner below. If you can't think of a specific person, create a mental picture of a Loving Parent and focus on that image for this exercise.
Instructions: Now list below the business succession and estate planning products most appealing to Loving Parents. (Refer to Figure 8.12 if you need to.)
Instructions: Next, write down the benefit Loving Parents are seeking from their business succession and estate plan. (Refer to Figure 8.11 if you need to.)
Instructions: Finally, write out some statements linking the specific features of the business succession and estate planning products Loving Parents are most interested in with the benefit they seek to achieve. For example, "I know it's hard to think about the day when you won't be running this business, but I also know you care a great deal that your family will be taken care of. There is much you can do today to protect the business for your family."

Empire Builders

Like the other family business owner segments, Empire Builders seek their own benefits in insurance services and products. In the case of business succession and estate planning, they respond most favorably to the benefit of enabling company growth. The positioning statement we created and tested was, "We have a business succession and estate plan to insure that the business will last and grow into the next century." Almost all Empire Builders said this was the most important reason they purchased business succession and estate planning, as shown in Figure 8.14. It is noteworthy that growth for growth's sake is not a high priority for the other family business owner segments.

Figure 8.14

POSITIONING STATEMENT: *WE HAVE A BUSINESS SUCCESSION AND ESTATE PLAN TO INSURE THAT THE BUSINESS WILL LAST AND GROW INTO THE NEXT CENTURY*

(Percent of family business owners with a business succession and estate plan who say this positioning statement is very important.)

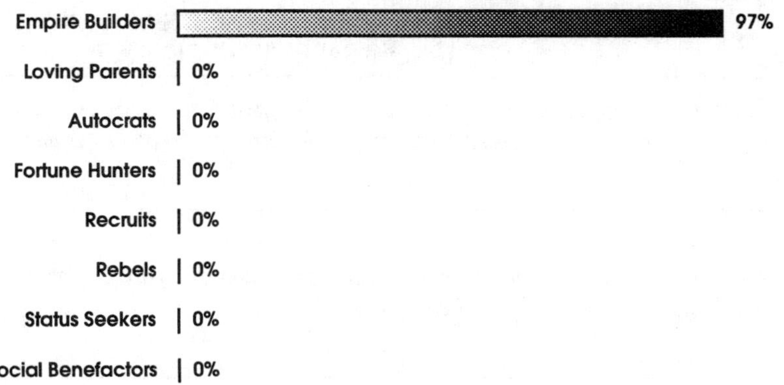

Number of Family Business Owners Who Recently Completed Business Succession or Estate Planning = 1,148

Empire Builders are not only very concerned that the business survive any transition, they want the business to continue to grow rapidly. Therefore, as Figure 8.15 illustrates, Empire Builders generally think that obtaining sufficient life insurance to pay estate taxes is extremely important and that creating all the necessary buy-sell agreements in advance is also important to assuring a smooth transition and future prosperity. Trust services are also important to Loving Parents because they can be used to safeguard resources the business might need at a future date. Written succession plans are relatively highly valued by this group. About half say succession plans are very important. Empire Builders prefer formal methods, so it is also not surprising that they are above average in relying on a formal training program for their heirs.

Figure 8.15

BUSINESS SUCCESSION AND ESTATE PLANNING PRODUCTS IMPORTANT TO EMPIRE BUILDERS

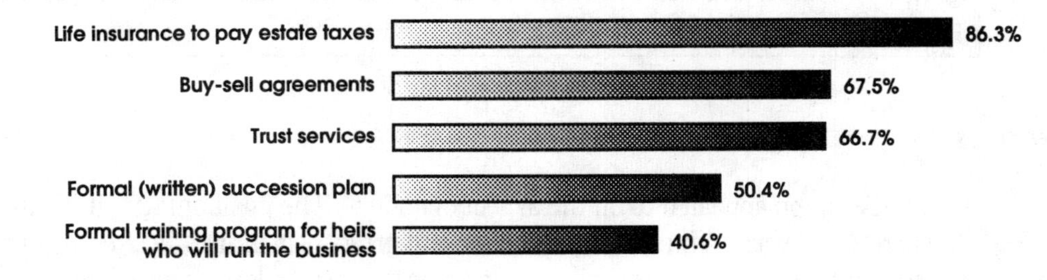

Number of Loving Parents = 261

Based on the response of Empire Builders to the positioning statement and knowledge of the products which most interest this segment, you are in a position to create your own sales track in Figure 8.16.

Figure 8.16

EMPIRE BUILDER/BUSINESS SUCCESSION AND ESTATE PLANNING SALES TRACK EXERCISE
Instructions: Write the name of an Empire Builder type of family business owner below. If you can't think of a specific person, create a mental picture of an Empire Builder and focus on that image for this exercise.
Instructions: Now list below the business succession and estate planning products most appealing to Empire Builders. (Refer to Figure 8.15 if you need to.)
Instructions: Next, write down the benefit Empire Builders are seeking from their business succession and estate plan. (Refer to Figure 8.14 if you need to.)
Instructions: Finally, write out some statements linking the specific features of the business succession and estate planning products Empire Builders are most interested in with the benefit they seek to achieve. For example, "Your goal for the business is growth, and I know you'll be interested to know that there are a lot of obstacles to growth that pop up around the time of transition. You can plan ahead to circumvent these obstacles and keep the business on its current growth trajectory."

Autocrats

Autocrats can be appealed to on the aspect of control. The positioning statement that we created and tested was, "A business succession and estate plan is an effective way of insuring and controlling how your business will be run when you are no longer here." As shown in Figure 8.17, this positioning statement was extremely appealing to Autocrats, primarily because they are oriented towards control, and somewhat appealing to a few Rebels, Empire Builders, and Loving Parents. Control is less appealing to the other family business owner segments.

Figure 8.17

POSITIONING STATEMENT: *THE BUSINESS SUCCESSION AND ESTATE PLAN IS AN EFFECTIVE WAY OF INSURING AND CONTROLLING HOW YOUR BUSINESS WILL BE RUN WHEN YOU ARE NO LONGER HERE*

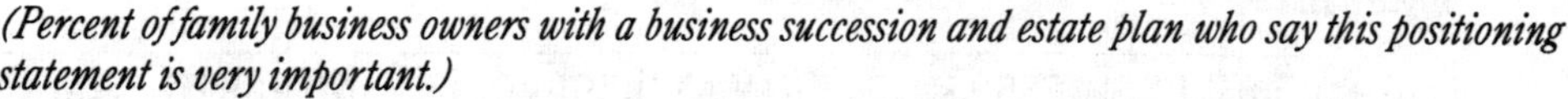

(Percent of family business owners with a business succession and estate plan who say this positioning statement is very important.)

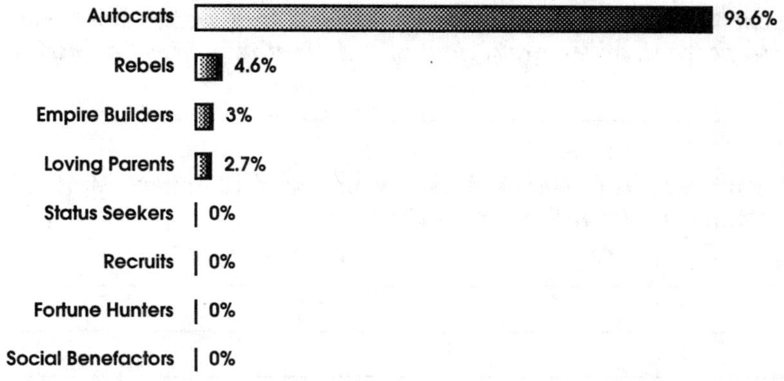

Number of Family Business Owners Who Recently Completed Business Succession or Estate Planning = 1,148

Autocrats are motivated by control over all aspects of their businesses and this motivation extends to their pattern of obtaining various business succession and estate planning services. The service deemed most important by this segment is trust services, as Figure 8.18 shows, because trusts can be created using terms and conditions which result in control by the individual creating the trust. Autocrats are also interested in life insurance to pay estate taxes. However, as could be expected, they have relatively little interest in written succession plans and buy-sell agreements, both of which require that the Autocrat name a successor and the process for making the transition. Autocrats retain more personal control if they keep people guessing about the successor and the succession process. For this same reason, few Autocrats have a formal training program for their heirs.

Figure 8.18

BUSINESS SUCCESSION AND ESTATE PLANNING PRODUCTS IMPORTANT TO AUTOCRATS

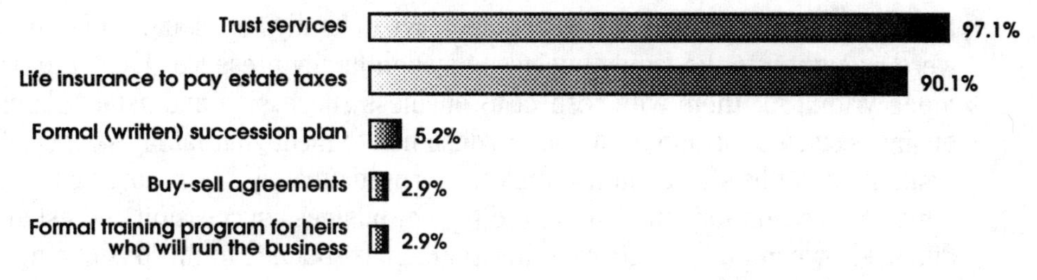

Number of Autocrats = 172

Based on the response of Autocrats to the positioning statement and knowledge of the products which most interest this segment, you are in a position to create your own sales track in Figure 8.19.

Figure 8.19

AUTOCRAT/BUSINESS SUCCESSION AND ESTATE PLANNING SALES TRACK EXERCISE
Instructions: Write the name of an Autocrat type of family business owner below. If you can't think of a specific person, create a mental picture of an Autocrat and focus on that image for this exercise.
Instructions: Now list below the business succession and estate planning products most appealing to Autocrats. (Refer to Figure 8.18 if you need to.)
Instructions: Next, write down the benefit Autocrats are seeking from their business succession and estate plan. (Refer to Figure 8.17 if you need to.)
Instructions: Finally, write out some statements linking the specific features of the business succession and estate planning products Autocrats are most interested in with the benefit they seek to achieve. For example, "The business has been successful because you control every aspect of it. I have some ideas here for you to be able to keep some important aspects of control even when the business passes to someone else."

Recruits

Recruits are people who are highly responsive to family needs and preferences because they were brought into the family business through family pressure. Thus, the positioning statement written for them with respect to business succession and estate planning was, "Your business succession and estate plan is designed to meet your family's expectations." Recruits responded to this statement favorable with approximately 81% reporting that it was the most important reason for establishing the type of business succession and estate plan that they did, as shown in Figure 8.20. No other segment responded to this positioning statement, with the exception of a few Status Seekers.

Figure 8.20

POSITIONING STATEMENT: *YOUR BUSINESS SUCCESSION AND ESTATE PLAN IS DESIGNED TO MEET YOUR FAMILY'S NEEDS*

(Percent of family business owners with a business succession and estate plan who say this positioning statement is very important.)

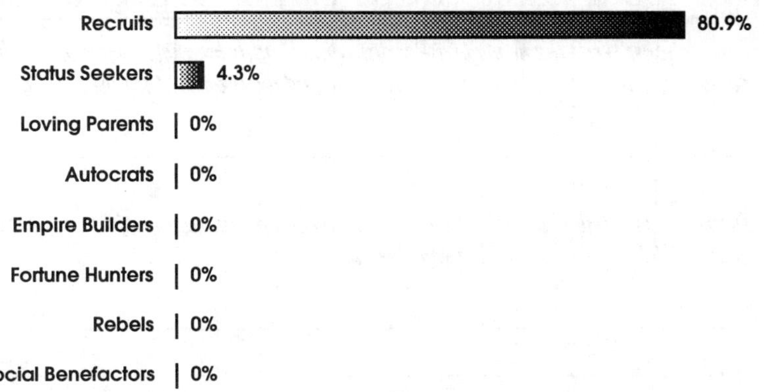

Number of Family Business Owners Who Recently Completed Business Succession or Estate Planning = 1,148

Recruits are very concerned that the business survive any transition because they feel responsible to the family for the business. Over half, therefore, believe that obtaining sufficient life insurance to pay estate taxes is important, as shown in Figure 8.21. Because Recruits were drafted into the business, they attach importance to both training programs for the heirs and a formal succession plan. Trust services are also important to some Recruits, as are buy-sell agreements.

Figure 8.21

BUSINESS SUCCESSION AND ESTATE PLANNING PRODUCTS IMPORTANT TO RECRUITS

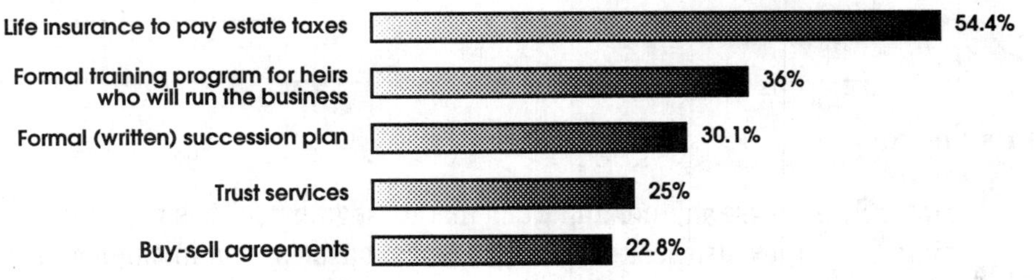

Number of Autocrats = 136

Based on the response of Recruits to the positioning statement and knowledge of the products which most interest this segment, you are in a position to create your own sales track in Figure 8.22.

Figure 8.22

RECRUIT/BUSINESS SUCCESSION AND ESTATE PLANNING SALES TRACK EXERCISE
Instructions: Write the name of a Recruit type of family business owner below. If you can't think of a specific person, create a mental picture of a Recruit and focus on that image for this exercise.
Instructions: Now list below the business succession and estate planning products most appealing to Recruits. (Refer to Figure 8.21 if you need to.)
Instructions: Next, write down the benefit Recruits are seeking from their business succession and estate plan. (Refer to Figure 8.20 if you need to.)
Instructions: Finally, write out some statements linking the specific features of the business succession and estate planning products Recruits are most interested in with the benefit they seek to achieve. For example, "You are interested in providing your successor with the best opportunity possible to continue this business successfully. There are some specific things you can do to accomplish this goal which I'd like to go over with you."

Status Seekers

Status Seekers are another important market segment for business succession and estate planning. Since they also seek different benefits, business continuation and wealth transfer products must be positioned differently with them. The positioning statement we tested with over a thousand recent purchasers of business succession and estate planning was, "Your business succession and estate plan is designed so that, in the future, you can have the same status you now enjoy." As Figure 8.23 shows, Status Seekers respond positively to this positioning statement, with about 70% agreeing that it was the most important reason for purchasing business succession and estate products. No members of any other segment cited this as an important reason. This means that insurance professionals selling to Status Seekers need to connect their products to social status, recognition and prestige in every way possible.

Figure 8.23

POSITIONING STATEMENT: *YOUR BUSINESS SUCCESSION AND ESTATE PLAN IS DESIGNED SO THAT, IN THE FUTURE, YOU CAN HAVE THE SAME STATUS YOU NOW ENJOY*

(Percent of family business owners with a business succession and estate plan who say this positioning statement is very important.)

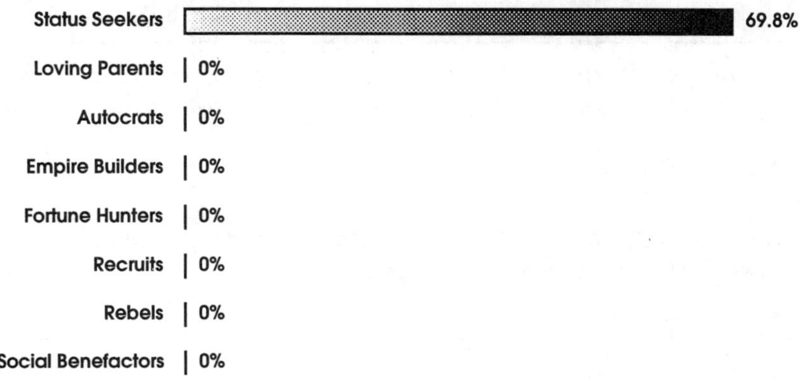

Number of Family Business Owners Who Recently Completed Business Succession or Estate Planning = 1,148

Status Seekers are also invested in having the business survive after them, and so most are interested in obtaining sufficient life insurance to pay estate taxes, as illustrated in Figure 8.24. Sizable proportions are also interested in trust services and buy-sell agreements in order to insure a smooth transition. Relatively few are interested in formal succession plans or in training heirs to the business in a formal way.

Figure 8.24

BUSINESS SUCCESSION AND ESTATE PLANNING PRODUCTS IMPORTANT TO STATUS SEEKERS

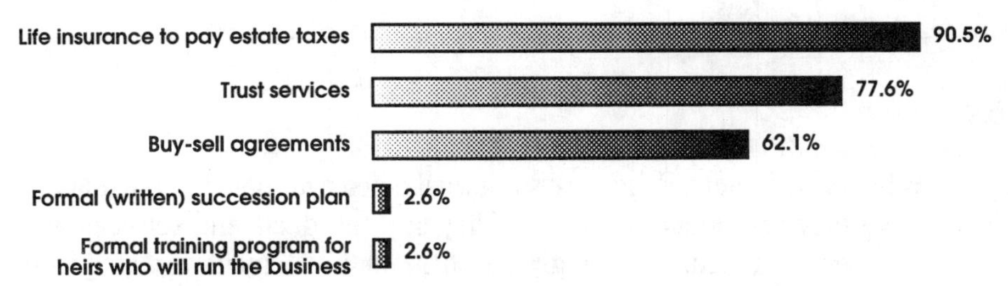

Number of Status Seekers = 116

Based on the response of Status Seekers to the positioning statement and knowledge of the products which most interest this segment, you are in a position to create your own sales track in Figure 8.25.

Figure 8.25

STATUS SEEKER/BUSINESS SUCCESSION AND ESTATE PLANNING SALES TRACK EXERCISE
Instructions: Write the name of a Status Seeker type of family business owner below. If you can't think of a specific person, create a mental picture of a Status Seeker and focus on that image for this exercise.
Instructions: Now list below the business succession and estate planning products most appealing to Status Seekers. (Refer to Figure 8.24 if you need to.)
Instructions: Next, write down the benefit Status Seekers are seeking from their business succession and estate plan. (Refer to Figure 8.23 if you need to.)
Instructions: Finally, write out some statements linking the specific features of the business succession and estate planning products Status Seekers are most interested in with the benefit they seek to achieve. For example, "Insuring the business in order to protect it through the time of transition will be important to keeping it the well respected business it is today. Here is our specific proposal that will let you do that."

Rebels

As business owners, Rebels are somewhat defensive about their managerial skills and eager to prove they are skilled managers. They seek products and services which will reflect their managerial acumen. Accordingly, the positioning statement we tested for this group was, "Your company's business succession and estate plan demonstrates your managerial skills." As expected, Rebels responded very favorably to this positioning statement. As shown in Figure 8.26, most Rebels stated that this was the most important reason they recently purchased business succession and estate planning products. A few Status Seekers also agreed, but being recognized for good managerial skills is not as relevant a benefit for the other family business owner segments.

Figure 8.26

POSITIONING STATEMENT: *YOUR COMPANY'S BUSINESS SUCCESSION AND ESTATE PLAN DEMONSTRATES YOUR MANAGERIAL SKILLS*

(Percent of family business owners with a business succession and estate plan who say this positioning statement is very important.)

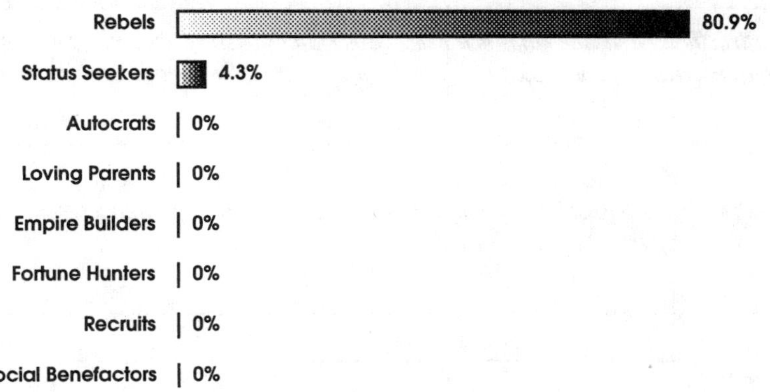

Number of Family Business Owners Who Recently Completed Business Succession or Estate Planning = 1,148

Like the other segments, Rebels are concerned that the business survive any transition and prosper in the future. Their self-image as professional business managers makes this imperative for them. Rebels therefore think obtaining sufficient life insurance to pay estate taxes is extremely important, as illustrated in Figure 8.27. Fewer agree that buy-sell agreements and trust services are very important. Like many other segments, specific programs for heirs such as a written succession plan or a formal training program are low in priority.

Figure 8.27

BUSINESS SUCCESSION AND ESTATE PLANNING PRODUCTS IMPORTANT TO REBELS

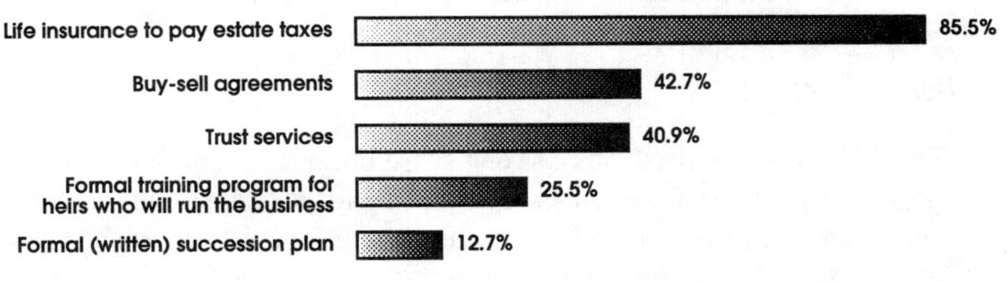

Number of Rebels = 110

Based on the response of Rebels to the positioning statement and knowledge of the products which most interest this segment, you are in a position to create your own sales track in Figure 8.28.

Figure 8.28

REBEL/BUSINESS SUCCESSION AND ESTATE PLANNING SALES TRACK EXERCISE
Instructions: Write the name of a Rebel type of family business owner below. If you can't think of a specific person, create a mental picture of a Rebel and focus on that image for this exercise.
Instructions: Now list below the business succession and estate planning products most appealing to Rebels. (Refer to Figure 8.27 if you need to.)
Instructions: Next, write down the benefit Rebels are seeking from their business succession and estate plan. (Refer to Figure 8.26 if you need to.)
Instructions: Finally, write out some statements linking the specific features of the business succession and estate planning products Rebels are most interested in with the benefit they seek to achieve. For example, "Running this business in as professional a way as possible has been important to you. That professionalism is also important when preparing the business for succession."

Social Benefactors

Family business owners with a strong sense of social responsibility are a small group. The positioning statement created for them was designed to appeal to this sense, "Your business succession and estate plan will insure the continuation of your social responsibility focus." As expected, the Social Benefactor segment responded well to this positioning statement for business succession and estate products, as shown in Figure 8.29. Most agreed that this was the most important reason for their recent decisions to buy business succession and estate products. Continuing a tradition of social responsibility is not important for the other family business owner segments.

Figure 8.29

POSITIONING STATEMENT: *YOUR BUSINESS SUCCESSION AND ESTATE PLAN WILL INSURE THE CONTINUATION OF YOUR SOCIAL RESPONSIBILITY FOCUS*

(Percent of family business owners with a business succession and estate plan who say this positioning statement is very important.)

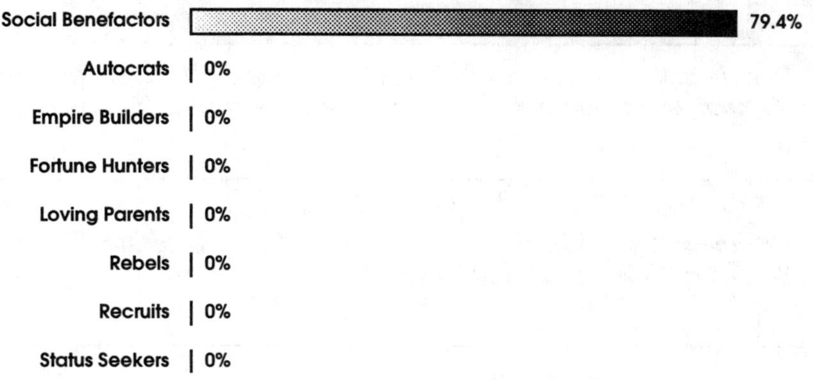

Number of Family Business Owners Who Recently Completed Business Succession or Estate Planning = 1,148

Social Benefactors are motivated to act ethically and fairly in business. They have a natural concern for the business and the people of the business after succession, and so tend to be above average in their interest in succession planning and estate planning. Social Benefactors generally believe that obtaining sufficient life insurance to pay estate taxes is extremely important, as illustrated in Figure 8.30. Quite a few also think trust services will help them meet goals of social responsibility. Social Benefactors take care of heirs, too. They are more likely than many other segments to attach importance to a written succession plan and a formal training program for heirs.

Figure 8.30

BUSINESS SUCCESSION AND ESTATE PLANNING PRODUCTS IMPORTANT TO SOCIAL BENEFACTORS

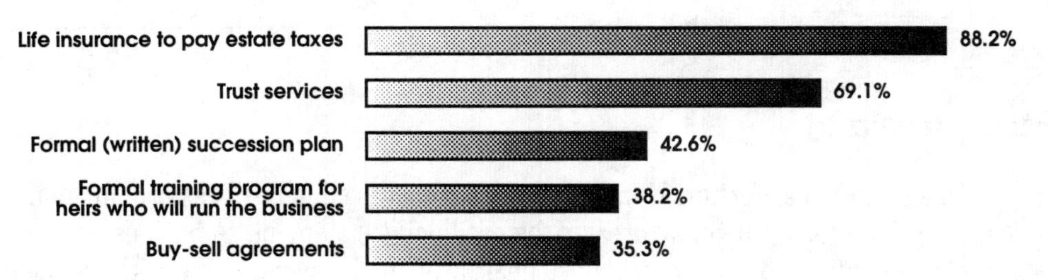

Number of Social Benefactors = 68

Based on the response of Social Benefactors to the positioning statement and knowledge of the products which most interest this segment, you are in a position to create your own sales track in Figure 8.31.

Figure 8.31

SOCIAL BENEFACTOR/BUSINESS SUCCESSION AND ESTATE PLANNING SALES TRACK EXERCISE
Instructions: Write the name of a Social Benefactor type of family business owner below. If you can't think of a specific person, create a mental picture of a Social Benefactor and focus on that image for this exercise.
Instructions: Now list below the business succession and estate planning products most appealing to Social Benefactors. (Refer to Figure 8.30 if you need to.)
Instructions: Next, write down the benefit Social Benefactors are seeking from their business succession and estate plan. (Refer to Figure 8.29 if you need to.)
Instructions: Finally, write out some statements linking the specific features of the business succession and estate planning products Social Benefactors are most interested in with the benefit they seek to achieve. For example, "You have been very responsible to your people all along, and now it's time to think about how to be responsible to them when the time comes to transfer the business. There are a number of things you can do that will protect the business for the family and the people associated with the business."

Fortune Hunters

Of all segments, Fortune Hunters were least interested in business continuation and estate planning. For this segment, we created the positioning statement, "A business succession and estate plan is configured to provide a substantial payout to the owners." We asked all the family business owners how important that reason was for obtaining the coverage that they did. As Figure 8.32 shows, this reason is extremely important to almost all Fortune Hunters because they are most interested in personal wealth. As Figure 8.32 also shows, this reason is of no importance to the other segments. This analysis shows, as do the preceding ones, the advantages of positioning business succession and estate planning in a specific way for each segment.

Figure 8.32

POSITIONING STATEMENT: *YOUR BUSINESS SUCCESSION AND ESTATE PLAN IS CONFIGURED TO PROVIDE A SUBSTANTIAL PAYOUT TO YOU*

(Percent of family business owners with a business succession and estate plan who say this positioning statement is very important.)

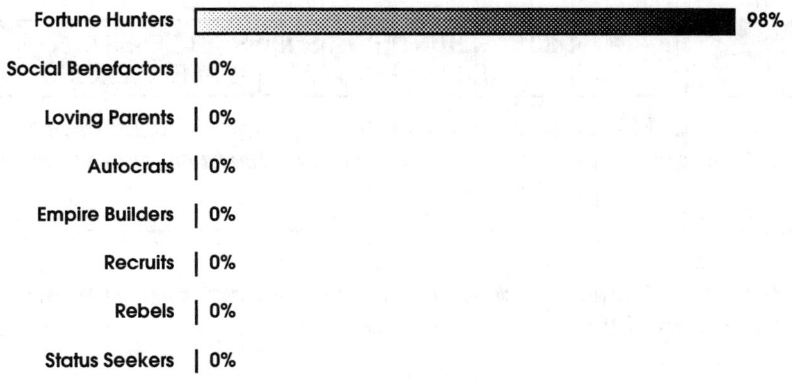

Number of Family Business Owners Who Recently Completed Business Succession or Estate Planning = 1,148

Although Fortune Hunters are the smallest segment for business succession and estate planning, when they decide it is important, they are quick to value individual plan components. For example, more than 90% of Fortune Hunters say insurance for estate taxes, buy-sell agreements, and trust services are all very important components of a business succession and estate plan, as shown in Figure 8.33. Because of the professionalism of their approach, they are also well above average in their belief that a succession plan is important.

Figure 8.33

BUSINESS SUCCESSION AND ESTATE PLANNING PRODUCTS IMPORTANT TO FORTUNE HUNTERS

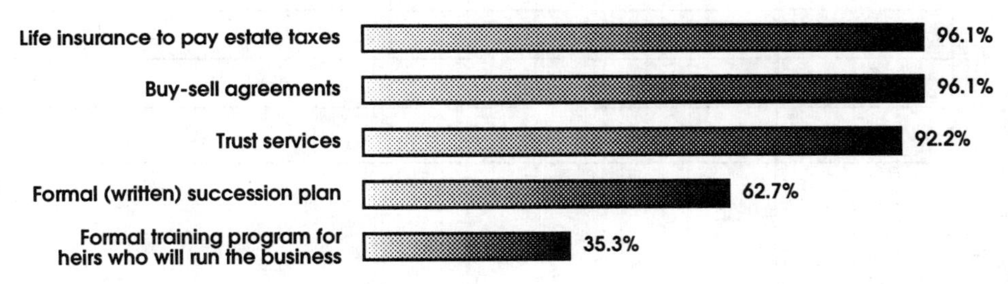

Number of Fortune Hunters = 51

Based on the response of Fortune Hunters to the positioning statement and knowledge of the products which most interest this segment, you are in a position to create your own sales track in Figure 8.34.

Figure 8.34

FORTUNE HUNTER/BUSINESS SUCCESSION AND ESTATE PLANNING SALES TRACK EXERCISE
Instructions: Write the name of a Fortune Hunter type of family business owner below. If you can't think of a specific person, create a mental picture of a Fortune Hunter and focus on that image for this exercise.
Instructions: Now list below the business succession and estate planning products most appealing to Fortune Hunters. (Refer to Figure 8.33 if you need to.)
Instructions: Next, write down the benefit Fortune Hunters are seeking from their business succession and estate plan. (Refer to Figure 8.32 if you need to.)
Instructions: Finally, write out some statements linking the specific features of the business succession and estate planning products Fortune Hunters are most interested in with the benefit they seek to achieve. For example, "It's important to you to be professional in all your dealings; you have been as successful as you have by being very rigorous. I know you'll want to be as rigorous when it comes to planning for the succession of this business, especially if you want to integrate this process into a retirement plan for yourself."

Your Action Plan

- Identify three current family business owner prospects for your services. Write their names in Figure 8.35.
- Specify which of the eight types of family business owners they are.
- Write down how you would position your services.
- Designate which products you would present to each client.

Figure 8.35

Family Business Owner	Family Business Owner Psychological Type	How I will position my services	Products I will emphasize
1.			
2.			
3.			

CHAPTER 9
ASSET PROTECTION PLANNING

Richard Bentley has just completed an estate plan for the Lovells. "I had them pinned as Loving Parent types," he thought. "Doing estate planning is a piece of cake for Loving Parents; you just position everything in terms of how it will help ease things for the children and take care of the grandchildren."

As a result of getting close to the Lovells and their way of doing business, Bentley had the sense that they might not have sufficient coverage from an asset protection point of view. "Estate planning for Loving Parents was a snap, but now I don't know if this approach works. I'm not sure I understand asset protection planning from a Loving Parent's perspective."

Asset protection planning is critical to family business owners. Having accumulated personal and business assets, it is a continuing challenge to protect those assets against many threats. (One of the most significant is litigation.) Family business owners vary in the extent to which they are aware of their exposure from an asset protection point of view and they also vary in the benefits they seek to fulfill when considering asset protection planning.

The Importance of Asset Protection Planning

An asset protection program involves the use of a number of specific risk management techniques and insurance products ranging from trusts (domestic and off-shore) to personal and directors liability insurance.

Prevalence of Asset Protection Products

Family business owners as a group tend to agree that some of these are more important than others. Check your knowledge of the market in the Asset Protection Products Exercise in Figure 9.01.

Figure 9.01

ASSET PROTECTION PRODUCTS EXERCISE			
Instructions: Check whether family business owners as a group feel that each of these asset protection products is very important, somewhat important or less important.			
Asset Protection Product	**Very Important**	**Somewhat Important**	**Less Important**
Off-shore trusts	❑	❑	❑
Property and casualty insurance	❑	❑	❑
Personal liability insurance	❑	❑	❑
Officers and directors insurance	❑	❑	❑
Use of trusts to protect assets	❑	❑	❑

Most family business owners agree that property and casualty insurance and personal liability insurance are important elements of an asset protection plan, as illustrated in Figure 9.02. These products are sold more widely than some of the other asset protection arrangements.

About two thirds feel the same way about the use of trusts to protect assets and officers and directors insurance. These asset protection products are increasing in importance and prevalence among family business owners.

Relatively few family business owners feel that off-shore trusts are important items in a comprehensive asset protection program. This represents an emerging market opportunity among family business owners as they seek out global markets to insulate themselves against the risks of the US market.

Figure 9.02

IMPORTANCE OF ASSET PROTECTION PLAN COMPONENTS

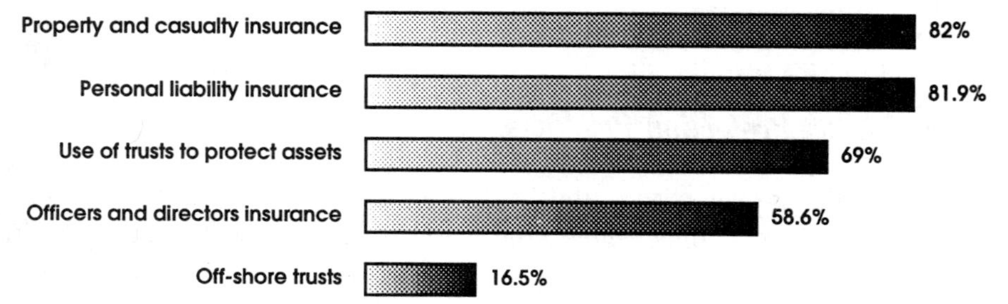

Number of Family Business Owners Who Recently Purchased An Asset Protection Product = 701

Obtaining sufficient property and casualty insurance for asset protection is seen as generally important by all family business owner segments, as Figure 9.03 shows. A third or more of all segments (and 90% or more of all but two segments) think property and casualty insurance is a critical component of any asset protection plan. Only Fortune Hunters and Status Seekers are less likely to attach great importance to this type of asset protection product, probably because both these segments emphasize consumption and private assets.

Figure 9.03

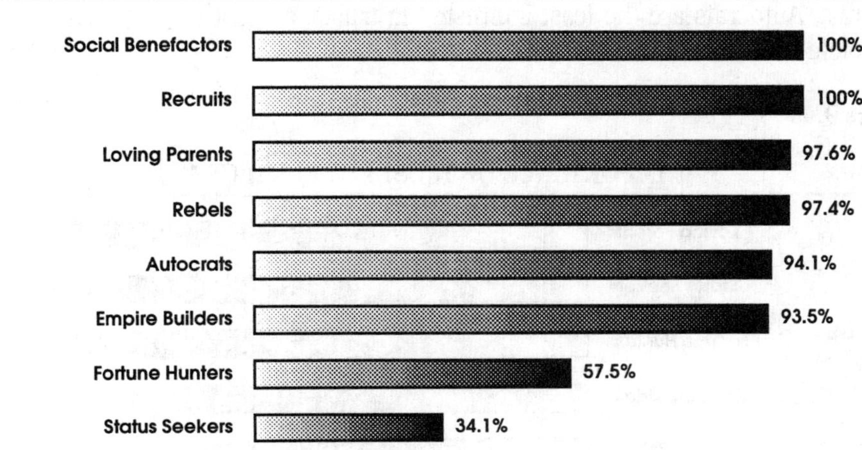

Number of Family Business Owners Who Recently Purchased An Asset Protection Product = 701

Although personal liability insurance is generally thought to be important in connection with asset protection planning, there is considerable variation across the family business segments. As Figure 9.04 illustrates, some segments, such as the Autocrats, Status Seekers, and Fortune Hunters are very committed to personal liability insurance. This is because this type of insurance is an effective vehicle for asset protection, a benefit which has particular appeal to these segments.

Figure 9.04

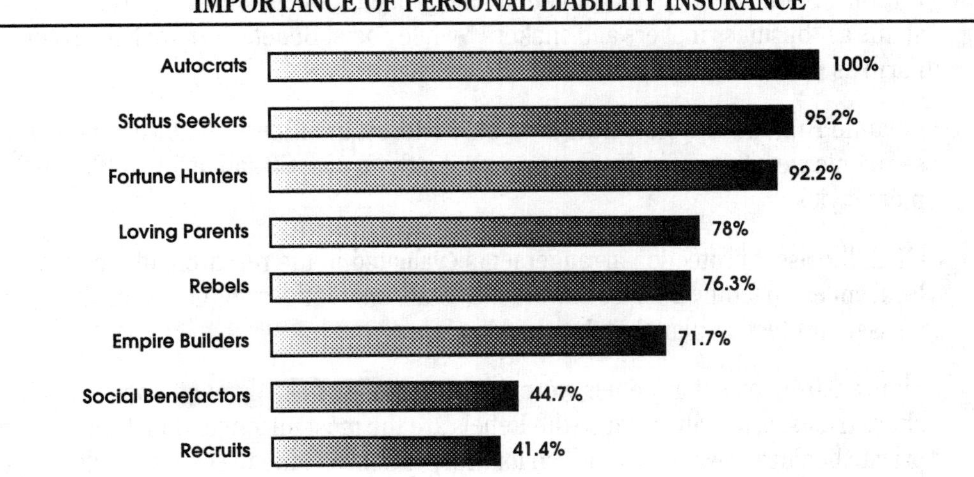

Number of Family Business Owners Who Recently Purchased An Asset Protection Product = 701

Interests in personal liability insurance among the family business owner types drops somewhat after these three segments. Less than 80% of Loving Parents, Rebels, and Empire Builders are very interested in personal liability insurance, as are less than half of Social Benefactors and Recruits.

When it comes to the use of trusts to protect assets, the product preferences of the various segments reflect their underlying beliefs and motivations. As could be predicted from their interest in preserving the business for the use of the family, Loving Parents are the most interested in trusts for asset protection, as Figure 9.05 shows. Status Seekers also find trusts appealing, as do Fortune Hunters because they contribute to personal asset maximization. By contrast, Autocrats are the least interested in trusts, at least in part because they can lose complete control over the assets.

Figure 9.05

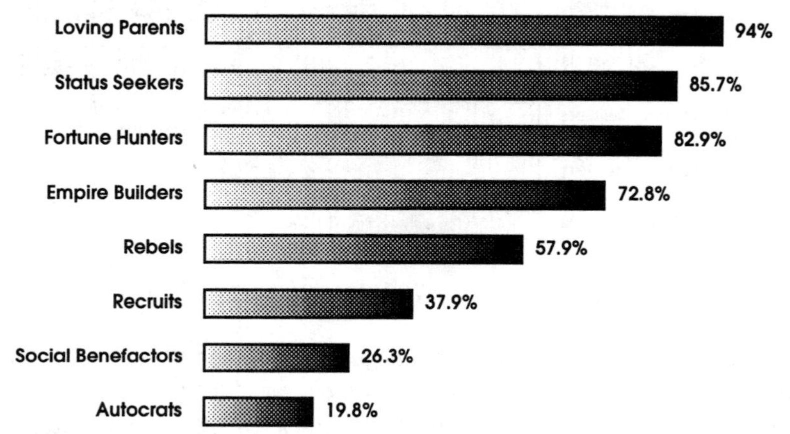

Number of Family Business Owners Who Recently Purchased An Asset Protection Product = 701

As Figure 9.06 illustrates, family firms are not generally agreed on the importance of officers and directors insurance as a part of a comprehensive asset protection. Some segments are very much in favor, including Status Seekers and Social Benefactors, although for different reasons. Status Seekers tend to adopt insurance products which will reflect well upon their status as "business movers and shakers," while Social Benefactors wish to protect others from harm as much as possible.

Fortune Hunters and Autocrats have little interest in officers and directors insurance. These segments view this type of insurance as something of a frill and of little utility in their management styles.

Of all the asset protection arrangements evaluated in the research, off-shore trusts have the least appeal to family business owners. Overall, only 16.5% said they were an important part of an asset protection plan that they had in place.

Figure 9.07 shows that Rebels were the most likely of all segments to have an interest in off-shore trusts, primarily because the Rebels are the most unconventional segment who became private business owners in a search for independence. Status Seekers are also on the high side in their interest in such trusts because they are interested in the prestige value of trusts generally and off-shore trusts have an exotic flavor. A portion of Fortune Hunters are attracted to

Figure 9.06

IMPORTANCE OF OFFICERS AND DIRECTORS INSURANCE

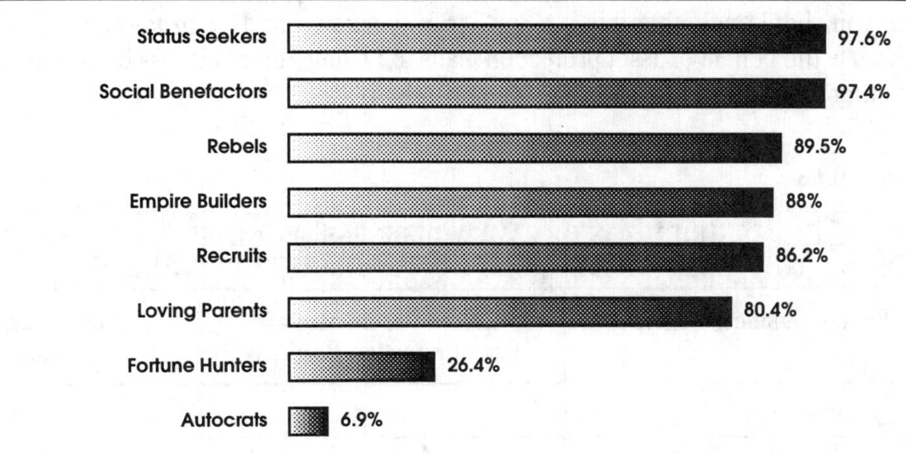

Number of Family Business Owners Who Recently Purchased An Asset Protection Product = 701

off-shore trusts because they hold out the promise of a greater return (less subject to taxes). However, many segments have little or no interest, among them Loving Parents, Autocrats, Empire Builders, Social Benefactors, and Recruits.

Figure 9.07

IMPORTANCE OF OFF-SHORE TRUSTS IN ASSET PROTECTION

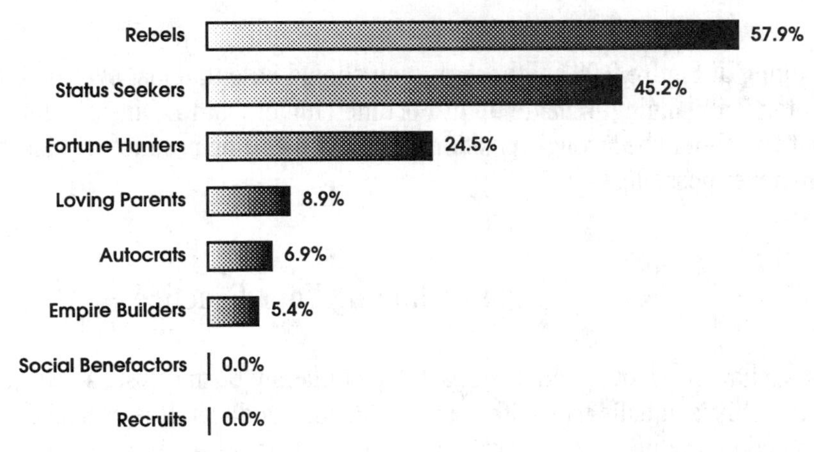

Number of Family Business Owners Who Recently Purchased An Asset Protection Product = 701

Key Market Segments for Asset Protection Plans

Based on their values and attitudes, not all family business segments are interested in asset protection plans to the same degree. This is easy to see when a profile of recent buyers is compared to the national distribution of family business owner segments, as shown in Figure 9.08. For example, Fortune Hunters make up 27.5% of all buyers of asset protection plan products, but make up only 8.9% of family business owners nationwide. The reason for this is obvious. Fortune Hunters are most interested in building their personal wealth. They would clearly be interested in and highly motivated to buy products which help them retain and protect their personal assets. The second largest segment of asset protection buyers are Loving Parents, but you should note that this is a smaller proportion than Loving Parents nationally. This is because the benefit of asset protection plans to Loving Parents is less direct than the benefits of other forms of insurance.

Figure 9.08

DISTRIBUTION OF FAMILY BUSINESS SEGMENTS: BUYERS OF ASSET PROTECTION PLAN PRODUCTS AND NATIONALLY		
Family Business Segment	**Recent Purchasers of Asset Protection Products**	**National Distribution of Segments**
Loving Parents	24.0%	34.1%
Autocrats	14.2%	19.2%
Empire Builders	13.1%	13.0%
Fortune Hunters	27.5%	8.9%
Recruits	4.1%	7.8%
Rebels	5.4%	6.5%
Status Seekers	6.0%	5.7%
Social Benefactors	5.4%	4.8%
Number of Family Business Owners Who Recently Purchased An Asset Protection Product = 701		

Looking at Figure 9.08 another way, you should note that just over half the market for asset protection planning is made up of Fortune Hunters and Loving Parents alone. This implies that you should be strongly positioning asset protection products against these two segments whenever possible.

Positioning Your Practice

As we have seen over and over, each type of family business sees insurance products differently. This is equally true with asset protection products. It is crucial that you position asset protection products properly with each family business segment. You can begin with the asset protection plan positioning exercise in Figure 9.09.

In the sections below you will be able to compare your positioning statements against those we created and tested with hundreds of family business owners.

Figure 9.09

POSITIONING ASSET PROTECTION PRODUCTS EXERCISE	
Instructions: Write out a phrase which describes a key benefit of asset protection planning in words especially meaningful to each family business owner segment.	
Fortune Hunters	
Loving Parents	
Autocrats	
Empire Builders	
Status Seekers	
Rebels	
Social Benefactors	
Recruits	

Fortune Hunters

Fortune Hunters are interested in current wealth rather than business growth or taking care of the family. For this reason, Fortune Hunters are the most promising asset protection planning segment. For Fortune Hunters, we created the positioning statement, "My asset protection plan is designed to protect me and my wealth," and asked all the family business owners how important this reason was for obtaining the coverage that they did. As Figure 9.10 shows, this reason is extremely important to almost all Fortune Hunters because they are most interested in personal wealth. As Figure 9.10 also shows, this reason is of little or no importance to the other segments. You can see the advantages of positioning asset protection planning in this way to this segment. You can also see that positioning asset protection products in this way to any other segment would be a waste of time.

Figure 9.10

POSITIONING STATEMENT: *MY ASSET PROTECTION PLAN IS DESIGNED TO PROTECT ME AND MY WEALTH*

(Percent of family business owners with an asset protection plan who say this positioning statement is very important for them.)

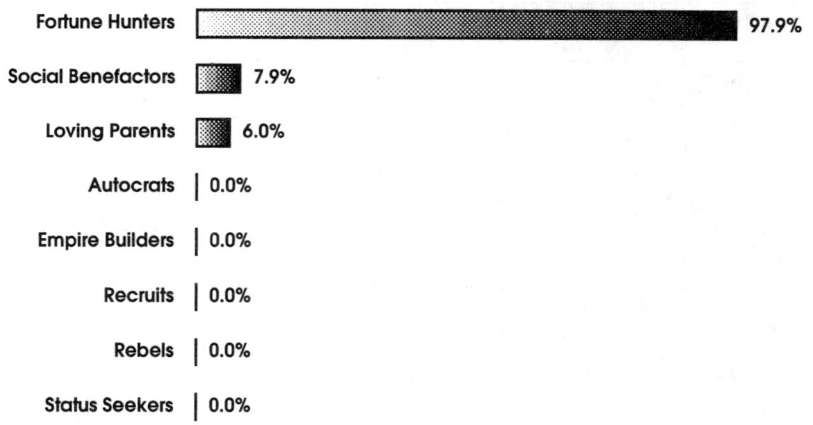

Number of Family Business Owners Who Recently Purchased An Asset Protection Product = 701

As shown in Figure 9.11, almost all Fortune Hunters are very interested in two forms of asset protection planning: personal liability insurance and the use of trusts to protect assets. Property and casualty insurance is important to about half of the Fortune Hunters. Off-shore trusts are not considered important by this segment at the current time, perhaps because of a lack of awareness.

Now that you have a sense of how to position asset protection products with this segment and an idea of which products are most meaningful to this segment, you are in a position to create your own sales track in Figure 9.12.

Figure 9.11

ASSET PROTECTION PLANNING PRODUCTS IMPORTANT TO FORTUNE HUNTERS

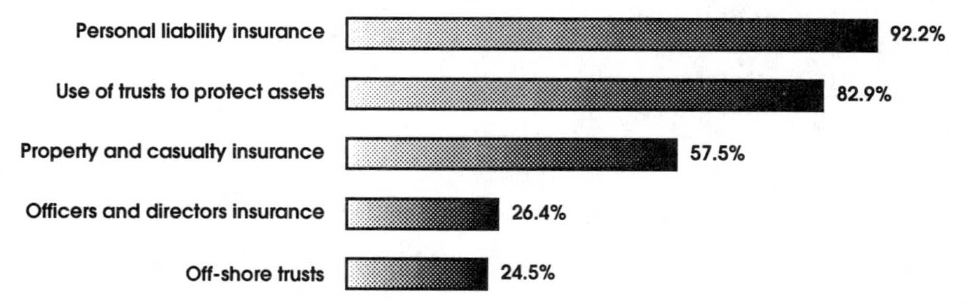

Number of Fortune Hunters = 193

Figure 9.12

FORTUNE HUNTER/ASSET PROTECTION PLANNING SALES TRACK EXERCISE
Instructions: Write the name of a Fortune Hunter type of family business owner below. If you can't think of a specific person, create a mental picture of a Fortune Hunter and focus on that image for this exercise.
Instructions: Now list below the asset protection planning products most appealing to Fortune Hunters. (Refer to Figure 9.11 if you need to.)
Instructions: Next, write down the benefit Fortune Hunters are seeking from their asset protection plans. (Refer to Figure 9.10 if you need to.)
Instructions: Finally, write some statements linking the specific features of asset protection planning Fortune Hunters are most interested in with the benefit they seek to achieve. For example: "I know you believe you should enjoy today the fruits of your labor. Protecting the assets you have worked so hard to obtain is critical. I have some specific suggestions of how you can use trusts to do that."

Loving Parents

The second most important segment for asset protection products is Loving Parents. For this segment, we created the positioning statement, "An asset protection plan designed explicitly to protect family members from litigation." For Loving Parents, the key benefit of all products is care and protection of the family. Since it is possible to see asset protection products as ways to increase the level of protection for the family, we tested this positioning approach which proved to be extremely effective with Loving Parents, as Figure 9.13 shows. Almost all of the Loving Parents who have recently purchased asset protection products said that this statement is a very important reflection of their reason for doing so. Note also that this reason is not relevant for any other segment.

Figure 9.13

POSITIONING STATEMENT: *AN ASSET PROTECTION PLAN DESIGNED EXPLICITLY TO PROTECT FAMILY MEMBERS FROM LITIGATION*

(Percent of family business owners with an asset protection plan who say this positioning statement is very important for them.)

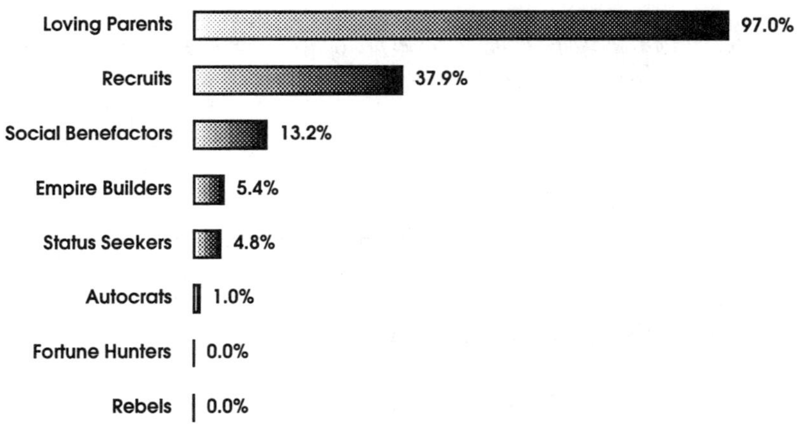

Number of Family Business Owners Who Recently Purchased An Asset Protection Product = 701

Because of their highly conservative nature and because they share a goal of protecting the assets of the business, Loving Parents are a good target for asset protection planning as shown in Figure 9.14. Most display considerable interest in property and casualty insurance, the use of trusts to protect assets, officers and directors insurance, and personal liability insurance. Off-shore trusts are not considered important by Loving Parents at the current time, perhaps because of a lack of awareness.

Figure 9.14

ASSET PROTECTION PLANNING PRODUCTS IMPORTANT TO LOVING PARENTS

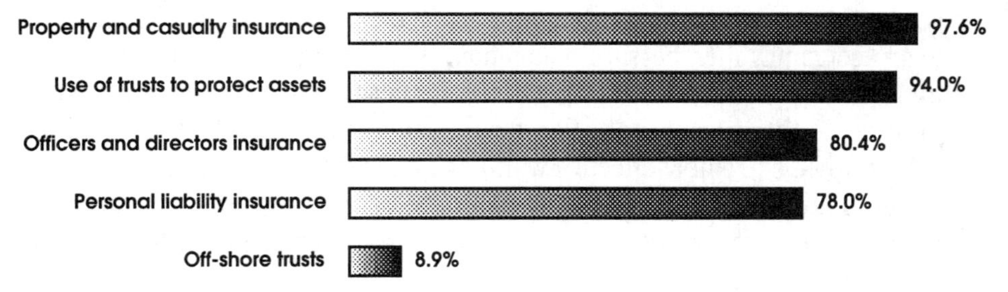

Number of Loving Parents = 168

Now that you have a sense of how to position asset protection products to this segment and an idea of which products are most meaningful to this segment, you are in a position to create your own sales track with in Figure 9.15.

Figure 9.15

LOVING PARENT/ASSET PROTECTION PLANNING SALES TRACK EXERCISE
Instructions: Write the name of a Loving Parent type of family business owner below. If you can't think of a specific person, create a mental picture of a Loving Parent and focus on that image for this exercise.
Instructions: Now list below the asset protection planning products most appealing to a Loving Parent. (Refer to Figure 9.14 if you need to.)
Instructions: Next, write down the benefit Loving Parents are seeking from their asset protection plans. (Refer to Figure 9.13 if you need to.)
Instructions: Finally, write some statements linking the specific features of asset protection planning Loving Parents are most interested in with the benefit they seek to achieve. For example: "Keeping the business safe for the next generation is your highest goal. There are some specific programs which can help you do just that."

Autocrats

While the proportion of the other segments is not as absolutely large as the first two, they are still good prospects for asset protection plan products. Autocrats, for example, can be appealed to on the basis of control. The positioning statement we created and tested was, "An asset protection plan is an effective way for you to control the risks facing the business." As shown in Figure 9.16, this positioning statement was extremely appealing to Autocrats, because they are oriented towards control, but did not reflect the views of the other family business owner segments.

Figure 9.17 shows that almost all Autocrats are very interested in two forms of asset protection planning: personal liability insurance and property and casualty insurance. Relatively few are interested in trusts to protect assets, off-shore trusts or officers and directors insurance.

Figure 9.16

POSITIONING STATEMENT: *THE ASSET PROTECTION PLAN IS AN EFFECTIVE WAY FOR YOU TO CONTROL THE RISK FACING THE BUSINESS*

(Percent of family business owners with an asset protection plan who say this positioning statement is very important for them.)

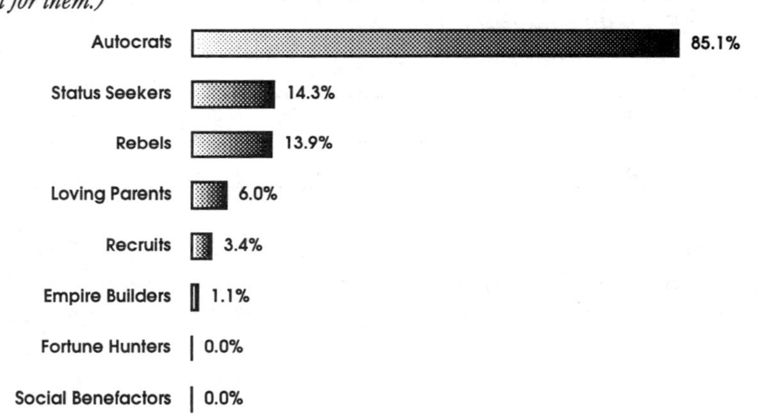

Number of Family Business Owners Who Recently Purchased An Asset Protection Product = 701

Figure 9.17

ASSET PROTECTION PLANNING PRODUCTS IMPORTANT TO AUTOCRATS

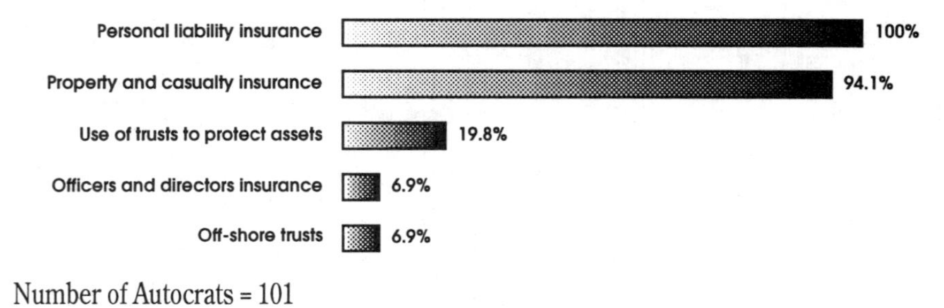

Number of Autocrats = 101

Now that you have a sense of how to position asset protection products to this segment and an idea of which products are most meaningful to this segment, you are in a position to create your own sales track in Figure 9.18.

Figure 9.18

AUTOCRAT/ASSET PROTECTION PLANNING SALES TRACK EXERCISE
Instructions: Write the name of an Autocrat type of family business owner below. If you can't think of a specific person, create a mental picture of an Autocrat and focus on that image for this exercise.
Instructions: Now list below the asset protection planning products most appealing to Autocrats. (Refer to Figure 9.17 if you need to.)
Instructions: Next, write down the benefit Autocrats are seeking from their asset protection plans. (Refer to Figure 9.16 if you need to.)
Instructions: Finally, write some statements linking the specific features of asset protection planning Autocrats are most interested in with the benefit they seek to achieve. For example: "Controlling risks is critical for a person in your position. Personal liability insurance is an excellent way of getting more control over uncontrollable risk elements."

Empire Builders

Like the other family business owner segments, Empire Builders seek their own benefits in insurance products. In the case of asset protection planning, they respond most favorably to the benefit of enabling company growth. The positioning statement we created and tested was, "We have an asset protection plan to insure that the unexpected doesn't hamper the company's growth." Almost all Empire Builders said this was the most important reason they purchased asset protection planning, as shown in Figure 9.19. It is noteworthy that growth for growth's sake is not a high priority of the other family business owner segments.

Figure 9.19

POSITIONING STATEMENT: *WE HAVE AN ASSET PROTECTION PLAN TO INSURE THAT THE UNEXPECTED DOESN'T HAMPER THE COMPANY'S GROWTH*

(Percent of family business owners with an asset protection plan who say this positioning statement is very important for them.)

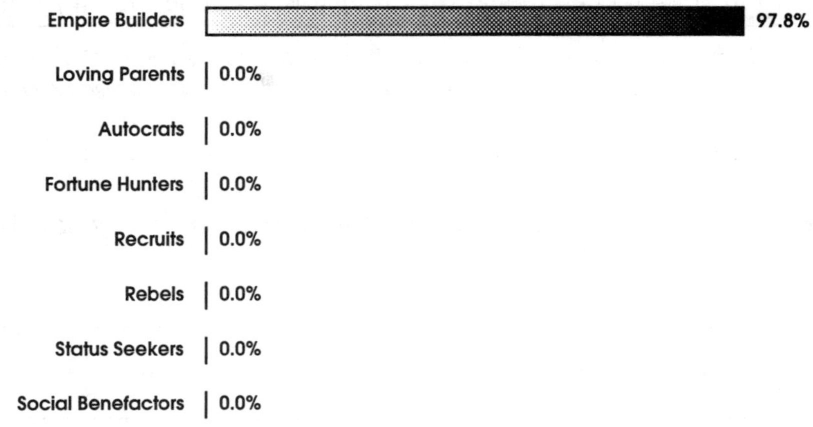

Number of Family Business Owners Who Recently Purchased An Asset Protection Product = 701

As Figure 9.20 shows, Empire Builders are good prospects for four forms of asset protection planning: property and casualty insurance, officers and directors insurance, the use of trusts to protect assets, and personal liability insurance. Off-shore trusts are not considered important by this segment at the current time.

Now that you have a sense of how to position asset protection products to this segment and an idea of which products are most meaningful to this segment, you are in a position to create your own sales track in Figure 9.21.

Figure 9.20

ASSET PROTECTION PLANNING PRODUCTS IMPORTANT TO EMPIRE BUILDERS

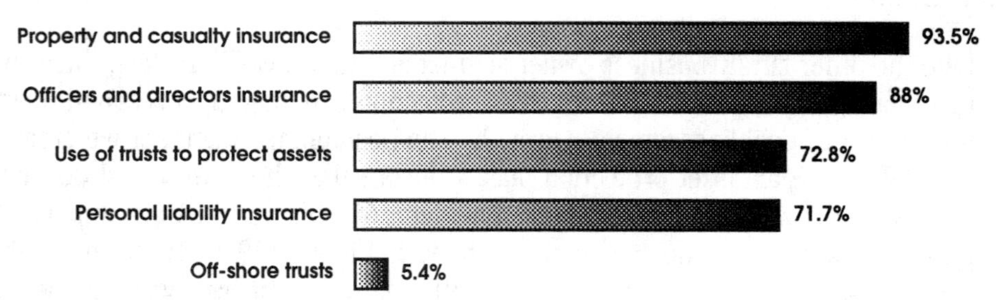

Number of Empire Builders = 92

Figure 9.21

EMPIRE BUILDER/ASSET PROTECTION PLANNING SALES TRACK EXERCISE
Instructions: Write the name of an Empire Builder type of family business owner below. If you can't think of a specific person, create a mental picture of a Empire Builder and focus on that image for this exercise.
Instructions: Now list below the asset protection planning products most appealing to Empire Builders. (Refer to Figure 9.20 if you need to.)
Instructions: Next, write down the benefit Empire Builders are seeking from their asset protection plans. (Refer to Figure 9.19 if you need to.)
Instructions: Finally, write some statements linking the specific features of asset protection planning Empire Builders are most interested in with the benefit they seek to achieve. For example: "You will be able to increase the odds of growing this business if you insulate it against outside threats that could stop its growth. For example, a lawsuit could divert resources you have set aside for expansion. I have a plan which will protect your business and enable it to grow."

Status Seekers

Status Seekers are another small, but important, market segment for asset protection planning. They, too, seek different benefits and therefore the product must be positioned differently to them. The positioning statement we tested with seven hundred recent purchasers of asset protection planning was, "Your asset protection plan is designed to make certain the unexpected doesn't interfere with the status you have achieved." Status Seekers responded very positively to this positioning. Fully 90% agreed strongly that it was the most important rationale for purchasing asset protection products while none of the members of the other segments cited this as an important reason, as shown in Figure 9.22. This means that insurance professionals selling to Status Seekers need to connect their products to social status, recognition and prestige in every way possible.

Figure 9.22

POSITIONING STATEMENT: *YOUR ASSET PROTECTION PLAN IS DESIGNED TO MAKE CERTAIN THE UNEXPECTED DOESN'T INTERFERE WITH THE STATUS YOU HAVE ACHIEVED*

(Percent of family business owners with an asset protection plan who say this positioning statement is very important for them.)

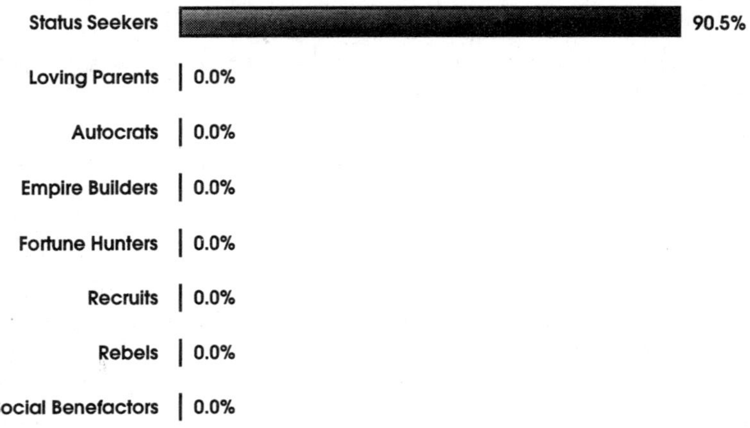

Number of Family Business Owners Who Recently Purchased An Asset Protection Product = 701

Status Seekers like "visible" products, the kind that can be talked about and which sound important. For this reason, they are among the most interested of all segments in officers and directors insurance which can be discussed with their boards, as shown in Figure 9.23. They are also above average in their interest in personal liability insurance because the dollar amount of the umbrella coverage sounds impressive. Certain types of trusts are also prestigious and Status Seekers are interested in using trusts to protect assets. Although their interest is lower for off-shore trusts, they are among the most interested of all segments in this asset protection alternative, again, because it confers prestige to refer to off-shore holdings. Significantly, property and casualty insurance is lowest on their list.

Figure 9.23

ASSET PROTECTION PLANNING PRODUCTS IMPORTANT TO STATUS SEEKERS

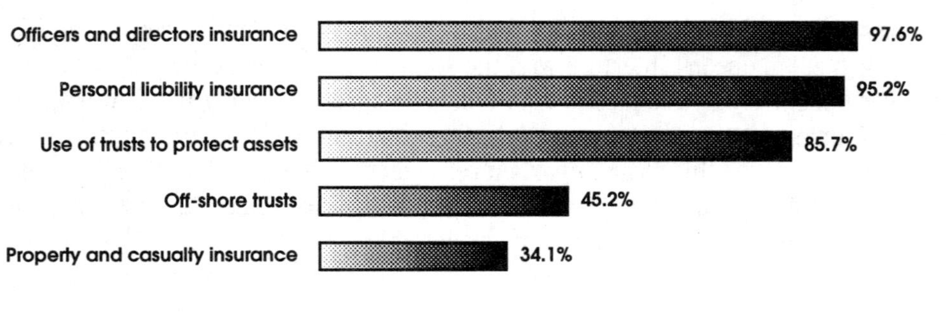

Number of Status Seekers = 41

Now that you have a sense of how to position asset protection products to this segment and an idea of which products are most meaningful to this segment, you are in a position to create your own sales track in Figure 9.24.

Figure 9.24

STATUS SEEKER/ASSET PROTECTION PLANNING SALES TRACK EXERCISE
Instructions: Write the name of a Status Seeker type of family business owner below. If you can't think of a specific person, create a mental picture of a Status Seeker and focus on that image for this exercise.
Instructions: Now list below the asset protection planning products most appealing to Status Seekers. (Refer to Figure 9.23 if you need to.)
Instructions: Next, write down the benefit Status Seekers are seeking from their asset protection plans. (Refer to Figure 9.22 if you need to.)
Instructions: Finally, write some statements linking the specific features of asset protection planning Status Seekers are most interested in with the benefit they seek to achieve. For example: "I know you rely on your board. I think you should consider reevaluating your officers and directors insurance for that group. They'll respect you for thinking of it; it's the kind of business practice that is usual for well-thought-of corporations."

Rebels

Rebels are business owners who are defensive about their managerial skills and eager to prove they are competent managers. They seek products and services which will reflect this. Accordingly, the positioning statement we tested for this group was, "Your company's asset protection plan demonstrates your managerial skills." As expected, Rebels responded very favorably to this positioning statement. As shown in Figure 9.25, almost all Rebels stated that this

Figure 9.25

POSITIONING STATEMENT: *YOUR COMPANY'S ASSET PROTECTION PLAN DEMONSTRATES YOUR MANAGERIAL SKILLS*

(Percent of family business owners with an asset protection plan who say this positioning statement is very important to them.)

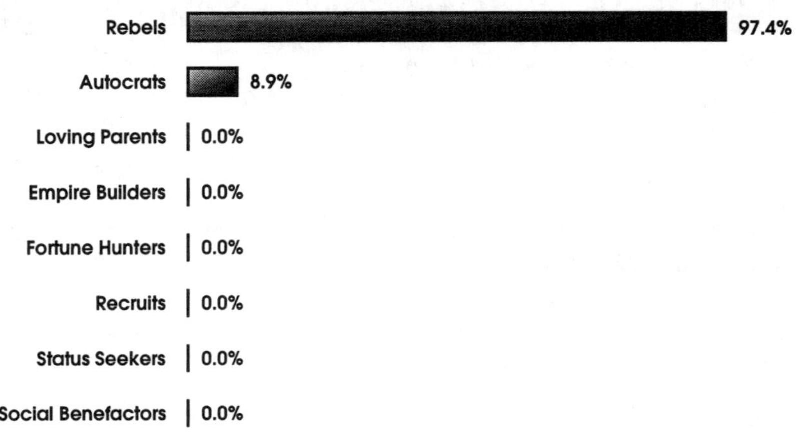

Number of Family Business Owners Who Recently Purchased An Asset Protection Product = 701

was the most important reason they recently purchased asset protection planning products. A few Autocrats concurred, but being recognized for good managerial skills is not as relevant a benefit for the other family business owner segments.

Because they are interested in products which reinforce their self-image as professional managers, Rebels are good prospects for a range of asset protection plans, as shown in Figure 9.26. Almost all Rebels are very interested in property and casualty insurance, officers and directors insurance, and personal liability insurance. Many are also interested in the use of trusts to protect assets and in off-shore trusts.

Figure 9.26

ASSET PROTECTION PLANNING PRODUCTS IMPORTANT TO REBELS

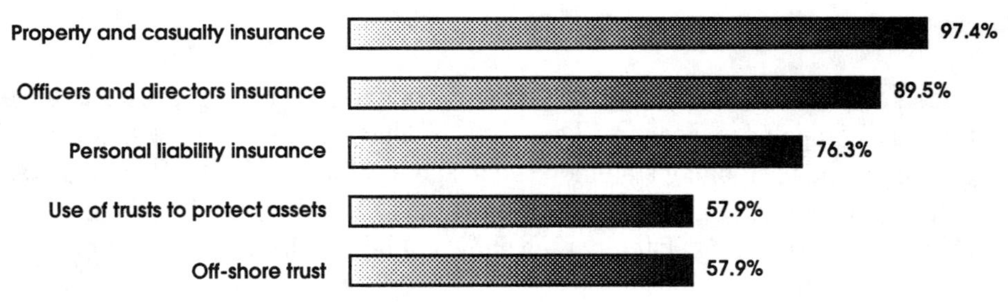

Number of Rebels = 38

Now that you have a sense of how to position asset protection products to this segment and an idea of which products are most meaningful to this segment, you are in a position to create your own sales track in Figure 9.27.

Figure 9.27

REBEL/ASSET PROTECTION PLANNING SALES TRACK EXERCISE
Instructions: Write the name of a Rebel type of family business owner below. If you can't think of a specific person, create a mental picture of a Rebel and focus on that image for this exercise.
Instructions: Now list below the asset protection planning products most appealing to Rebels. (Refer to Figure 9.26 if you need to.)
Instructions: Next, write down the benefit Rebels are seeking from their asset protection plans. (Refer to Figure 9.25 if you need to.)
Instructions: Finally, write some statements linking the specific features of asset protection planning Rebels are most interested in with the benefit they seek to achieve. For example: "I know you are constantly aware of the need to manage this business in as professional and as safe a manner as possible. Protecting the personal assets you have worked so hard for is also very important. I have some specific suggestions of how you can do that."

Social Benefactors

Family business owners with a strong sense of social responsibility are a small but highly differentiated group. The positioning statement created for them was designed to appeal to this sense, "Your asset protection plan is a good expression of your sense of social responsibility." As expected, the Social Benefactor segment responded well to this positioning of asset protection products, as shown in Figure 9.28. Almost all agreed that this was the most important reason for their recent decision to buy asset protection products. Social responsibility — whether it is directed at employees, other stakeholders or the community at large — is not important to the other family business owner segments.

Figure 9.28

POSITIONING STATEMENT: *YOUR ASSET PROTECTION PLAN IS A GOOD EXPRESSION OF YOUR SENSE OF SOCIAL RESPONSIBILITY*

(Percent of family business owners with an asset protection plan who say this positioning statement is very important for them.)

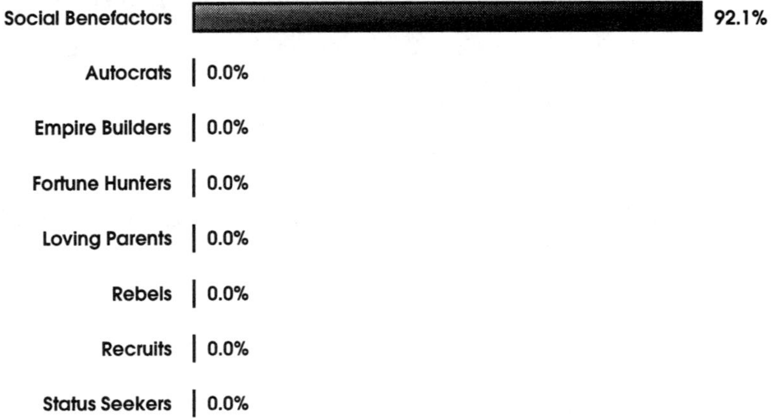

Number of Family Business Owners Who Recently Purchased An Asset Protection Product = 701

As Figure 9.29 illustrates, Social Benefactors are most interested in asset protection products which also help them follow through on their perceived responsibility to others in their social groups. For example, they are the most interested of all segments in officers and directors insurance because this product helps them protect people who are supporting them in their business. They are also interested in property and casualty insurance because it reduces risks for the people in the business. They are far less interested in products which protect personal assets such as trusts.

Now that you have a sense of how to position asset protection products to this segment and an idea of which products are most meaningful to this segment, you are in a position to create your own sales track in Figure 9.30.

Figure 9.29

ASSET PROTECTION PLANNING PRODUCTS IMPORTANT TO SOCIAL BENEFACTORS

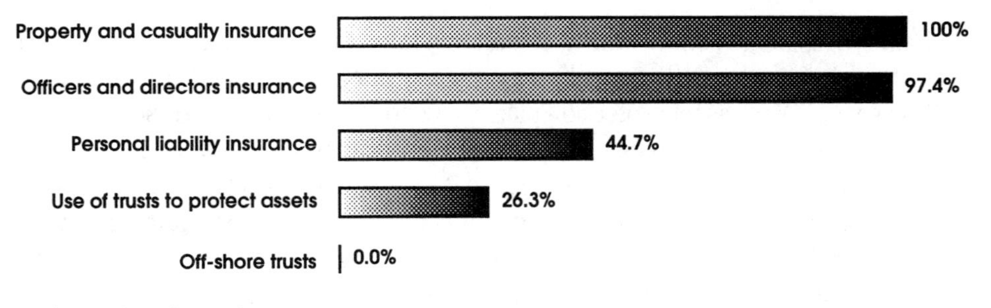

Number of Social Benefactors = 30

Figure 9.30

SOCIAL BENEFACTOR/ASSET PROTECTION PLANNING SALES TRACK EXERCISE
Instructions: Write the name of a Social Benefactor type of family business owner below. If you can't think of a specific person, create a mental picture of a Social Benefactor and focus on that image for this exercise.
Instructions: Now list below the asset protection planning products most appealing to Social Benefactors. (Refer to Figure 9.29 if you need to.)
Instructions: Next, write down the benefit Social Benefactors are seeking from their asset protection plans. (Refer to Figure 9.28 if you need to.)
Instructions: Finally, write some statements linking the specific features of asset protection planning Social Benefactors are most interested in with the benefit they seek to achieve. For example: "Being responsible for the people who care for you and support you in the business is important. Officers and directors insurance is an effective way you can reciprocate to your officers and directors for all the support they provide you in the business."

Recruits

Recruits are the family business owners brought into the family business through family pressure. They are people who are highly responsive to family needs and preferences. Thus, the positioning statement written for them with respect to asset protection planning was, "Your asset protection plan was established because of family preferences and needs." Recruits responded to this statement, with 96.6% saying it was the most important reason for establishing the type of asset protection plan they did, as shown in Figure 9.31. It is noteworthy that a fair proportion of Loving Parents, a group which is closely linked to the dynamics of the family, also responded to this statement.

Figure 9.31

POSITIONING STATEMENT: *YOUR ASSET PROTECTION PLAN WAS ESTABLISHED BECAUSE OF FAMILY PREFERENCES AND NEEDS*

(Percent of family business owners with an asset protection plan who say this positioning statement is very important for them.)

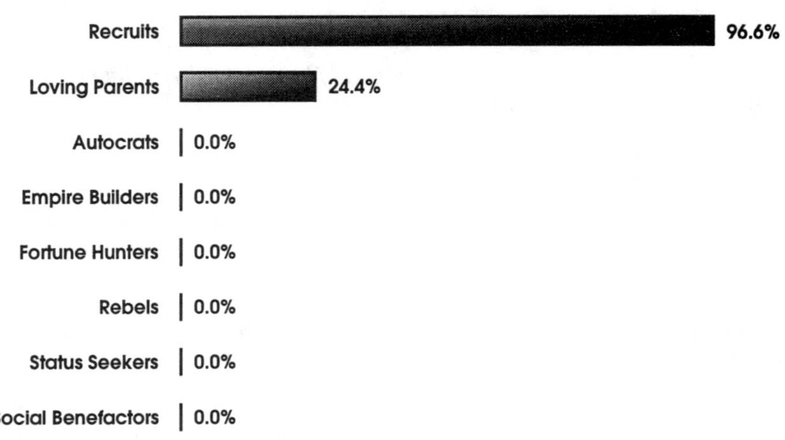

Number of Family Business Owners Who Recently Purchased An Asset Protection Product = 701

As shown in Figure 9.32, almost all Recruits are very interested in two forms of asset protection planning: property and casualty insurance and officers and directors insurance. Personal liability insurance and the use of trusts to protect assets are important to some. Off-shore trusts are not considered important by this segment at the current time, perhaps because of a lack of awareness.

Figure 9.32

ASSET PROTECTION PLANNING PRODUCTS IMPORTANT TO RECRUITS

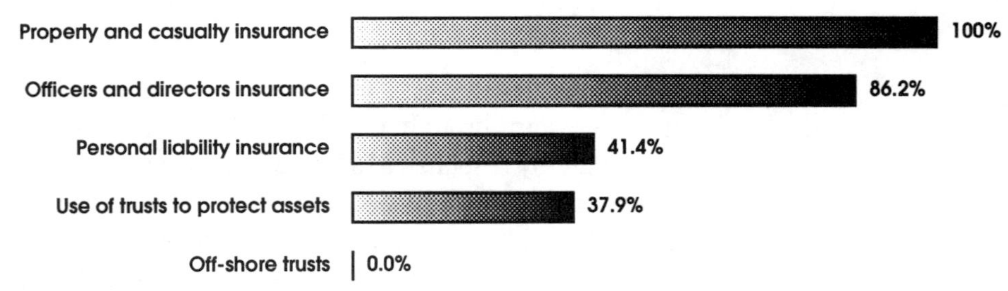

Number of Recruits = 29

Now that you have a sense of how to position asset protection products to this segment and an idea of which products are most meaningful to this segment, you are in a position to create your own sales track in Figure 9.33.

Figure 9.33

RECRUIT/ASSET PROTECTION PLANNING SALES TRACK EXERCISE
Instructions: Write the name of a Recruit type of family business owner below. If you can't think of a specific person, create a mental picture of a Recruit and focus on that image for this exercise.
Instructions: Now list below the asset protection planning products most appealing to Recruits. (Refer to Figure 9.32 if you need to.)
Instructions: Next, write down the benefit Recruits are seeking from their asset protection plans. (Refer to Figure 9.31 if you need to.)
Instructions: Finally, write some statements linking the specific features of asset protection planning Recruits are most interested in with the benefit they seek to achieve. For example: "When you manage the business on behalf of a family, you must feel you have a responsibility to protect the assets of the business. I have a number of ways you can be responsive to your family's expectations."

Your Action Plan

- Identify three current family business owner prospects for your services. Write their names in Figure 9.34.
- Specify which of the eight types of family business owners they are.
- Write down how you would position your services.
- Designate which products you would present to each client.

Figure 9.34

Family Business Owner	Family Business Owner Psychological Type	How I will position my services	Products I will emphasize
1.			
2.			
3.			

CHAPTER 10
INVESTMENT MANAGEMENT

Richard Bentley smiled to himself. "I've got this system down now," he thought. "Vince is a Fortune Hunter, sure as I'm sitting here. That man is purely interested in getting wealthy. Well, next to making the money, investing it well is how wealth is made. I bet he'd be interested in some of the high performance investment management services I can provide, especially if I emphasize potential for returns."

Owners of successful businesses must handle investment management decisions. They may obtain these services from life insurance professionals like yourself or from other financial services providers such as the private banking departments of banks, stock brokers or other financial services providers. All of these providers compete directly and indirectly for the business owner investment management dollar.

For investment management, we looked most closely at the four leading investment management services available from insurance professionals and/or other financial services professionals. They are mutual funds, variable products (including variable life insurance and variable annuities), discretionary investment accounts (professional management of the portfolio) and wrap accounts.

The Importance of Investment Management

As explored here, investment management includes a range of services. It is important to explore which forms of investment management are currently important to family business owners and which particular segments are interested in each type of investment management service.

Prevalence of Investment Management

Family business owners, as a group, tend to agree that some investment management programs are more appealing, more relevant to their circumstances, and more important than others. They have a greater interest in buying these. Check your knowledge of the investment management market among family business owners in Figure 10.1.

Figure 10.01

INVESTMENT MANAGEMENT EXERCISE			
Instructions: Check whether family business owners as a group feel that each of these investment management structures is very important, somewhat important or less important.			
Investment Management	**Very Important**	**Somewhat Important**	**Less Important**
Mutual funds	❑	❑	❑
Variable products	❑	❑	❑
Discretionary investment accounts	❑	❑	❑
Wrap accounts	❑	❑	❑

As Figure 10.2 shows, as an investment management option, mutual funds are significantly more important to family business owners than any other type of investment management service. More than 75% of family business owners say that mutual funds are a very important part of their investment portfolio.

By comparison, the other investment management options are very important to smaller proportions of the family business owner market. For example, less than a quarter say variable products such as variable life insurance and variable annuities are very important to them. Even fewer are interested in discretionary investment accounts or wrap accounts.

When mutual funds are looked at, Bentley is indeed right. Mutual funds, as a form of investment management product, are most important to the Fortune Hunter personality type, as

Figure 10.02

IMPORTANCE OF INVESTMENT MANAGEMENT PRODUCTS

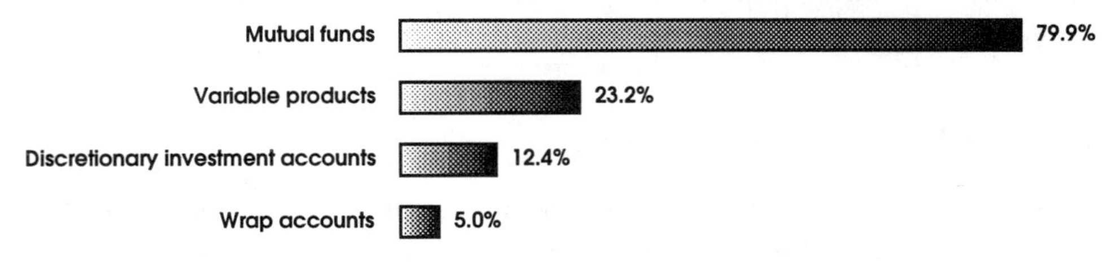

Number of Family Business Owners Who Recently Purchased Investment Management = 878

shown in Figure 10.3. However, it is important to note that this form of investment management service is likely to be of interest to all family business owner segments, at least to some degree, in view of the widespread availability of mutual funds.

Figure 10.03

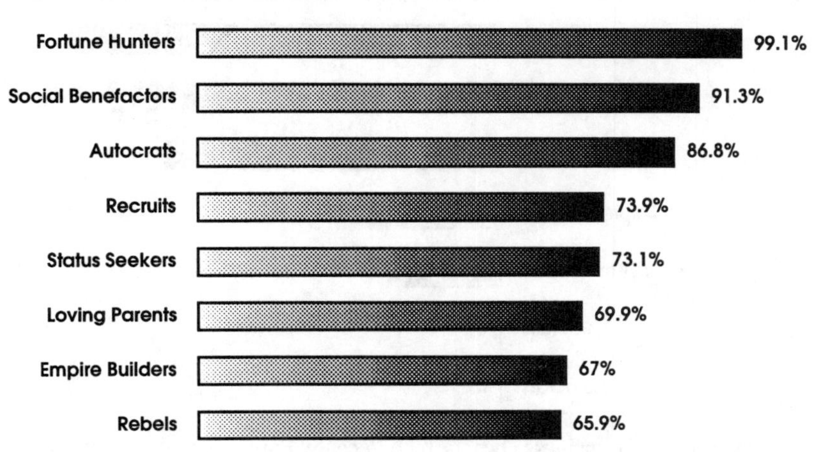

Number of Family Business Owners Who Recently Purchased Investment Management = 878

Interest in variable products is somewhat lower. Of all segments, Empire Builders and Loving Parents seem to be the better prospects since 40.5% and 30.9%, respectively, feel that variable products are an important component of their investment portfolios, as illustrated in Figure 10.4.

Figure 10.04

IMPORTANCE OF VARIABLE PRODUCTS

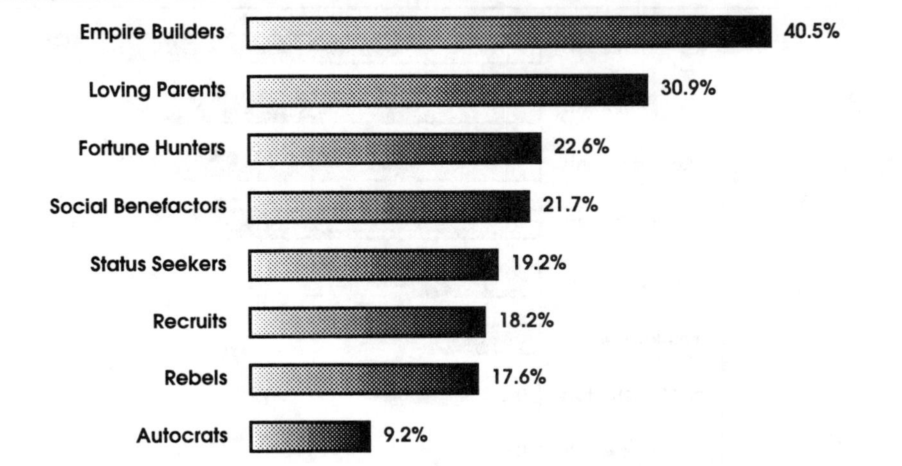

Number of Family Business Owners Who Recently Purchased Investment Management = 878

Compared to mutual funds, and even to variable products, there is little interest in discretionary investment accounts, as Figure 10.5 shows.

Figure 10.05

IMPORTANCE OF DISCRETIONARY ADVISORY ACCOUNTS

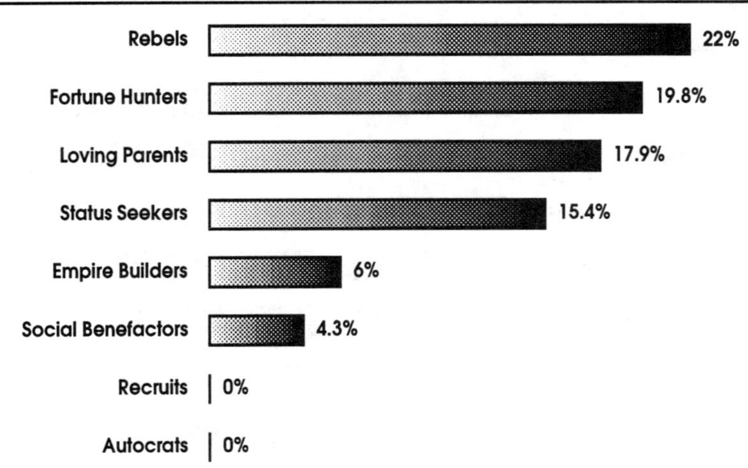

Number of Family Business Owners Who Recently Purchased Investment Management = 878

Wrap accounts are, relatively speaking, newer innovations among investment management products and they are not often sold by life insurance professionals. The low importance rating for wrap accounts among family business owners may be due to a lack of awareness. It may also be that many business owners are investing in the business rather than extracting assets for personal investing. It's hard to tell which at this time. What is the case is that relatively few family business owners feel that wrap accounts are a very important part of their investment management program, as shown in Figure 10.6.

Figure 10.06

IMPORTANCE OF WRAP ACCOUNTS

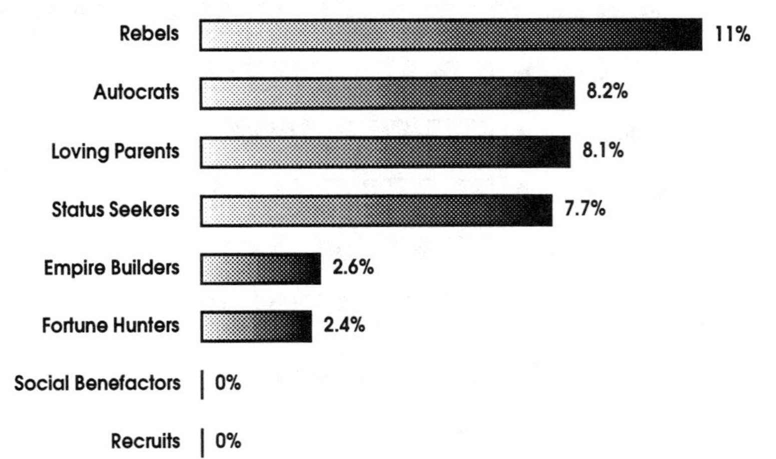

Number of Family Business Owners Who Recently Purchased Investment Management = 878

Key Market Segments for Investment Management Products

The market for investment management products is spread across all the personality types. The largest segment, Loving Parents, has less than 20% and the smallest has less than 10%, as shown in Figure 10.07. Some segments are more predisposed to investment management than their distribution in the population would indicate. Included here are Empire Builders, Recruits, Fortune Hunters, Rebels, Status Seekers, and Social Benefactors. The interesting exception is Loving Parents, as shown in Figure 10.07.

Although Loving Parents account for one in three business owners nationally, they make up a smaller proportion of those interested in investment management products. Autocrats are also under-represented (11.2% as compared to 19.2%). Heads of business-owning families in these two groups are attached to the power and role that status gives them within the family. They like control over their children's lives and that control only exists to the extent they remain head of the business as well as head of the family.

Figure 10.07

DISTRIBUTION OF FAMILY BUSINESS SEGMENTS: BUYERS OF INVESTMENT MANAGEMENT PRODUCTS AND NATIONALLY		
Family Business Segment	**Recent Purchasers of Investment Management**	**National Distribution of Segments**
Fortune Hunters	24.1%	8.9%
Loving Parents	14.0%	34.1%
Empire Builders	13.2%	13.0%
Status Seekers	11.8%	5.7%
Autocrats	11.2%	19.2%
Rebels	10.4%	6.5%
Recruits	10.0%	7.8%
Social Benefactors	5.2%	4.8%

Number of Family Business Owners Who Recently Purchased Investment Management = 878

Positioning Your Practice

As we have seen with respect to executive benefits in Chapter 6 and with respect to retirement benefits in Chapter 7, each type of family business owner sees insurance and other financial products differently. That is, each has a unique set of needs and wants and, therefore, each personality type sees a different benefit. Clearly, emphasizing a benefit that is especially appealing and relevant to a family business owner will be more likely to be successful than emphasizing one which is not relevant to that segment. Knowing exactly which benefits appeal to each segment is critical to successful investment management sales. It is crucial that you position investment management properly with each family business segment. You can begin with the positioning investment management exercise in Figure 10.8.

Figure 10.08

POSITIONING INVESTMENT MANAGEMENT EXERCISE	
Instructions: Write out a phrase which describes investment management in words especially meaningful to each family business owner segment.	
Fortune Hunters	
Loving Parents	
Empire Builders	
Status Seekers	
Autocrats	
Rebels	
Recruits	
Social Benefactors	

In the sections below you will be able to compare your positioning statements against those we created and tested with eight hundred family business owners.

Fortune Hunters

Because Fortune Hunters are characterized by the desire to accumulate wealth, they are relatively disinterested in the goals of other family business owners such as caring for the family or leaving the business as a family legacy. Taking this into account, the positioning statement we created and tested with over eight hundred recent purchasers of investment management was, "Your goal in investing is to become rich." Fortune Hunters, as expected, responded very positively to this positioning statement, as shown in Figure 10.9. Over 90% agreed strongly that it was the most important rationale in their purchase of investment management services. This positioning statement had a slight appeal to Loving Parents but none at all for members of other segments. This means that life insurance professionals selling investment management services and products to Fortune Hunters need to emphasize the investment performance of their products and make explicit connections between those products and wealth accumulation.

Fortune Hunters are a good market for specific types of investment management products, as Figure 10.10 shows. They are especially interested in mutual funds, in part because of the investment record of these funds. Their interest extends to variable products and discretionary investment accounts as well. Given the orientation of this segment, there might be more interest in wrap accounts if there were greater awareness of this investment option.

Figure 10.09

POSITIONING STATEMENT: *YOUR GOAL IN INVESTING IS TO BECOME RICH*

(Percent of family business owners with investment management who say this positioning statement is very important to them.)

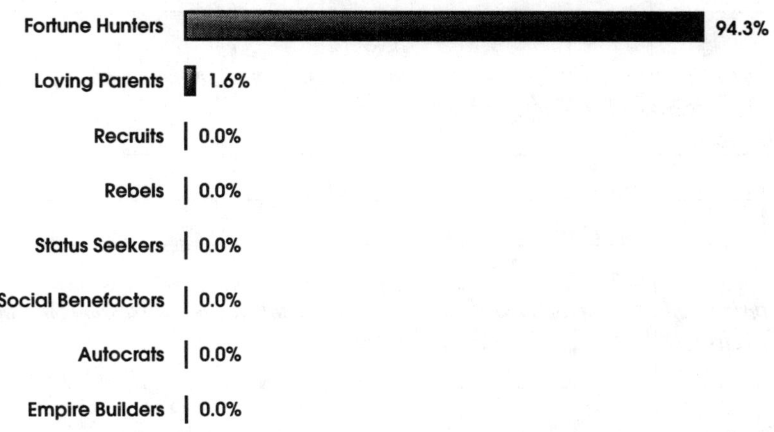

Number of Family Business Owners Who Recently Purchased Investment Management = 878

Figure 10.10

INVESTMENT MANAGEMENT PRODUCTS IMPORTANT TO FORTUNE HUNTERS

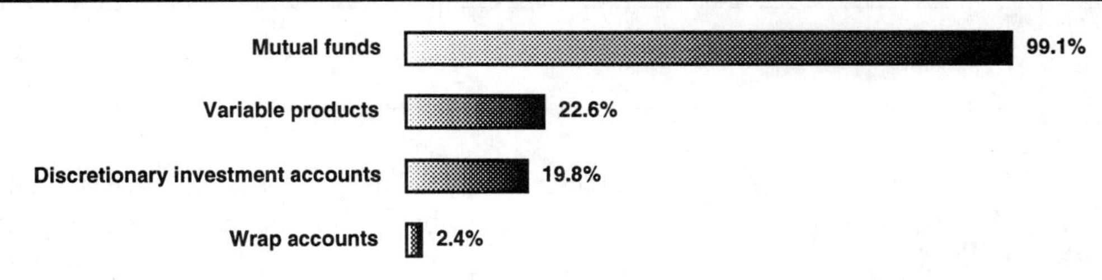

Number of Fortune Hunters = 212

This information should enable you to create effective sales presentations of investment management services to the Fortune Hunter type of family business owner. The exercise in Figure 10.11 will enable you to do so easily by bringing together the information in this section and assisting you in creating your own sales track.

Figure 10.11

FORTUNE HUNTER/INVESTMENT MANAGEMENT SALES TRACK EXERCISE
Instructions: Write the name of a Fortune Hunter type of family business owner below. If you can't think of a specific person, create a mental picture of a Fortune Hunter and focus on that image for this exercise.
Instructions: Now list below the investment management services most appealing to Fortune Hunters. (Refer to Figure 10.10 if you need to.)
Instructions: Next, write down the benefit Fortune Hunters are seeking from their investment management services. (Refer to Figure 10.09 if you need to.)
Instructions: Finally, write out some statements linking the specific features of the investment management products Fortune Hunters are most interested in with the benefit they seek to achieve. For example: "I agree that the main objective of investment management services should be the creating of significant incremental wealth for you. I have selected these funds for you based on their long-term results."

Loving Parents

Loving Parents seek, above all, to safeguard their families. The family business is the cornerstone of this effort. Investments are an important part of the overall strategy of protecting the family. For Loving Parents, we created the positioning statement, "You invest primarily so you can take care of the family." All the family business owners in the study were asked to rate how important this reason was for them personally in selecting investment management services.

As Figure 10.12 shows, this reason is extremely important to almost all Loving Parents because they are most interested in taking care of their families now and in later generations. Because Loving Parents manage the business as a legacy for their families, they respond positively to investment management services positioned to help them maintain the economic security of the family. As Figure 10.12 also illustrates, this reason is of little or no importance to the other segments. You can see the advantages of positioning investment management as a way of taking care of the family to Loving Parents. You can also see that this approach has little appeal to any other segment.

Figure 10.12

POSITIONING STATEMENT: *YOU INVEST PRIMARILY SO YOU CAN TAKE CARE OF THE FAMILY*

(Percent of family business owners with investment management who say this positioning statement is very important for them.)

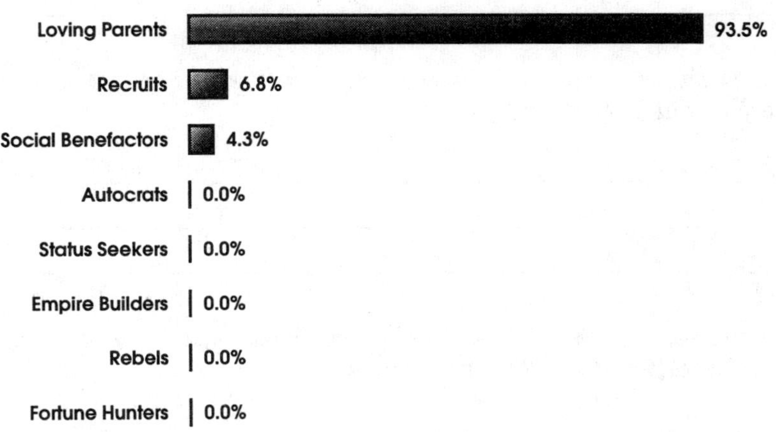

Number of Family Business Owners Who Recently Purchased Investment Management = 878

Among the different investment management alternatives, most Loving Parents say mutual funds are important to them, as shown in Figure 10.13. Loving Parents are also good prospects for other investment services. Although the proportions are smaller, their interest is above average for variable products, discretionary investment accounts and even wrap accounts. Life insurance professionals who connect these products to the core value of safeguarding the family will find Loving Parents good prospects.

Based on the information so far, you should be able to create effective sales presentations positioning investment management effectively to Loving Parents. The exercise in Figure 10.14 will enable you to do so easily by integrating the products and benefit information in this section and preparing you to create your own sales track.

Figure 10.13

INVESTMENT MANAGEMENT PRODUCTS IMPORTANT TO LOVING PARENTS

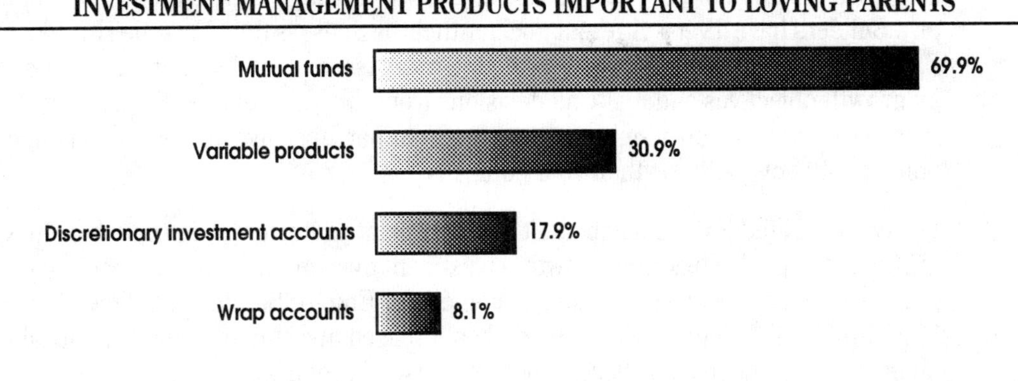

Number of Loving Parents = 123

Figure 10.14

LOVING PARENT/INVESTMENT MANAGEMENT SALES TRACK EXERCISE
Instructions: Write the name of of a Loving Parent type of family business owner below. If you can't think of a specific person, create a mental picture of a Loving Parent and focus on that image for this exercise.
Instructions: Now list below the investment management services most appealing to Loving Parents. (Refer to Figure 10.13 if you need to.)
Instructions: Next, write down the benefit Loving Parents are seeking from their investment management services. (Refer to Figure 10.12 if you need to.)
Instructions: Finally, write out some statements linking the specific features of the investment management products Loving Parents are most interested in with the benefit they seek to achieve. For example: "Wrap accounts are a way other close families in business that I know take care of each other. Your investment programs will enable you to use your resources to safeguard your family."

Empire Builders

The third most important segment for investment management is the Empire Builders. Empire Builders have a very different goal for their businesses than Fortune Hunters and Loving Parents. Empire Builders want to create big businesses — business empires. They are driven by growth objectives and make all decisions from this perspective. Accordingly, for this segment we created the positioning statement, "Your personal investments are an important component in the overall growth of your company."

For Empire Builders, the key benefit of all financial and insurance products is how they contribute to the goal of business growth. Investment management can be a boon to growth. This is an extremely effective positioning statement for Empire Builders, as shown in Figure 10.15. Most Empire Builders who have recently purchased investment management said this statement is a very important reflection of their reason for doing so. Note, also, that this reason is not particularly relevant for any other segment.

Figure 10.15

POSITIONING STATEMENT: *YOUR PERSONAL INVESTMENTS ARE AN IMPORTANT COMPONENT IN THE OVERALL GROWTH OF YOUR COMPANY*

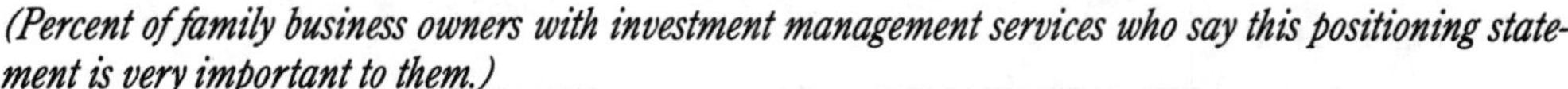
(Percent of family business owners with investment management services who say this positioning statement is very important to them.)

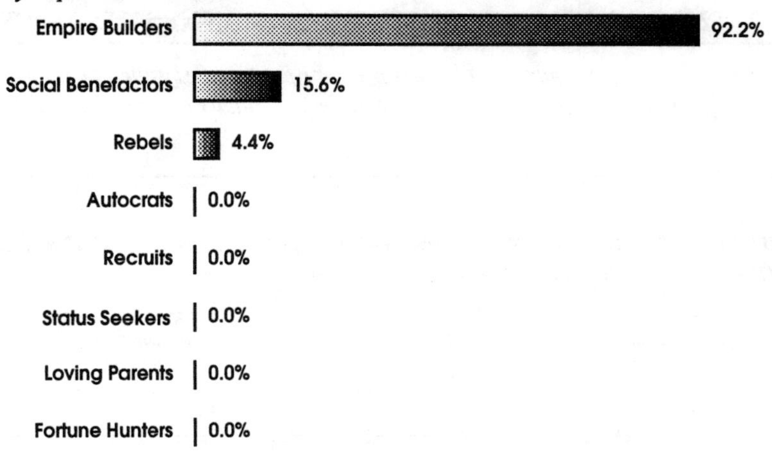

Number of Family Business Owners Who Recently Purchased Investment Management = 878

As Figure 10.16 illustrates, Empire Builders are the segment most interested in variable life insurance and annuities. Just under half of Empire Builders say such products are very important to them, the highest proportion of any segment. Overall, most Empire Builders are interested in mutual funds, but this segment is not particularly interested in discretionary investment accounts or wrap accounts.

Figure 10.16

INVESTMENT MANAGEMENT PRODUCTS IMPORTANT TO EMPIRE BUILDERS

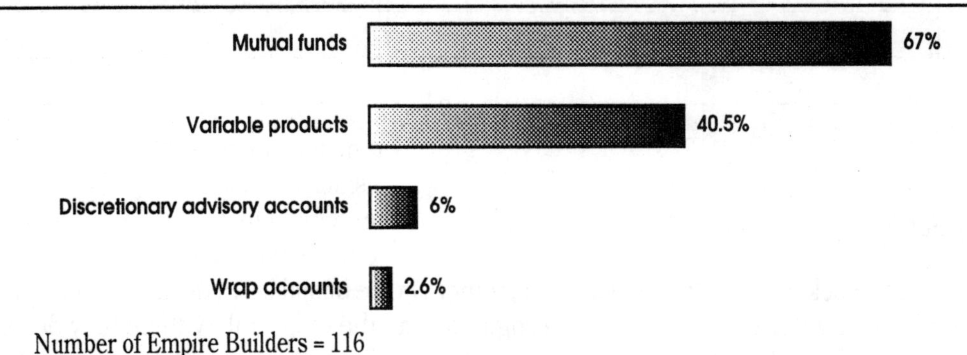

Number of Empire Builders = 116

Based on the information so far, you should be able to create effective sales presentations of investment management to Empire Builders. The exercise in Figure 10.17 will enable you to do so easily.

Figure 10.17

EMPIRE BUILDER/INVESTMENT MANAGEMENT SALES TRACK EXERCISE
Instructions: Write the name of a Empire Builder type of family business owner below. If you can't think of a specific person, create a mental picture of a Empire Builder and focus on that image for this exercise.
Instructions: Now list below the investment management services most appealing to Empire Builders. (Refer to Figure 10.16 if you need to.)
Instructions: Next, write down the benefit Empire Builders are seeking from their investment management services. (Refer to Figure 10.15 if you need to.)
Instructions: Finally, write out some statements linking the specific features of the investment management products Empire Builders are most interested in with the benefit they seek to achieve. For example: "Certain kinds of investment management products have been effective for other business owners I know whose goal is aggressive business growth."

Status Seekers

Status Seekers are interested in having others in the business, in the family and in the community at large give them the social recognition and the respect they think they deserve. Status Seekers are interested in appearances and image. The positioning statement created for them was designed to appeal to this sense, "Your investing enables you to achieve social recognition and status." As expected, the Status Seeker segment responded well to this positioning of investment management. Almost all agreed that this was the most important reason for their recent decisions to buy investment management products. Status Seeking motivations are not important to any of the other family business owner segments, as shown in Figure 10.18.

Figure 10.18

POSITIONING STATEMENT: *YOUR INVESTING ENABLES YOU TO ACHIEVE SOCIAL RECOGNITION AND STATUS*

(Percent of family business owners with investment management who say this positioning statement is very important for them.)

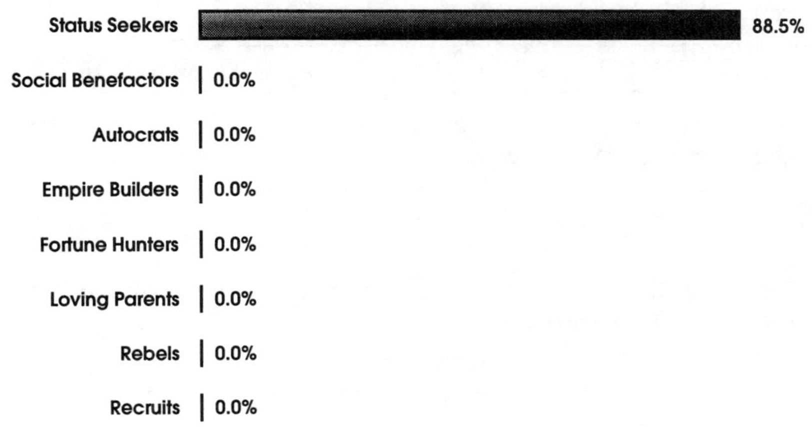

Number of Family Business Owners Who Recently Purchased Investment Management = 878

Although Status Seekers are a small segment, they can be a good market for some investment management products, especially mutual funds, as Figure 10.19 shows. Less than a quarter are interested in variable products, discretionary investment accounts, and wrap accounts, although this disinterest may be from a lack of awareness.

Figure 10.19

INVESTMENT MANAGEMENT PRODUCTS IMPORTANT TO STATUS SEEKERS

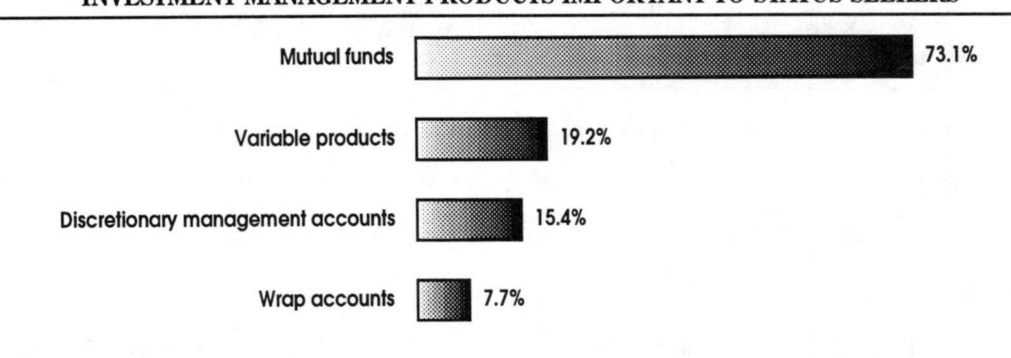

Number of Status Seekers = 104

This information should enable you to create effective sales presentations of investment management to the Status Seeker type of family business owner. The exercise in Figure 10.20 will enable you to do so easily by bringing together the information in this section and enabling you to create your own sales track.

Figure 10.20

STATUS SEEKER/INVESTMENT MANAGEMENT SALES TRACK EXERCISE
Instructions: Write the name of a Status Seeker type of family business owner below. If you can't think of a specific person, create a mental picture of a Status Seeker and focus on that image for this exercise.
Instructions: Now list below the investment management services most appealing to Status Seekers. (Refer to Figure 10.19 if you need to.)
Instructions: Next, write down the benefit Status Seekers are seeking from their investment management services. (Refer to Figure 10.18 if you need to.)
Instructions: Finally, write out some statements linking the specific features of the investment management products Status Seekers are most interested in with the benefit they seek to achieve. For example: "I've found that business owners who run their businesses most professionally earn the respect of their peers. The most respected business owners I know have the kind of investments I'm about to show you."

Autocrats

Autocrats can be appealed to on the aspect of control. They are individuals who are highly self confident and who believe that they are competent to make most business decisions unilaterally. The positioning statement we created and tested with over eight hundred recent investment management service purchasers was, "You can control others because they one day expect to inherit your invested assets." As shown in Figure 10.21, this positioning statement was extremely appealing to Autocrats because they are oriented towards control. You should note that this positioning approach is not at all appealing to any other segment. If you were to emphasize the use of investment management in controlling family members to any other segment you would probably not succeed in motivating them to buy.

Figure 10.21

POSITIONING STATEMENT: *YOU CAN CONTROL OTHERS BECAUSE THEY ONE DAY EXPECT TO INHERIT YOUR INVESTED ASSETS*

(Percent of family business owners with investment management who say this positioning statement is very important for them.)

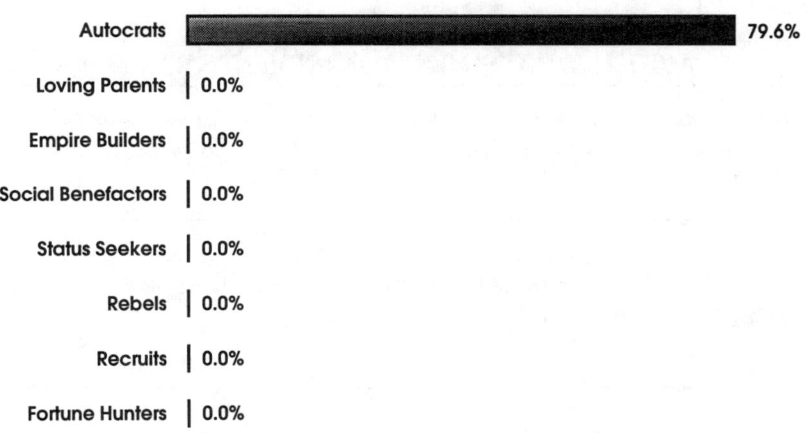

Number of Family Business Owners Who Recently Purchased Investment Management = 878

Autocrats have a highly restricted set of preferences when it comes to investment management services. They are high and above average in their preference for mutual funds. They are below average in their interest in variable products and discretionary investment accounts. Finally, they have little overall interest in wrap accounts as Figure 10.22 illustrates.

Figure 10.22

INVESTMENT MANAGEMENT PRODUCTS IMPORTANT TO AUTOCRATS

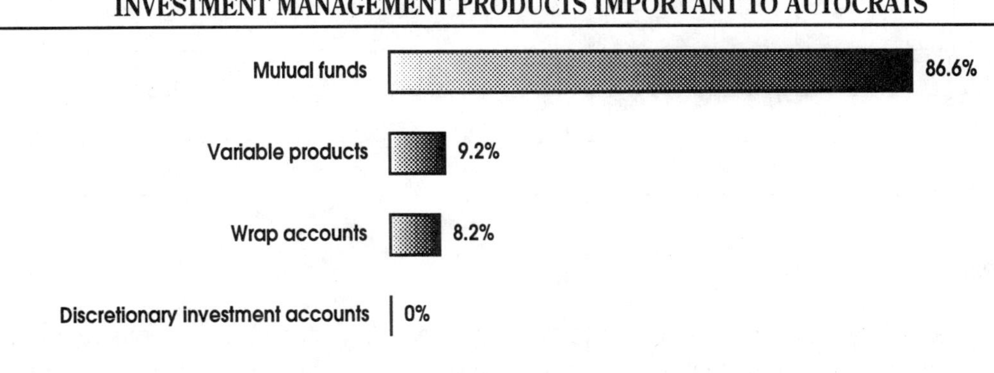

Number of Autocrats = 98

Based on the information so far, you should be able to create effective sales presentations for investment management services for the Autocrat type of family business owner. The exercise in Figure 10.23 will enable you to do so easily by bringing together the information in this section and enabling you to create your own sales track.

Figure 10.23

AUTOCRAT/INVESTMENT MANAGEMENT SALES TRACK EXERCISE
Instructions: Write the name of a Autocrat type of family business owner below. If you can't think of a specific person, create a mental picture of a Autocrat and focus on that image for this exercise.
Instructions: Now list below the investment management services most appealing to Autocrats. (Refer to Figure 10.22 if you need to.)
Instructions: Next, write down the benefit Autocrats are seeking from their investment management services. (Refer to Figure 10.21 if you need to.)
Instructions: Finally, write out some statements linking the specific features of the investment management products Autocrats are most interested in with the benefit they seek to achieve. For example: "Since control of family members while you are running a business is so critical, consider ways you could use your investments as a part of that process. I have some suggestions."

Rebels

Rebels are typically ex-corporate employees who are striving to demonstrate that they are professional, competent, and independent managers. They tend to use large corporations as their reference point when making business decisions. Making investment decisions is part of this same pattern. As a result, the positioning statement we tested for this group was, "Your investing is an expression of your independence." As expected, Rebels responded very favorably to this positioning approach. As shown in Figure 10.24, most Rebels agreed that this was the most important reason they recently purchased the investment management they did. A few Empire Builders concurred, but no one from the other segments agreed.

Figure 10.24

POSITIONING STATEMENT: *YOUR INVESTING IS AN EXPRESSION OF YOUR INDEPENDENCE*

(Percent of family business owners with investment management who say this positioning statement is very important for them.)

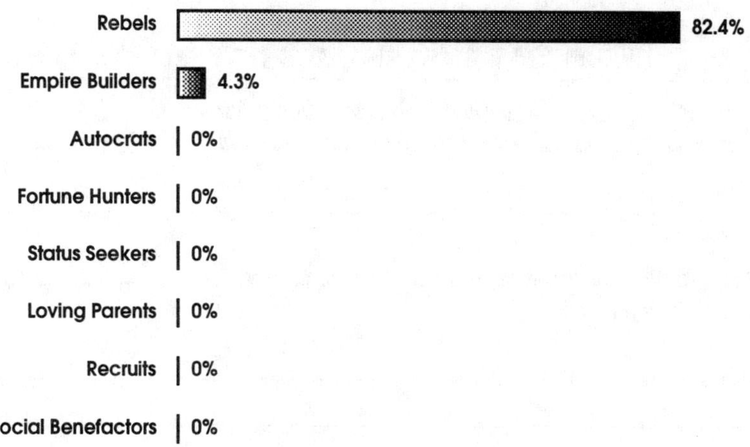

Number of Family Business Owners Who Recently Purchased Investment Management = 878

Like the other segments, Rebels are more interested in mutual funds than they are in the other forms of investment management, as Figure 10.25 illustrates. Fewer are interested in variable products, discretionary investment accounts, or wrap accounts.

Figure 10.25

INVESTMENT MANAGEMENT PRODUCTS IMPORTANT TO REBELS

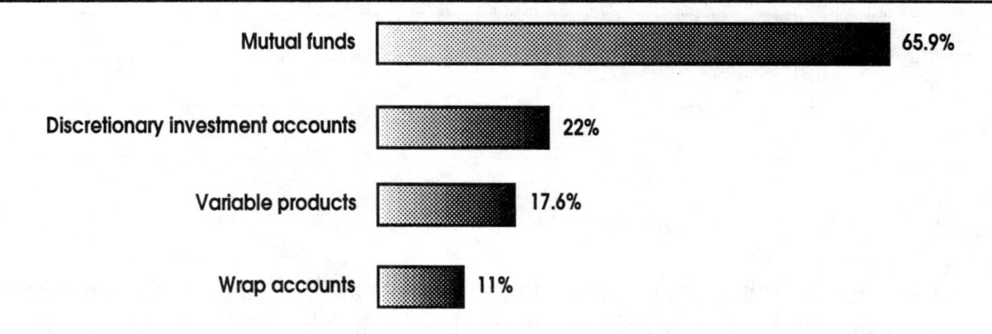

Number of Rebels = 91

This information should enable you to create effective sales presentations of investment management for the Rebel family business owner personality. The exercise in Figure 10.26 will enable you to do so by bringing together the information in this section so that you can create your own sales track.

Figure 10.26

REBEL/INVESTMENT MANAGEMENT SALES TRACK EXERCISE
Instructions: Write the name of a Rebel type of family business owner below. If you can't think of a specific person, create a mental picture of a Rebel and focus on that image for this exercise.
Instructions: Now list below the investment management services most appealing to Rebels. (Refer to Figure 10.25 if you need to.)
Instructions: Next, write down the benefit Rebels are seeking from their investment management services. (Refer to Figure 10.24 if you need to.)
Instructions: Finally, write out some statements linking the specific features of the investment management products Rebels are most interested in with the benefit they seek to achieve. For example: "Professionally run corporations are aggressive about obtaining professional investment management services. We can provide the same professional services to you. Here's how."

Recruits

Because Recruits were brought into the business by their families, they share a need to take care of these families by running the business on their behalf. Thus, the positioning statement we created and tested which was designed to appeal especially to Recruits read, "Your investing is strongly influenced by family expectations." Almost all Recruits said this was the most important reason they purchased investment management, as shown in Figure 10.27. This positioning approach has no appeal for any other segment.

Figure 10.27

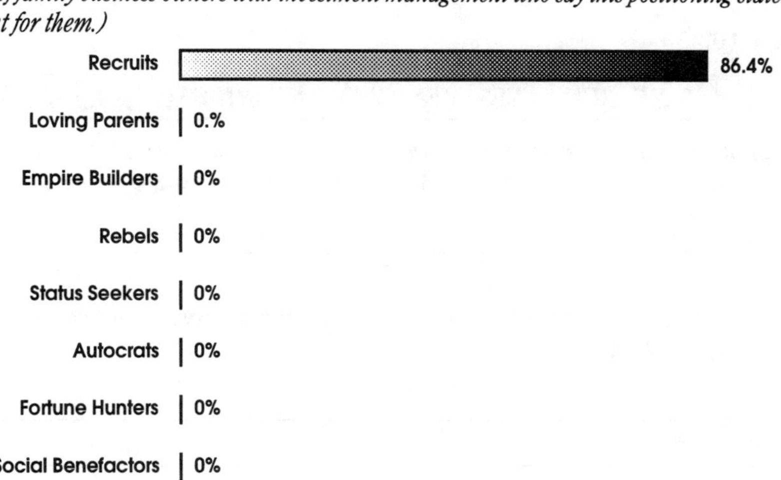

Number of Family Business Owners Who Recently Purchased Investment Management = 878

Recruits are generally conservative in their selection of investment management services. For example, as illustrated in Figure 10.28, none say that either discretionary investment accounts or wrap accounts are important to them. Most feel mutual funds are very important and a smaller proportion of Recruits say the same thing about variable products.

Figure 10.28

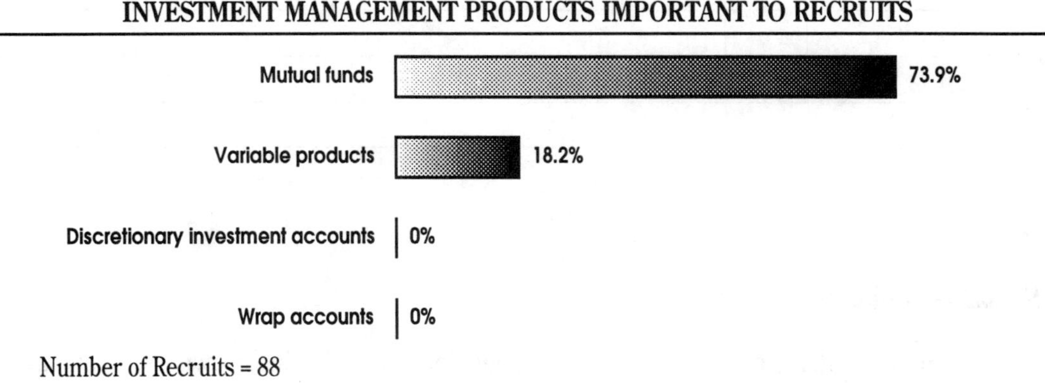

Number of Recruits = 88

This information should enable you to create effective sales presentations of investment management for the Recruit family business owner personality type. The exercise in Figure 10.29 will enable you to do so easily by bringing together the information in this section and creating your own sales track.

Figure 10.29

RECRUIT/INVESTMENT MANAGEMENT SALES TRACK EXERCISE
Instructions: Write the name of a Recruit type of family business owner below. If you can't think of a specific person, create a mental picture of a Recruit and focus on that image for this exercise.
Instructions: Now list below the investment management services most appealing to Recruits. (Refer to Figure 10.28 if you need to.)
Instructions: Next, write down the benefit Recruits are seeking from their investment management services. (Refer to Figure 10.27 if you need to.)
Instructions: Finally, write out some statements linking the specific features of the investment management products Recruits are most interested in with the benefit they seek to achieve. For example: "A comprehensive investment management program like this one used in major corporations will help you meet your family's expectations."

Social Benefactors

Social Benefactors are the socially responsible family business owners. They have a concern for the impact of their businesses on the lives of others and on the communities of which they are a part. Accordingly, the positioning statement written for them with respect to investment management was, "You take socially responsible criteria into account when investing." Social Benefactors responded to this statement readily. Fully 95% said it was the most important reason for establishing the type of investment management plan they did, as shown in Figure 10.30.

Figure 10.30

POSITIONING STATEMENT: *YOU TAKE SOCIALLY RESPONSIBLE CRITERIA INTO ACCOUNT WHEN INVESTING*

(Percent of family business owners with investment management plan who say this positioning statement is very important for them.)

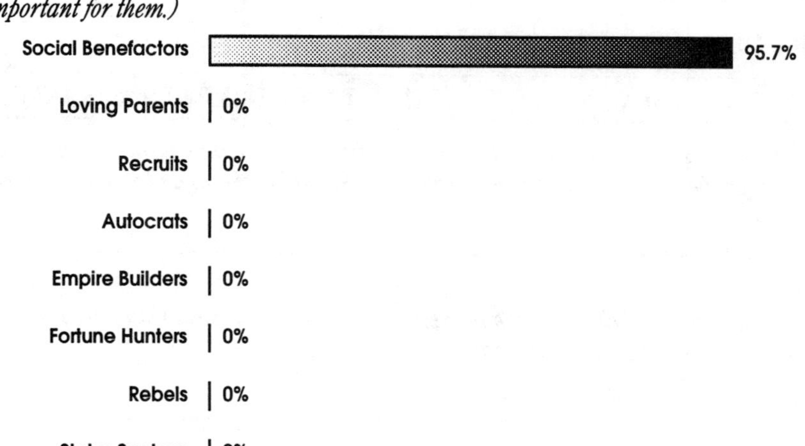

Number of Family Business Owners Who Recently Purchased Investment Management = 878

Although Social Benefactors are the smallest segment, they are an important one for investment management programs which enable them to express their feelings of social responsibility. As Figure 10.31 shows, mutual funds have the strongest appeal while only a fifth are interested in variable products.

Figure 10.31

INVESTMENT MANAGEMENT PRODUCTS IMPORTANT TO SOCIAL BENEFACTORS

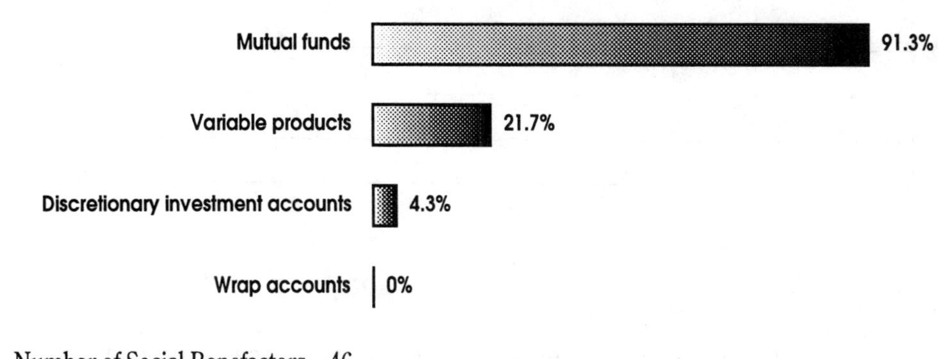

Number of Social Benefactors = 46

This information should enable you to create effective sales presentations of investment management for the Social Benefactor type of family business owner. The exercise in Figure 10.32 will enable you to do so easily by bringing together the information in this section and creating your own sales track.

Figure 10.32

SOCIAL BENEFACTOR/INVESTMENT MANAGEMENT SALES TRACK EXERCISE
Instructions: Write the name of a Social Benefactor type of family business owner below. If you can't think of a specific person, create a mental picture of a Social Benefactor and focus on that image for this exercise.
Instructions: Now list below the investment management services most appealing to Social Benefactors. (Refer to Figure 10.31 if you need to.)
Instructions: Next, write down the benefit Social Benefactors are seeking from their investment management services. (Refer to Figure 10.30 if you need to.)
Instructions: Finally, write out some statements linking the specific features of the investment management products Social Benefactors are most interested in with the benefit they seek to achieve. For example: "You have said that using your business to create a more socially responsible world is important to you. So is investing, and I have for you some exciting investment opportunities all of which meet social responsibility criteria."

Your Action Plan

- Identify three current family business owner prospects for your services. Write their names in the Figure 10.33.
- Specify which of the eight types of family business owners they are.
- Write down how you would position your services.
- Designate which products you would present to each client.

Figure 10.33

Family Business Owner	Family Business Owner Psychological Type	How I will position my services	Products I will emphasize
1.			
2.			
3.			

CHAPTER 11
CHARITABLE ESTATE PLANNING

Richard Bentley got to know James Terhune when both were raising funds for their college. Bentley knew Terhune came from the family that owned the Terhune Works, one of the last privately-owned manufacturing firms in the city. In addition to being wealthy, Terhune was well known for his charitable works in the community. He was on the board of trustees of the hospital, the area community foundation and the local museum. "You have a responsibility to give it back," Terhune was fond of saying. "This community has given a lot to me and my family and it is only right that we give back to the community."

Bentley had handled a few minor insurance matters for Terhune and, after a meeting to arrange for a coverage increase on one of the policies, Bentley raised the topic of charitable estate planning. He explained that charitable estate planning involved using certain tax provisions to make gifts to charities which also had significant benefits for the Terhune business interests and his family. Terhune was responsive. He had the sense that there were things he could do, but hadn't known where to start. He scheduled a time to sit down with Bentley to get the charitable estate planning process started.

Charitable estate planning is critical to many family business owners. If an owner is a first generation family business owner, he has built the business up and has a high personal stake in seeing it successfully conveyed to the next generation. A second (or later) generation family business owner sees the businesses as a form of trusteeship and feels morally responsible to insure its safe transition along family lines. Either way, family business owners are generally highly motivated to insure the safe succession of their businesses. The only obstacle is that many family business owners think they will live forever.

Thus, the whole area of transition or succession planning, which includes charitable estate planning, is one of the most difficult areas to work in with a family business owner. There are additional reasons it is difficult. Estate planning issues which are already fairly complex become even more so when the principal asset is a closely-held business. Issues of how best to insure business continuity as well as wealth transfer can be clouded by interpersonal issues among family members. The technical and sales skills of the life insurance professional are often severely tested. The reason for taking on such cases is that they are among the most profitable available.

The Importance of Charitable Estate Planning

A charitable estate planning program for the closely-held business can involve one or more financial strategies, including charitable remainder trusts, private foundations, charitable bequests, donor advised funds, charitable lead trusts, pooled income funds, charitable gift annuities and life insurance. Few donors will incorporate more than two of these into their estate plan. But, virtually all owners of closely-held businesses could benefit from including one or more of these options in their estate plans. Charitable estate planning is the process which systematically explores these options on behalf of the prospect.

Prevalence of Charitable Estate Strategies

Family business owners, as a group, tend to agree that some of these are more important than others. Check your knowledge of the market in the charitable estate strategies exercise in Figure 11.01.

Although these are family business owners who recently completed the charitable estate planning process, relatively few feel that each of these strategies is very important. There are reasons for this. Most insurance agents still feel uncomfortable with the technical complexi-

Figure 11.01

CHARITABLE ESTATE STRATEGIES EXERCISE

Instructions: Check whether family business owners as a group feel that each of these charitable estate strategies is very important, somewhat important or less important.

Charitable Estate Strategy	Very Important	Somewhat Important	Less Important
Charitable bequests	❑	❑	❑
Private family or corporate foundation	❑	❑	❑
Charitable remainder trusts	❑	❑	❑
Donor advised fund	❑	❑	❑
Charitable lead trusts	❑	❑	❑
Pooled income funds	❑	❑	❑
Charitable gift annuities	❑	❑	❑
Life insurance	❑	❑	❑

ties of these strategies and, thus, may not be able to present all of them to their clients. As a result, not all clients find each very important because they are not familiar with how it could be advantageous to them personally. The other reason is that a typical charitable estate plan will only include one or two of these options, customized to meet the client's needs. Clients are unlikely to rate as "very important" strategies which they decided against.

As shown in Figure 11.02, the component of charitable estate planning which most family business owners do agree is important is the charitable remainder trust. Charitable bequests are important to fewer business owners.

The other charitable estate planning products are very important to even smaller numbers, reflecting the fact that this market is in the early stages of development. Donor advised funds are very important to about 17%, while life insurance is important to about 11% and a private or corporate foundation is important to 9%. Charitable gift annuities, charitable lead trusts and pooled income funds are each very important to less than 5%.

Figure 11.02

IMPORTANCE OF CHARITABLE ESTATE PLAN STRATEGIES

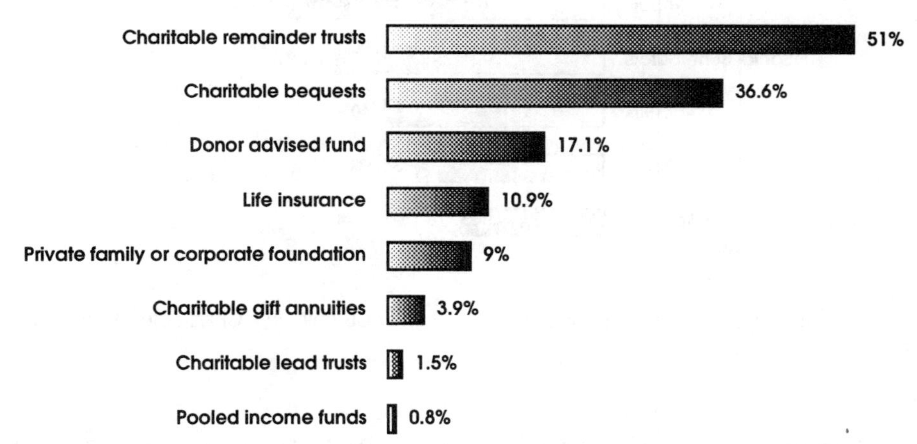

Number of Family Business Owners Who Recently Completed a Charitable Estate Plan = 907

The key to understanding markets for the various charitable estate planning products is understanding the way they are viewed by each of the eight family owner types. Based on their personalities, family business owners seek very different charitable estate planning products. By knowing in advance how each personality reacts to the different products you will be able to sell more effectively.

For example, when we look at how family business owners react to charitable remainder trusts, Figure 11.03 shows large differences. Because of their values, two business owner types are natural prospects for charitable remainder trusts, Loving Parents and Social Benefactors. When working with these types, it is essential to relate the features of the trust to the need that these two segments have for taking care of others — the family in the case of Loving Parents and the community or cause in the case of Social Benefactors.

Rebels and Recruits should be told about the benefits of charitable remainder trusts, since 58% and 40%, respectively, are very interested. Charitable remainder trusts could be explained to Empire Builders and Status Seekers along with other options, since a few of them are interested.

Among all segments, Fortune Hunters and Autocrats are most interested in charitable remainder trusts. This interest is prompted by the positive effect on personal financial planning in the case of Fortune Hunters and because of the possibilities for control in the case of Autocrats.

Figure 11.03

IMPORTANCE OF CHARITABLE REMAINDER TRUSTS IN CHARITABLE ESTATE PLANNING

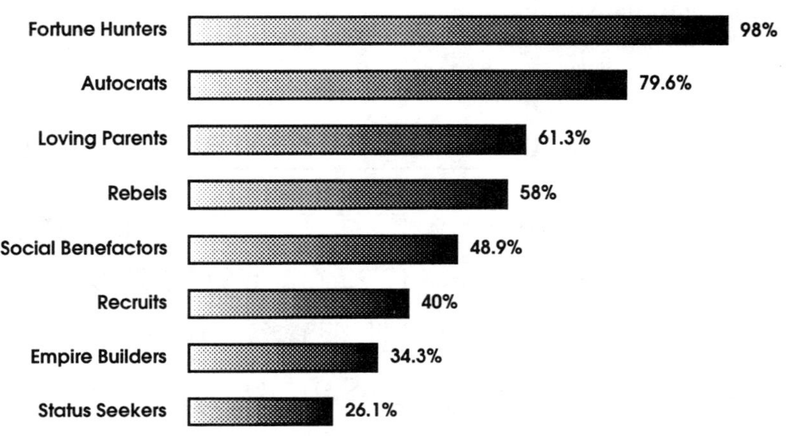

Number of Family Business Owners Who Recently Completed a Charitable Estate Plan = 907

As Figure 11.04 illustrates, Loving Parents and Social Benefactors head the list of segments interested in charitable bequests. This result might be expected given their values and goals in running their businesses. Other segments are comparatively less interested in the overall concept of charitable bequests in estate planning and will probably remain so unless the process is firmly connected to their goals and values as family business owners.

For example, Rebels, Recruits, and Empire Builders are lower in interest. Even fewer Status Seekers, Fortune Hunters, and Autocrats are interested in charitable bequests.

Donor advised funds appeal to a very specific group of family business owners. Donor advised funds allow donors to direct income to various charities while having the principal under management of a community foundation. Donor advised funds have particular appeal to Empire Builders, Status Seekers and Rebels, but for different reasons, as shown in Figure 11.05.

About a third of Empire Builders value donor advised funds. They like the ability such funds give them to support local institutions which, in turn, create a positive environment for their business.

Figure 11.04

IMPORTANCE OF CHARITABLE BEQUESTS IN CHARITABLE ESTATE PLANNING

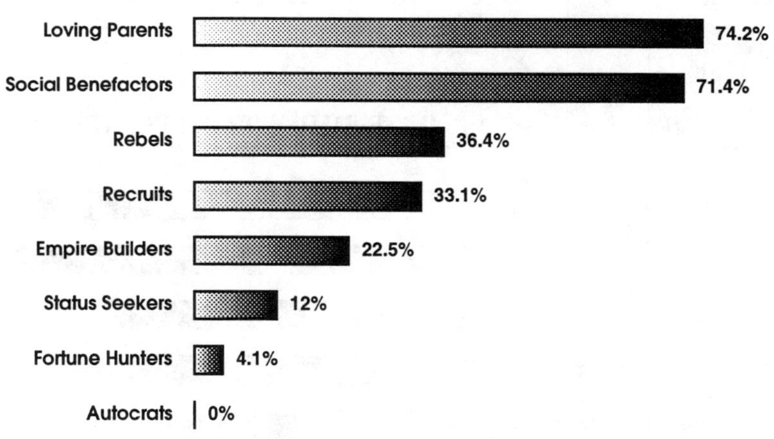

Number of Family Business Owners Who Recently Completed a Charitable Estate Plan = 907

Status Seekers also think donor advised funds are important. Status Seekers warm to the continuing social prestige that directing funds can bring. Rebels are the third group which should be targeted for donor advised funds. Rebels seek the acknowledgment of others that they are successful. Because of the context in which donor advised funds operate, Rebels anticipate that others will be aware of their role in allocating fund assets and be duly impressed with the fund itself.

Less than 10% of each of the other types feels that donor advised funds would be very important for their situations. Excellent sales professionals will sound out all prospects on the topic of donor advised funds, but usually will not push the issue if the donor is a Loving Parent, Recruit, Social Benefactor, Autocrat or Fortune Hunter.

Figure 11.05

IMPORTANCE OF DONOR ADVISED FUNDS IN CHARITABLE ESTATE PLANNING

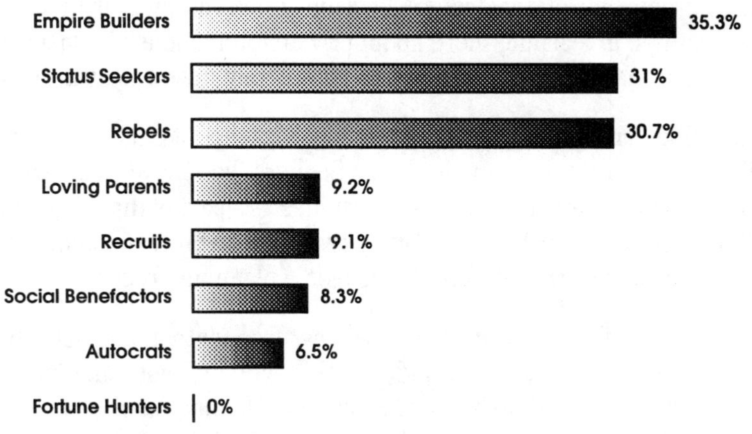

Number of Family Business Owners Who Recently Completed a Charitable Estate Plan = 907

In other research, we have confirmed the widespread interest family business owners have in private foundations. For these purposes, however, we asked only if a private foundation was "very important" to them in the creation of their recent charitable estate plan. Overall, private foundations did not play a large role, as shown in Figure 11.06.

Figure 11.06

IMPORTANCE OF A PRIVATE FAMILY OR CORPORATE FOUNDATION

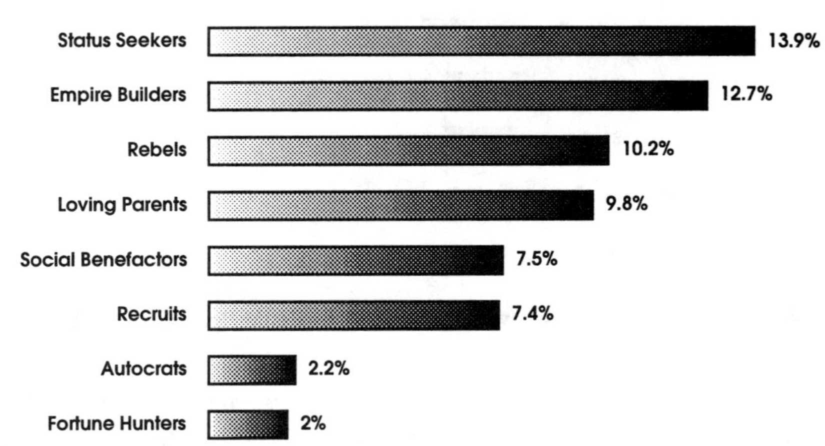

Number of Family Business Owners Who Recently Completed a Charitable Estate Plan = 907

More than 10% of each of three types felt private or corporate foundations were very important. Status Seekers felt private foundations were important because they conferred a social prestige on the founder. Empire Builders found the perpetual nature of a foundation appealing. Slightly more than 10% of Rebels think private foundations are important probably because Rebels appreciate the acknowledgment of their own skills that the creation of a private foundation implies.

Less than 10% of the other family business owners types feel that private foundations are an important part of their charitable estate planning efforts at this time. These groups include Loving Parents, Social Benefactors, Recruits, Autocrats and Fortune Hunters. Given the widespread interest in learning more about private foundations, life insurance sales professionals should be prepared to educate all interested family business owners on the option.

Gift annuities are not generally an important aspect of charitable estate planning. Only one family business owner segment, Status Seekers, had more than 10% who were interested in charitable estate planning and in gift annuities as a part of that plan, as shown in Figure 11.07. All other types of family business owners were relatively less inclined to consider gift annuities as a very important part of a charitable estate planning process.

Typically, charitable lead trusts are used less frequently than charitable remainder trusts. As a result, it is not surprising to find that this type of trust tends not to be a very important component of the charitable estate planning of family business owners, as shown in Figure 11.08. Empire Builders are the only segment which is relatively interested in the charitable lead trust.

Figure 11.07

IMPORTANCE OF GIFT ANNUITIES IN CHARITABLE ESTATE PLANNING

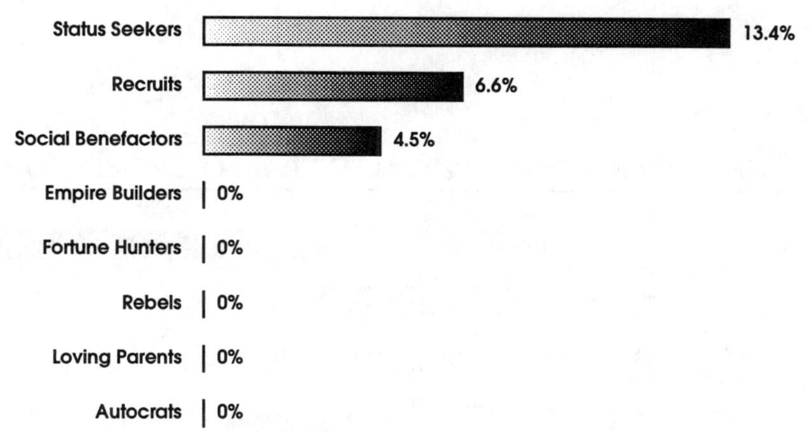

Number of Family Business Owners Who Recently Completed a Charitable Estate Plan = 907

Figure 11.08

IMPORTANCE OF CHARITABLE LEAD TRUSTS IN CHARITABLE ESTATE PLANNING

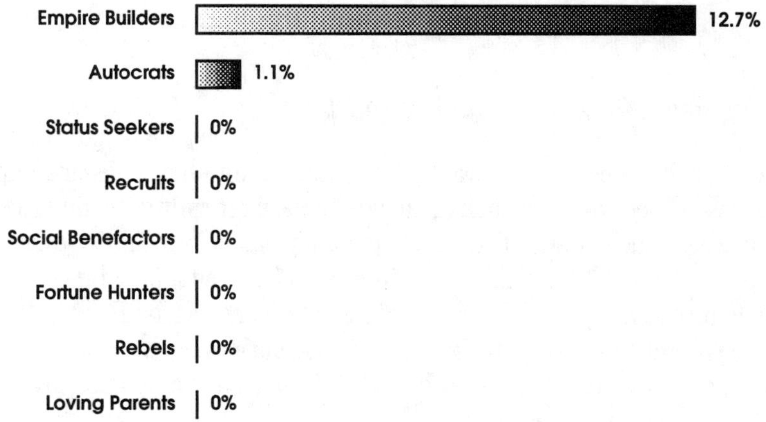

Number of Family Business Owners Who Recently Completed a Charitable Estate Plan = 907

Pooled income funds are very important to only a few family business owners, as shown in Figure 11.09. Recruits are slightly more interested than the other types, but insurance professionals should expect interest in pooled income funds to be low across the board.

Figure 11.09

IMPORTANCE OF POOLED INCOME FUNDS IN CHARITABLE ESTATE PLANNING

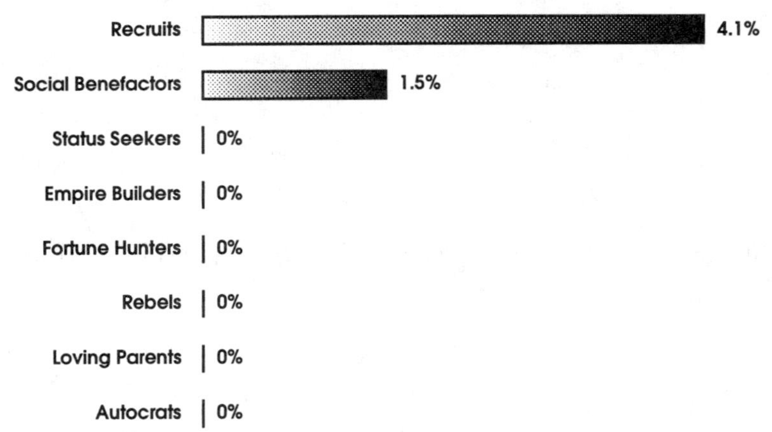

Number of Family Business Owners Who Recently Completed a Charitable Estate Plan = 907

Key Market Segments for Charitable Estate Plans

Some family business owners are better prospects for charitable estate planning than others. This is easy to see when a profile of those who have recently completed a charitable estate plan is compared to the national distribution of family business owner segments as shown in Figure 11.10. For example, Status Seekers comprise 5.7% of all family business owners but 17.4% of those who recent established charitable estate plans. Social Benefactors are just 4.8% of all family business owners but 14.7% of recent purchasers of charitable estate services. Recruits are also good prospects since they include 7.8% of all owners nationally but 13.3% of those who established charitable estate plans.

The largest segment for charitable estate plans are Loving Parents, but it should be noted that they are relatively under-represented. While they represent 34.1% of business owners nationally, they are just 18% of recent purchasers of charitable estate products.

Charitable estate planning is of somewhat less interest to Empire Builders, Autocrats, Rebels, and Fortune Hunters.

Another perspective on Figure 11.10 is that almost half of the market is comprised of Loving Parents, Status Seekers, and Social Benefactors. These three segments are the most philanthropically inclined or are more attuned to the social benefits of being thought philanthropic. Life insurance professionals should suggest charitable estate planning to these segments.

Figure 11.10

DISTRIBUTION OF FAMILY BUSINESS SEGMENTS: BUYERS OF CHARITABLE ESTATE PLAN PRODUCTS AND NATIONALLY		
Family Business Segment	**Recent Purchasers of Charitable Estate Products**	**National Distribution of Segments**
Loving Parents	18.0%	34.1%
Status Seekers	17.4%	5.7%
Social Benefactors	14.7%	4.8%
Recruits	13.3%	7.8%
Empire Builders	11.2%	13.0%
Autocrats	10.3%	19.2%
Rebels	9.7%	6.5%
Fortune Hunters	5.4%	8.9%
Number of Family Business Owners Who Recently Completed Business Succession or Estate Planning = 1,148		

Positioning Your Practice

As you appreciate by now, each type of family business owner sees insurance products and financial strategies differently. This is also true of charitable estate products. In order to be successful in promoting charitable estate planning, you must emphasize the specific benefits each segment associates with the process and the outcome. You can begin with the charitable estate plan positioning exercise in Figure 11.11.

Figure 11.11

POSITIONING CHARITABLE ESTATE PRODUCTS EXERCISE	
Instructions: Write out a phrase which describes a key benefit of charitable estate planning in words especially meaningful to each family business owner segment.	
Loving Parents	
Status Seekers	
Social Benefactors	
Recruits	
Empire Builders	
Autocrats	
Rebels	
Fortune Hunters	

In the sections below you can compare your positioning statement against those we created and tested with hundreds of family business owners.

Loving Parents

The most important business owner segment for charitable estate products is Loving Parents. For this segment, we created the positioning statement, "Charitable estate planning is a meaningful way to express your family's values." Loving Parents are driven by values. The value of taking care of their families comes first, of course, and the value of taking care of others in addition to the family is important to many as well. Since charitable estate products are an obvious manifestation of certain values, we tested this positioning statement and found that it was extremely effective with Loving Parents, as shown in Figure 11.12. Almost all Loving Parents who have recently purchased charitable estate products said this statement is a very important reflection of their reasons for doing so. Note also that this reason is much less important for other segments. Before selecting and using any positioning statement, you should be certain which type of family business owner you are working with.

Figure 11.12

POSITIONING STATEMENT: *CHARITABLE ESTATE PLANNING IS A MEANINGFUL WAY TO EXPRESS YOUR FAMILY'S VALUES*

(Percent of family business owners with a charitable estate plan who say this positioning statement is very important to them.)

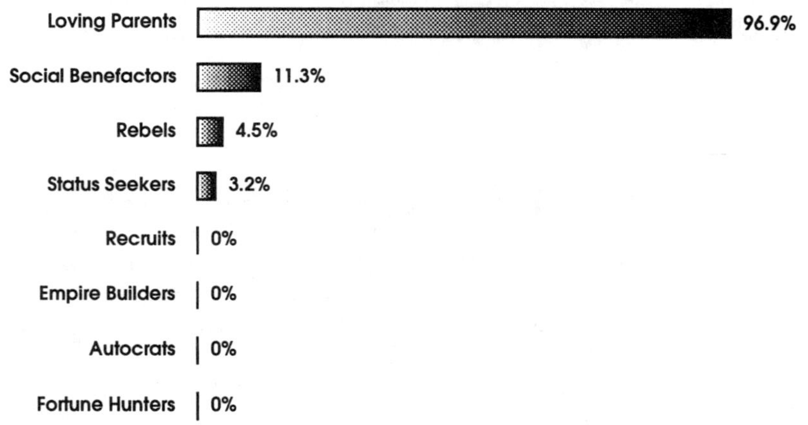

Number of Family Business Owners Who Recently Completed a Charitable Estate Plan = 907

As Figure 11.13 shows, Loving parents are primarily interested in charitable bequests and charitable remainder trusts. Less than 10% of Loving Parents are very interested in private family foundations, donor advised funds, life insurance, charitable lead trusts, pooled income funds or charitable gift annuities.

Based on the information so far, you should be able to create effective sales presentations of charitable estate planning products for Loving Parents. The exercise in Figure 11.14 will enable you to do so easily.

Figure 11.13

CHARITABLE ESTATE PLANNING PRODUCTS IMPORTANT TO LOVING PARENTS

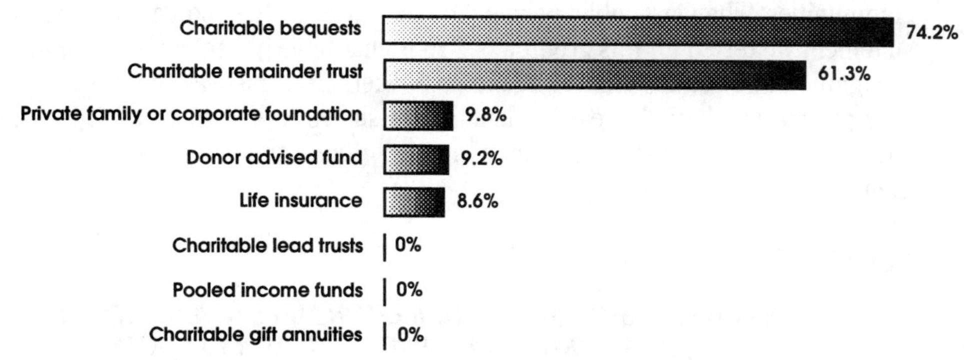

Number of Loving Parents = 163

Figure 11.14

LOVING PARENT/CHARITABLE ESTATE PLANNING SALES TRACK EXERCISE

Instructions: Write the name of a Loving Parent type of family business owner below. If you can't think of a specific person, create a mental picture of a Loving Parent and focus on that image for this exercise.

____

Instructions: Now list below the charitable estate planning products most appealing to Loving Parents. (Refer to Figure 11.13 if you need to.)

____

____

____

Instructions: Next, write down the benefit Loving Parents are seeking from charitable estate planning. (Refer to Figure 11.12 if you need to.)

____

____

____

Instructions: Finally, write out some statements linking the specific features of the charitable estate planning products Loving Parents are most interested in with the benefit they seek to achieve. For example: "When you are a parent, you have to think ahead to how best to protect your family over the long term. Charitable remainder trusts are a way you can protect some of the family's assets, ease the burden of the estate and also benefit charities which are important to the family."

____

____

____

Status Seekers

Status Seekers, as the name implies, seek the social approval and respect of others in their communities. They are public people who like to be in the spotlight. Thus, the positioning statement we tested for this group was, "Your charitable giving enables you to achieve social recognition and status." Almost all Status Seekers said this was the most important reason they purchased charitable estate planning, as shown in Figure 11.15. It is noteworthy that social recognition and status are not a high priority for the other family business owner segments.

Figure 11.15

POSITIONING STATEMENT: *YOUR CHARITABLE GIVING ENABLES YOU TO ACHIEVE SOCIAL RECOGNITION AND STATUS*

(Percent of family business owners with a charitable estate plan who say this positioning statement is very important to them.)

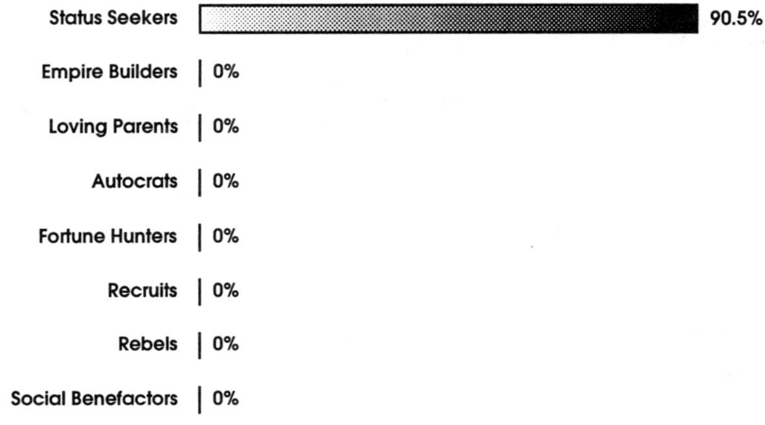

Number of Family Business Owners Who Recently Completed a Charitable Estate Plan = 907

Although they are a relatively large segment, Status Seekers are not particularly good prospects for charitable estate planning. Less than a third were very interested in any given charitable estate planning strategies, as shown in Figure 11.16. Status Seekers do prefer vehicles which give them prominence within the nonprofit community, such as donor advised funds, charitable remainder trusts and private foundations. Charitable lead trusts and pooled income funds do not interest the Status Seekers.

Based on the information so far, you should be able to create effective sales presentations of charitable estate planning products for Status Seekers. The exercise in Figure 11.17 will enable you to do so easily.

Figure 11.16

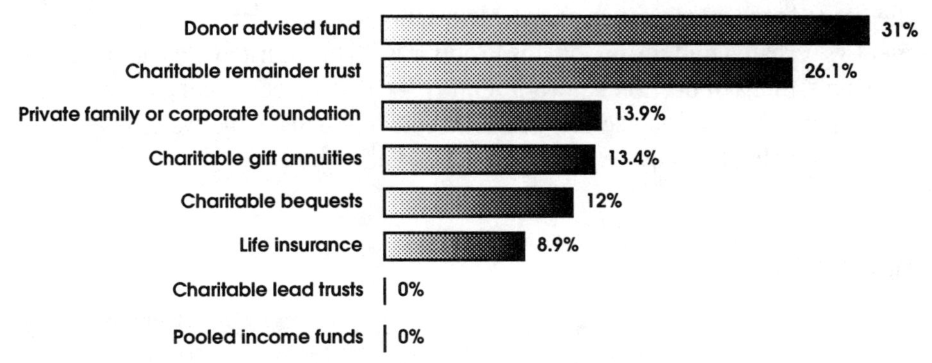

Number of Status Seekers = 158

Figure 11.17

STATUS SEEKER/CHARITABLE ESTATE PLANNING SALES TRACK EXERCISE

Instructions: Write the name of a Status Seeker type of family business owner below. If you can't think of a specific person, create a mental picture of a Status Seeker and focus on that image for this exercise.

____

Instructions: Now list below the charitable estate planning products most appealing to Status Seekers. (Refer to Figure 11.16 if you need to.)

____

____

____

Instructions: Next, write down the benefit Status Seekers are seeking from charitable estate planning. (Refer to Figure 11.15 if you need to.)

____

____

____

Instructions: Finally, write out some statements linking the specific features of the charitable estate planning products Status Seekers are most interested in with the benefit they seek to achieve. For example: "There are ways charitable giving can give you the status and recognition you deserve for all your contributions to the community over the years. Donor advised funds are a particularly good way to be a prominent giver."

____

____

____

Social Benefactors

Social Benefactors are oriented to consider the overall good of society. To find them high on the list of those interested in charitable estate planning is no surprise. The positioning statement we created and tested for this group was, "The charitable estate plan is the socially responsible thing to do." As shown in Figure 11.18, this positioning statement was extremely appealing to Social Benefactors. Philanthropic or altruistic motivations are less typical of the other family business owners, as Figure 11.18 also shows.

Figure 11.18

POSITIONING STATEMENT: *THE CHARITABLE ESTATE PLAN IS THE SOCIALLY RESPONSIBLE THING TO DO*

(Percent of family business owners with a charitable estate plan who say this positioning statement is very important to them.)

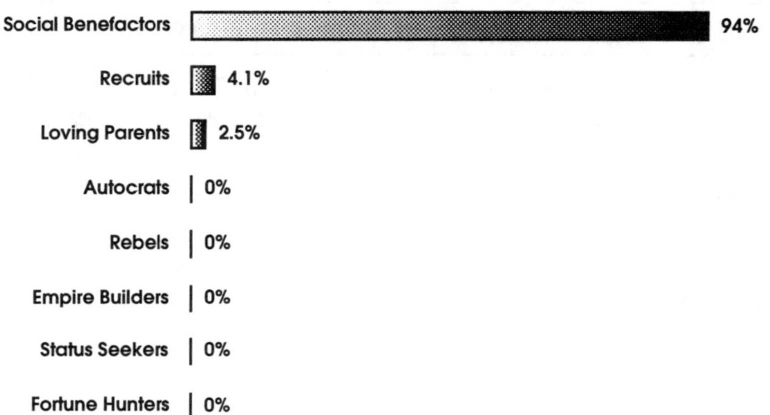

Number of Family Business Owners Who Recently Completed a Charitable Estate Plan = 907

Social Benefactors are mostly interested in charitable bequests and charitable remainder trusts, as shown in Figure 11.19. Less than a third of Social Benefactors are very interested in life insurance and even fewer are interested in donor advised funds, private family foundations, charitable lead trusts, pooled income funds and charitable gift annuities. Given the attitudes of this segment, it may be that these other products have not been promoted specifically to their needs. A larger market may exist here for other charitable estate planning products, if they are properly positioned.

Based on the information so far, you should be able to create effective sales presentations of charitable estate planning products for Social Benefactors. The exercise in Figure 11.20 will enable you to do so easily.

Figure 11.19

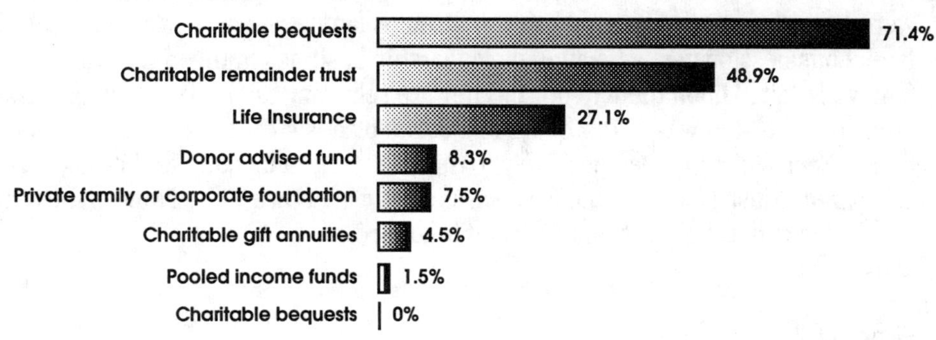

Number of Social Benefactors = 133

Figure 11.20

SOCIAL BENEFACTOR/CHARITABLE ESTATE PLANNING SALES TRACK EXERCISE

Instructions: Write the name of a Social Benefactor type of family business owner below. If you can't think of a specific person, create a mental picture of a Social Benefactor and focus on that image for this exercise.

____

Instructions: Now list below the charitable estate planning products most appealing to Social Benefactors. (Refer to Figure 11.19 if you need to.)

____

____

____

Instructions: Next, write down the benefit Social Benefactors are seeking from charitable estate planning. (Refer to Figure 11.18 if you need to.)

____

____

____

Instructions: Finally, write out some statements linking the specific features of the charitable estate planning products Social Benefactors are most interested in with the benefit they seek to achieve. For example: "Giving back to your community is important to you and there are a number of ways we can do this."

____

____

____

Recruits

Recruits are people who are highly responsive to family needs and preferences because they were brought into the family business through family pressure. As you recall, Recruits are family business owners who attained leadership positions in the family business because the family prevailed upon them to do so. They are reluctant CEOs. The positioning statement we created and tested was, "Your charitable estate plan is strongly influenced by family expectations." Recruits responded positively to this statement. Fully 97% said it was true for them, as compared to just 2.5% of Loving Parents, as shown in Figure 11.21. None of the other segments cite family expectations as an important influence.

Figure 11.21

POSITIONING STATEMENT: *YOUR CHARITABLE ESTATE PLAN IS STRONGLY INFLUENCED BY FAMILY EXPECTATIONS*

(Percent of family business owners with a charitable estate plan who say this positioning statement is very important to them.)

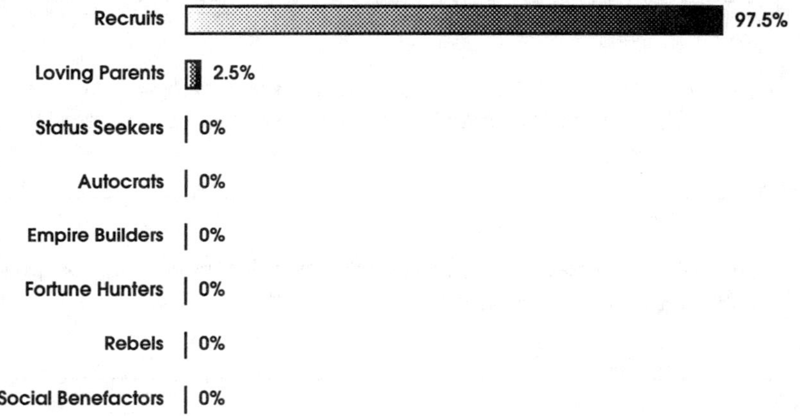

Number of Family Business Owners Who Recently Completed a Charitable Estate Plan = 907

Only a minority of Recruits are interested in the specific aspects of charitable estate planning. For example just 40% are interested in charitable remainder trusts and 33% in charitable bequests trusts. Less than 10% of Recruits are very interested in private family foundations, donor advised funds, charitable lead trusts, pooled income funds or charitable gift annuities, as shown in Figure 11.22.

Based on the information so far, you should be able to create effective sales presentations of charitable estate planning products for Recruits. The exercise in Figure 11.23 will enable you to do so easily.

Figure 11.22

CHARITABLE ESTATE PLANNING PRODUCTS IMPORTANT TO RECRUITS

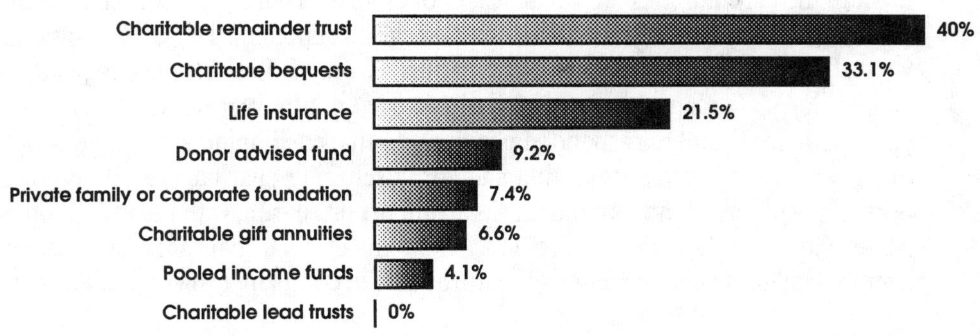

Number of Recruits = 121

Figure 11.23

RECRUIT/CHARITABLE ESTATE PLANNING SALES TRACK EXERCISE

Instructions: Write the name of a Recruit type of family business owner below. If you can't think of a specific person, create a mental picture of a Recruit and focus on that image for this exercise.

____

Instructions: Now list below the charitable estate planning products most appealing to Recruits. (Refer to Figure 11.22 if you need to.)

____

____

____

Instructions: Next, write down the benefit Recruits are seeking from charitable estate planning. (Refer to Figure 11.21 if you need to.)

____

____

____

Instructions: Finally, write out some statements linking the specific features of the charitable estate planning products Recruits are most interested in with the benefit they seek to achieve. For example: "When you manage a business on behalf of a family, as you do, you need to be conscious of their expectations as well as your own. Many prominent family-owned businesses can take advantage of charitable estate planning."

____

____

____

Empire Builders

Empire Builders seek to create a business that will grow and prosper over time. Their commitment to the communities their businesses operate in is purely instrumental. If the community is strong, it will provide employees, customers and suppliers. Thus, the positioning statement we tested with almost a thousand recent purchasers of charitable estate planning was, "Your charitable estate plan is designed to help your community grow, so you can grow your company." Empire Builders responded positively to this positioning statement, with 85% agreeing that it was the most important rationale for purchasing charitable estate products. No members of any other segments cited this as an important reason, with the exception of a few Social Benefactors, as shown in Figure 11.24. This means that insurance professionals selling to Empire Builders need to connect their products to company growth, both direct and indirect.

Figure 11.24

POSITIONING STATEMENT: *YOUR CHARITABLE ESTATE PLAN IS DESIGNED TO HELP YOUR COMMUNITY GROW, SO YOU CAN GROW YOUR COMPANY*

(Percent of family business owners with a charitable estate plan who say this positioning statement is very important to them.)

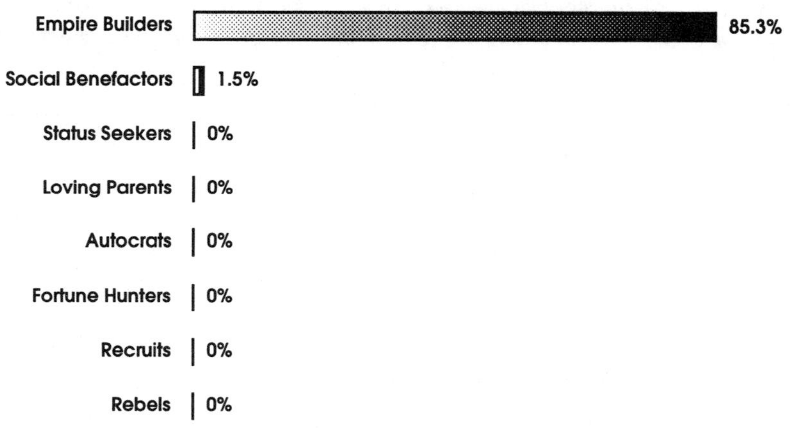

Number of Family Business Owners Who Recently Completed a Charitable Estate Plan = 907

Because Empire Builders understand the link between community growth and business growth, they give to nonprofit organizations which, in turn, create a more prosperous community. As Figure 11.25 shows, Empire Builders direct their charitable estate planning interests towards donor advised funds, charitable remainder trusts, and charitable bequests. They have less interest in private foundations and charitable lead trusts and express no interest in life insurance, pooled income funds or charitable gift annuities.

Based on the information so far, you should be able to create effective sales presentations of charitable estate planning products for Empire Builders. The exercise in Figure 11.26 will enable you to do so easily.

Figure 11.25

CHARITABLE ESTATE PLANNING PRODUCTS IMPORTANT TO EMPIRE BUILDERS

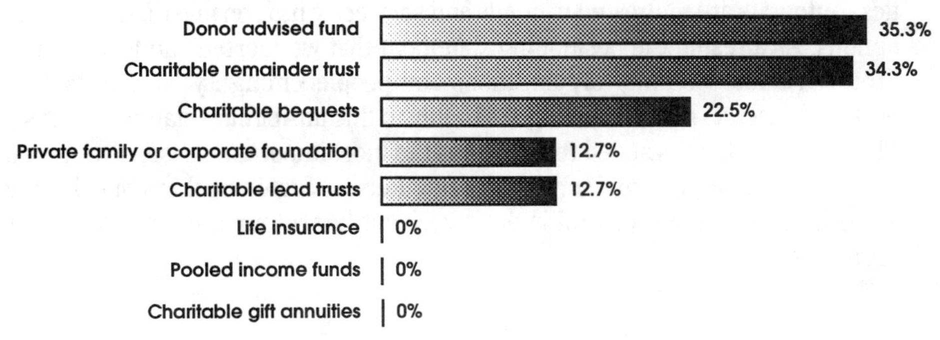

Number of Empire Builders = 102

Figure 11.26

EMPIRE BUILDER/CHARITABLE ESTATE PLANNING SALES TRACK EXERCISE

Instructions: Write the name of an Empire Builder type of family business owner below. If you can't think of a specific person, create a mental picture of an Empire Builder and focus on that image for this exercise.

____

Instructions: Now list below the charitable estate planning products most appealing to Empire Builders. (Refer to Figure 11.25 if you need to.)

____

____

____

Instructions: Next, write down the benefit Empire Builders are seeking from charitable estate planning. (Refer to Figure 11.24 if you need to.)

____

____

____

Instructions: Finally, write out some statements linking the specific features of the charitable estate planning products Empire Builders are most interested in with the benefit they seek to achieve. For example: "I appreciate how dependent our community is on your business and how much you appreciate that the business is dependent on the community. I know about some ways you can continue your support of local nonprofits now and in the future, but with greater tax advantages."

____

____

____

Autocrats

Autocrats seek control over their people and environments. They are authoritarian personalities. Autocrats are interested in goods and services which enable them to expand their control options. As a result, the positioning statement that we created and tested for this group was, "You can influence other organizations and people through your charitable giving." As expected, Autocrats responded very favorably to this positioning statement. As shown in Figure 11.27, most Autocrats stated that this was the most important reason they recently purchased charitable estate planning services. A few Rebels, Status Seekers and Loving Parents also agreed, but extending control is not a relevant benefit for the other family business owner segments.

Figure 11.27

POSITIONING STATEMENT: *YOU CAN INFLUENCE OTHER ORGANIZATIONS AND PEOPLE THROUGH YOUR CHARITABLE GIVING*

(Percent of family business owners with a charitable estate plan who say this positioning statement is very important to them.)

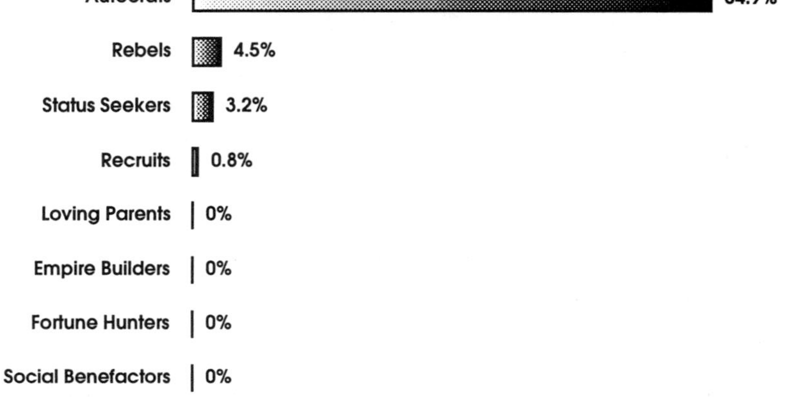

Number of Family Business Owners Who Recently Completed a Charitable Estate Plan = 907

Autocrats are primarily interested in charitable remainder trusts. Less than 10% of Autocrats are very interested in any of the other charitable estate planning products, as shown in Figure 11.28.

Based on the information so far, you should be able to create effective sales presentations of charitable estate planning products for Autocrats. The exercise in Figure 11.29 will enable you to do so easily.

Figure 11.28

CHARITABLE ESTATE PLANNING PRODUCTS IMPORTANT TO AUTOCRATS

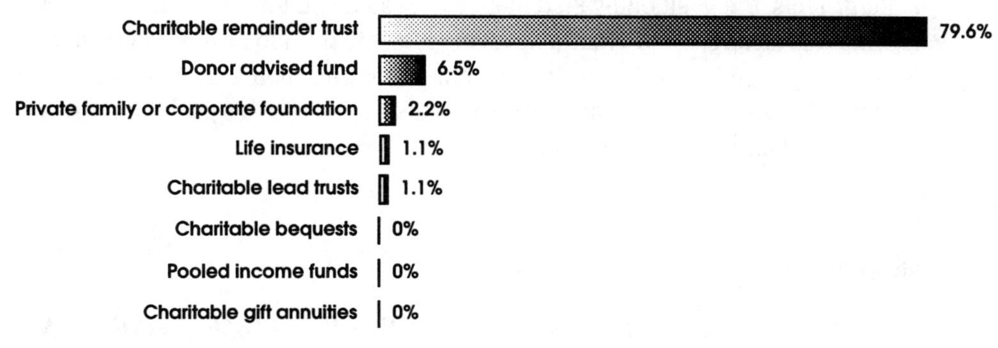

Number of Autocrats = 93

Figure 11.29

AUTOCRAT/CHARITABLE ESTATE PLANNING SALES TRACK EXERCISE

Instructions: Write the name of an Autocrat type of family business owner below. If you can't think of a specific person, create a mental picture of an Autocrat and focus on that image for this exercise.

____

Instructions: Now list below the charitable estate planning products most appealing to Autocrats. (Refer to Figure 11.28 if you need to.)

____

____

____

Instructions: Next, write down the benefit Autocrats are seeking from charitable estate planning. (Refer to Figure 11.27 if you need to.)

____

____

____

Instructions: Finally, write out some statements linking the specific features of the charitable estate planning products Autocrats are most interested in with the benefit they seek to achieve. For example: "I know it is your style to manage everything very closely. Control is important, even when giving to nonprofits. CRTs enable you to achieve your financial, tax and philanthropic objectives and still have a great measure of control."

____

____

____

Rebels

Rebels need to feel independent. Typically, they left corporate employment because it was stifling. Thus, the positioning statement we created and tested for this group was designed to tap into this feeling, "Your charitable giving is an expression of your independence." Almost all Rebels responded favorably to this statement, but no member of any other segment did as shown in Figure 11.30. Insurance professionals should use this positioning approach only with this type of family business owner.

Figure 11.30

POSITIONING STATEMENT: *YOUR CHARITABLE GIVING IS AN EXPRESSION OF YOUR INDEPENDENCE*

(Percent of family business owners with a charitable estate plan who say this positioning statement is very important to them.)

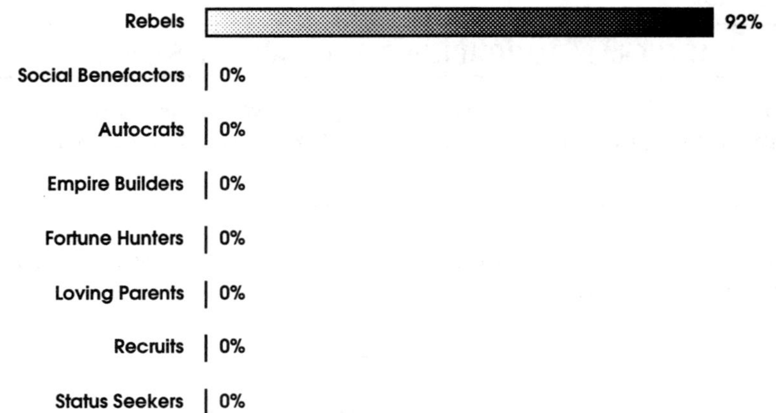

Number of Family Business Owners Who Recently Completed a Charitable Estate Plan = 907

As illustrated in Figure 11.31, Rebels are mostly interested in charitable remainder trusts because their state-of-the-art sophistication and complexity is appealing to this group. To a lesser extent, they are interested in charitable bequests and donor advised funds. Of the Rebels, 10% or less are interested in private family foundations, life insurance, charitable lead trusts, pooled income funds or charitable gift annuities.

Based on the information so far, you should be able to create effective sales presentations of charitable estate planning products for Rebels. The exercise in Figure 11.32 will enable you to do so easily.

Figure 11.31

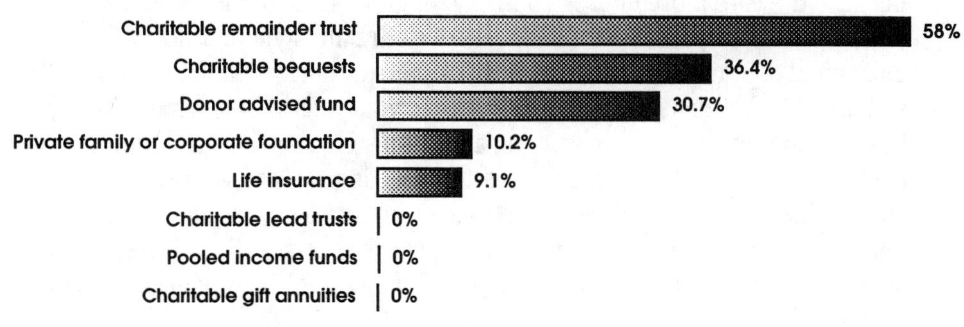

Number of Rebels = 88

Figure 11.32

REBEL/CHARITABLE ESTATE PLANNING SALES TRACK EXERCISE

Instructions: Write the name of a Rebel type of family business owner below. If you can't think of a specific person, create a mental picture of a Rebel and focus on that image for this exercise.

____

Instructions: Now list below the charitable estate planning products most appealing to Rebels. (Refer to Figure 11.31 if you need to.)

____

____

____

Instructions: Next, write down the benefit Rebels are seeking from charitable estate planning. (Refer to Figure 11.30 if you need to.)

____

____

____

Instructions: Finally, write out some statements linking the specific features of the charitable estate planning products Rebels are most interested in with the benefit they seek to achieve. For example: "Managing the business professionally is very important to you. You should consider the most sophisticated products. While CRTs are complex, they offer the professional business manager the best combination of financial benefits and management controls."

____

____

____

Fortune Hunters

Of all segments, Fortune Hunters were least interested in charitable estate planning, probably because they are more interested in enjoying the fruits of their labors now. Fortune Hunters are interested in personal wealth and a wealthy life style and not in creating assets for the enjoyment of future generations. We attempted to appeal to their interests with the positioning statement, "You focus on the tax benefits of your charitable giving." As Figure 11.33 shows, this reason is extremely important to all Fortune Hunters because they are most interested in personal wealth and are accustomed to analyzing tax considerations. As Figure 11.33 also shows, this reason is of some importance to Empire Builders and Autocrats and of little or no importance to the other segments. This analysis shows, as do the preceding ones, the advantages of positioning charitable estate planning in a specific way to each segment.

Figure 11.33

POSITIONING STATEMENT: *YOU FOCUS ON THE TAX BENEFITS OF YOUR CHARITABLE GIVING*

(Percent of family business owners with a charitable estate plan who say this positioning statement is very important to them.)

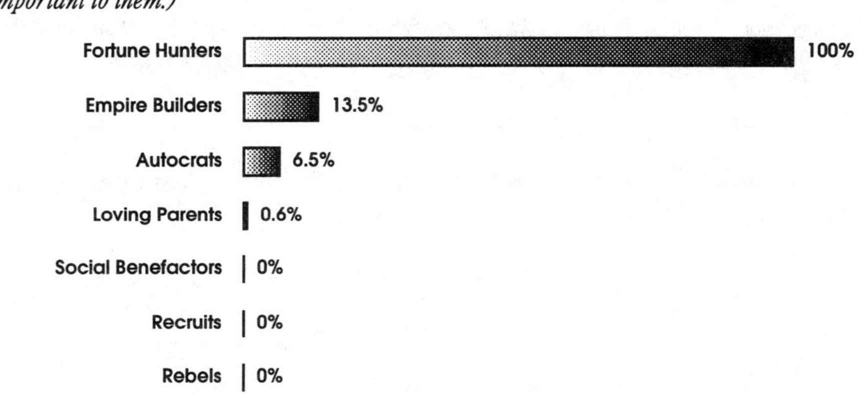

Number of Family Business Owners Who Recently Completed a Charitable Estate Plan = 907

Of all family business owner segments, Fortune Hunters are the most interested in charitable remainder trusts. This fits well with their focus on the tax advantages of charitable estate planning. They have little or no interest in the other charitable estate planning products, perhaps out of the perception that charitable remainder trusts offer the greatest financial and tax advantages, as shown in Figure 11.34.

Based on the information so far, you should be able to create effective sales presentations of charitable estate planning products for Fortune Hunters. The exercise in Figure 11.35 will enable you to do so easily.

Figure 11.34

CHARITABLE ESTATE PLANNING PRODUCTS IMPORTANT TO FORTUNE HUNTERS

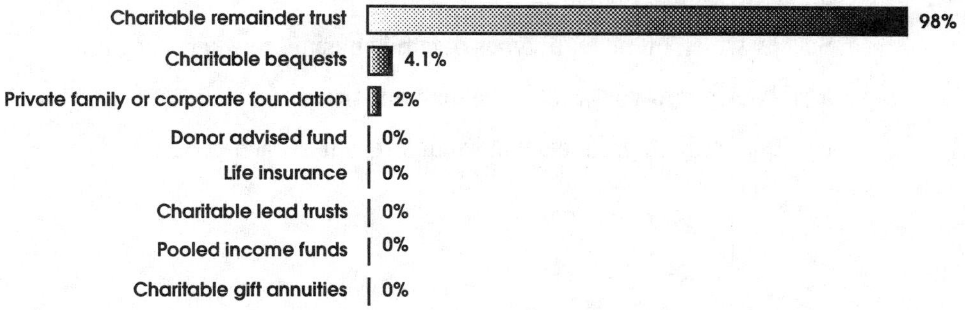

Product	Percentage
Charitable remainder trust	98%
Charitable bequests	4.1%
Private family or corporate foundation	2%
Donor advised fund	0%
Life insurance	0%
Charitable lead trusts	0%
Pooled income funds	0%
Charitable gift annuities	0%

Number of Fortune Hunters = 163

Figure 11.35

FORTUNE HUNTER/CHARITABLE ESTATE PLANNING SALES TRACK EXERCISE

Instructions: Write the name of a Fortune Hunter type of family business owner below. If you can't think of a specific person, create a mental picture of a Fortune Hunter and focus on that image for this exercise.

___

Instructions: Now list below the charitable estate planning products most appealing to Fortune Hunters. (Refer to Figure 11.34 if you need to.)

___

___

___

Instructions: Next, write down the benefit Fortune Hunters are seeking from charitable estate planning. (Refer to Figure 11.33 if you need to.)

___

___

___

Instructions: Finally, write out some statements linking the specific features of the charitable estate planning products Fortune Hunters are most interested in with the benefit they seek to achieve. For example: "Using every possible tax advantage is an important strategy for you. CRTs offer exceptional tax advantages to people in your position and can provide current income as well."

___

___

___

Your Action Plan

- Identify three current family business owner prospects for your services. Write their names in Figure 11.36.
- Specify which of the eight types of family business owners they are.
- Write down how you would position your services.
- Designate which products you would present to each client.

Figure 11.36

Family Business Owner	Family Business Owner Psychological Type	How I will position my services	Products I will emphasize
1.			
2.			
3.			

Section IV

Marketing To Family Businesses

CHAPTER 12
FINDING THEM

Richard Bentley knows there are lots of ways to get in front of wealthy family business owners. However, not all of them seem to work equally well. Richard has spent over $20,000 on direct mail pieces promoting his expertise. He has spent an additional $10,000 on local advertising. He has concluded that these approaches aren't very cost effective. Richard knows that there are lots of ways of creating interest for his services and products. The question is, "Which ways work best with wealthy family business owners?" He knows some ways work better than others. He has learned this lesson the hard way having wasted considerable sums on sure fire approaches that didn't get him anywhere.

Bentley knows that he isn't the only one who has tried things that brought limited results. He therefore raised the issue to his study group. He wanted to hear which approaches produce the best results from other financial services professionals who are targeting family businesses.

Prospecting for family business owners is often seen as the most difficult component of the entire marketing process. Expert life insurance professionals tend to feel that once they can get in front of a wealthy family business owner they are in a good position to make a sale. The key is finding them.

Different wealthy segments, such as inherited wealth and corporate executives, use different sources of information when making choices about life insurance professionals. While there is a fair amount of consistency among affluent family business owners, even the eight personalities will emphasize different sources of information.

You need to understand which of the various sources of information are likely to get you in front of a family business owner and which ones are not. Then you need to heavily stress those approaches which produce the best results.

Sure Fire Ways To Find Them

There are a number of ways you can generate interest in your offerings. The key is knowing which ways affluent family business owners respond to most often. Bear in mind, that every possible approach to making contact has been attempted. Roberta Kipling has even tried marketing her financial planning and investment management services over the Internet. The problem she found is that the family businesses she was able to interest were recently-established firms. They had not been in business long and the owners were certainly not wealthy. The wealthy family business owners tend to be older and are generally uncomfortable with technology. Therefore, at the present time, the Internet is not one of the best means of communicating with them.

Among the more conventional approaches, it is clear that some work well and some do not. You need to spend your time and money on what works well. The two most effective approaches are:

- Referrals from satisfied clients; and
- Referrals from advisors.

To the greatest extent possible, you should use both these approaches. The other approaches discussed below will also result in new business. However, nothing is better for making contact with family business owners then these approaches.

Client Referrals

For Carl Brown, the wealthy family business clients come in on their own. Carl has been providing estate and succession planning services before they were commonly tied together or as he puts it, "When the dinosaurs still ruled the earth."

Carl has learned the hard way how to manage the relationship with business owners. We say the hard way because when Carl first started out in business, he lost lots of clients and was unable to get referrals for a long time. He wasn't doing a very good job of relationship management.

Now things have changed. Carl is proficient at managing relationships with family business owners. His clients are satisfied with both the products and services he sells as well as with the way he relates to them. When you effectively manage the relationship with existing clients, you will probably get referrals from them.

Principle: The most effective way to get family business owners as new clients is by getting referrals from existing satisfied clients.

Not every financial services provider will have things work out like Carl. Most of the time prospects will not keep walking in on their own. Instead, you are going to have to prime the pump. This means you are going to have to keep asking for referrals from your family business owner clients.

This may sound obvious, but the research and our experience working with top-of-the-line financial service providers tell us differently. The more common situation is where the financial service provider doesn't ask for a referral. An insurance agent once explained that he didn't think his clients knew other wealthy family business owners so he never bothered to ask. We know that isn't the case. Well-established family business owners do indeed know each other. Asking for referrals will lead you to other clients.

Another insurance agent said she didn't want to pressure her clients so she didn't ask for referrals. And she didn't get any. If you skillfully ask for referrals, satisfied clients, by and large, are more than happy to provide them.

The critical link is client satisfaction. Very satisfied clients will reciprocate by helping you. They will also ask you for additional services over time, as illustrated in Figure 12.01.

Figure 12.01

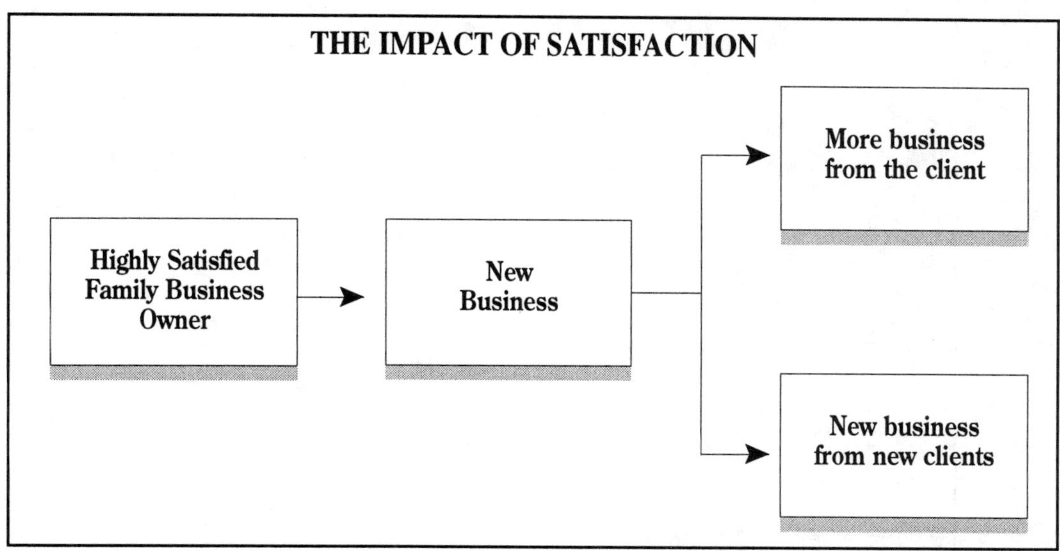

Creating very satisfied clients is like the golden goose in the children's fairy tale. If you have a golden goose, it keeps on laying golden eggs providing you with an ongoing stream of riches. Very satisfied family business owner clients are like that. They will provide you with referrals to their peers. They will also come back to you time and again for additional services. This dynamic is illustrated in the "Golden Goose" model in Figure 12.02.

Clients who are only somewhat satisfied will think the exchange with you has already been pretty even and will not be very helpful.

Dissatisfied clients will, of course, not help you identify new clients and they will not work with you again on their own matters. It's easy to see the implications of dissatisfaction among clients when you compare the "Golden Goose" model in Figure 12.02 to the "Laying an Egg" model in Figure 12.03. Bluntly put, every time you "lay an egg" in providing service to a family business owner client, you create a potential "golden goose" for someone else.

Figure 12.02

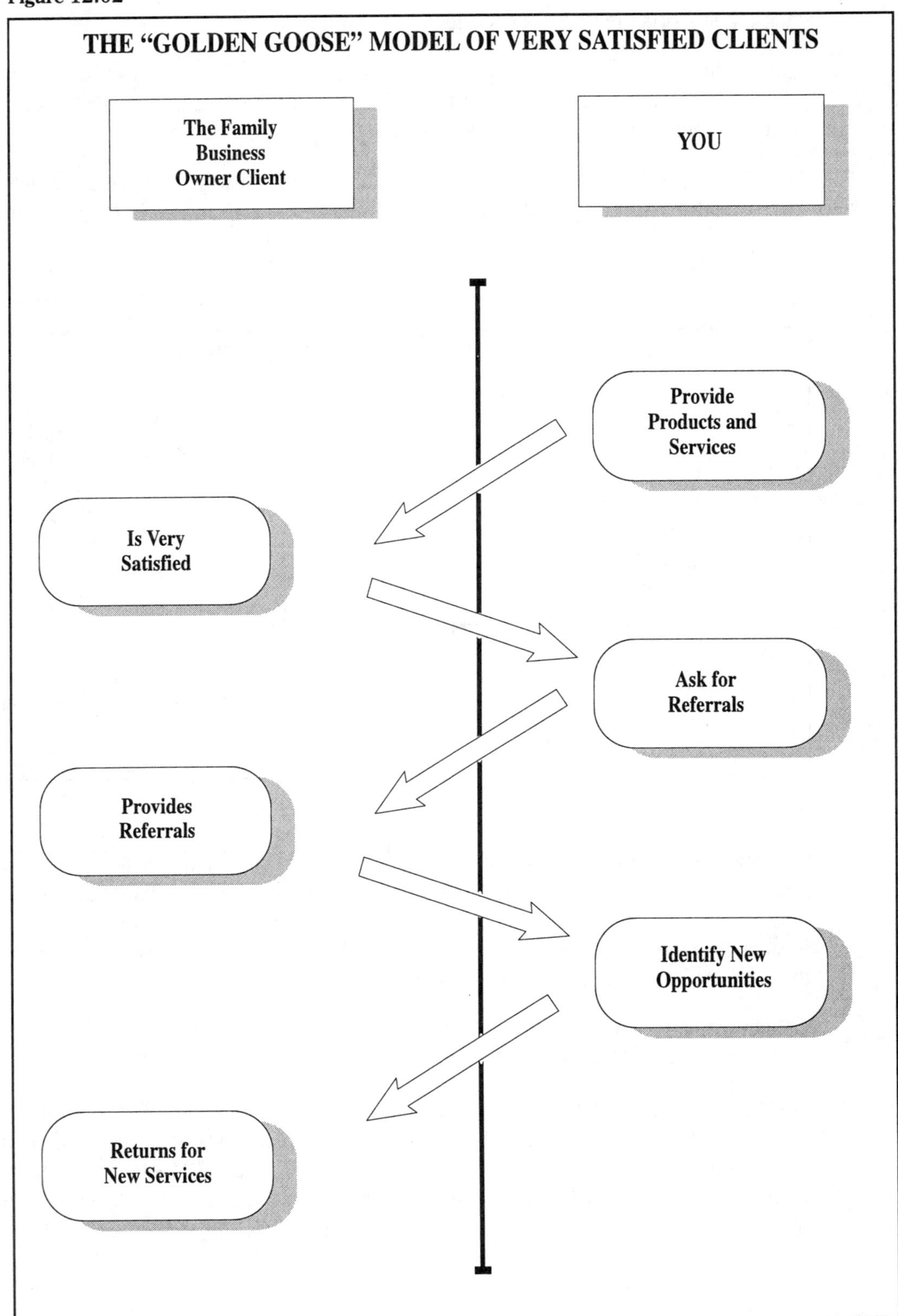
THE "GOLDEN GOOSE" MODEL OF VERY SATISFIED CLIENTS
The Family Business Owner Client
YOU
Provide Products and Services
Is Very Satisfied
Ask for Referrals
Provides Referrals
Identify New Opportunities
Returns for New Services

Figure 12.03

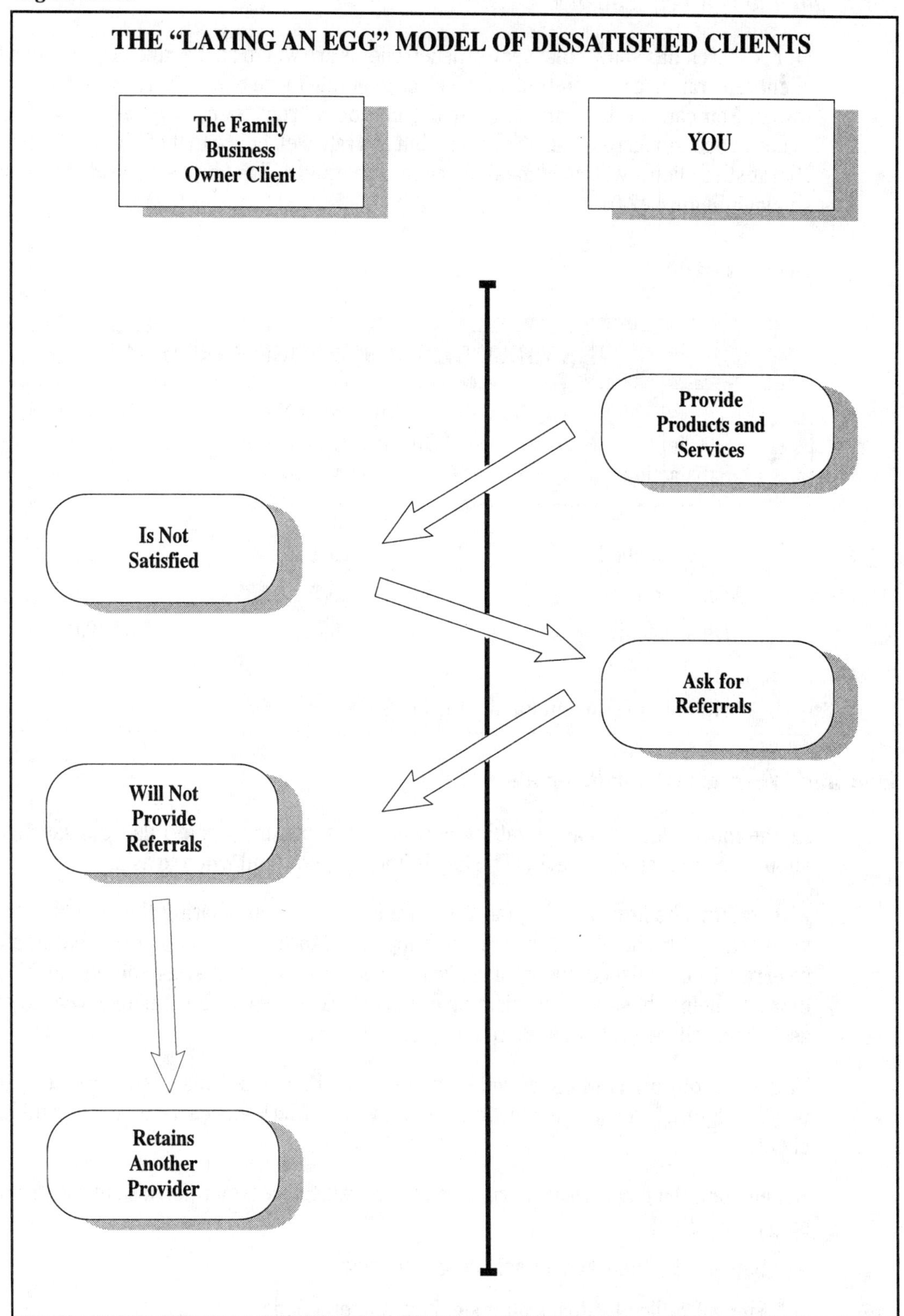
THE "LAYING AN EGG" MODEL OF DISSATISFIED CLIENTS
The Family Business Owner Client
YOU
Provide Products and Services
Is Not Satisfied
Ask for Referrals
Will Not Provide Referrals
Retains Another Provider

How Valuable is a Very Satisfied Client?

Our research has shown that very satisfied clients are worth an average of more than two new client referrals in a year and will themselves generate more business from the family business owner. You can see how dramatically the numbers drop; clients who are only satisfied will make an occasional referral, on average, but at a rate well below that of highly satisfied clients. Dissatisfied clients will avoid making any referrals and will not be a source of new business, as shown in Figure 12.04.

Figure 12.04

THE VALUE OF A VERY SATISFIED CLIENT		
Client Satisfaction	Number of New Business Opportunities in a Year	Number of Referrals in a Year
Very Satisfied	0.9	2.1
Satisfied	0.1	0.4
Dissatisfied	0.0	0.0
Number of Affluent Family Business Owners = 433		

How and When to Ask for Referrals

As the most effective way of getting new business, obtaining referrals from satisfied clients should be emphasized heavily. The key is knowing how and when to ask.

How to ask: The key to asking for a referral is to talk about sharing the benefits of your services with your client's associates and suppliers. Mark Bewquine is excellent at asking for referrals from satisfied clients. He always positions the request as something his client is doing to help a business associate or friend. Mark makes sure his clients realize that their associates will be grateful to them for referring Mark.

This way not only is Mark provided with qualified leads but his clients are seen in a very positive light. It's a win-win situation for everyone – Mark, his current clients, and his future clients.

Asking for a referral is an art anyone can learn well. Successful referrals emerge from a seven step process:

Step #1: Set the stage for soliciting feedback

Step #2: Solicit feedback after significant interactions

Step #3: Client review of the process

Step #4: Asking for the referral

Step #5: Thanking them for the referral

Step #6: Providing process feedback

Step #7: Thank them again

As you practice these steps, your own personal style will develop.

When to ask: You should only ask for a referral when the affluent family business owner is likely to give you one. When is this? When they feel you have done an excellent job for them. Consider the example of Tim Scalli, an excellent estate planner. After the family business owner client has signed all the documents, Tim takes them to lunch and he asks for referrals. Tim says that nine out of ten times he gets a very warm lead.

Tim also will periodically review the estate planning issues for his clients. He makes it a point not to ask for referrals every time he sees them. Instead he makes sure that he only asks maybe once in every three or four meetings. This way he usually walks away with the name of a new family business owner to call on.

Before reading on, take a moment to complete the exercise in Figure 12.05.

Referrals from Advisors

Bethany Sands targets the most effective intermediary to successful family business owners – accountants. She regularly holds seminars for accountants where they can learn about the latest tax laws that will affect their wealthy business owner clients. At these seminars the accountants receive continuing education credits which helps fill up the room. Beth also spends a lot of time with accountants one-to-one discussing the different ways insurance can help wealthy business owners meet their goals. There are many innovative ways insurance can be used by family business owners. The accountants are always looking for new ideas that will help their clients. Beth is a major source of those ideas. Therefore, the accountants are a major source of clients for Beth.

Figure 12.05

WHEN TO ASK FOR REFERRALS EXERCISE	
Instructions: List three current clients who you believe are very satisfied with your services. Then decide when is the next naturally occurring point that they will be particularly aware of how pleased they are with your services.	
Current Clients	**When I Will Ask For Referrals**
1.	
2.	
3.	

Principle: Accountants are the most influential advisor to successful family businesses.

Beth receives a great deal of support from her primary insurance company. More than other types of financial institutions, the insurance companies have recognized the gate-keeping role accountants play when it comes to family business owners.

Accountants are regularly called upon by family business owners to help evaluate the merits of various financial strategies. By targeting the accountants directly, you're targeting what is generally considered the most important financial advisor to affluent family businesses.

If you are to be effective generating referrals from accountants, you must be aware of the primary reasons they will make referrals to you. These are:

- You are providing referrals to them.
- You are providing them with useful information.
- You have a recognized unique expertise in demand by successful business owners.

Cross-referrals: The accountants are sending you business and they are interested in you doing the same. While this is a good strategy, it can become problematic. It is probably impossible to guarantee a *quid pro quo* relationship. You want to get as many accountants as possible sending you potential family business clients. Unfortunately, it is likely that you will not be able to provide all the accountants you are targeting with new business. Therefore, it is often wise to be in a position to provide them with information they can use.

Providing information: There are two types of information that accountants are interested in. So interested, in fact, that you can build solid relationships that will result in new business for you.

One type of information is of a technical nature. How are the new tax laws affecting wealthy family business owners? How can life insurance be used creatively? What kinds of retirement programs work best under what situations? These are the types of issues traditionally addressed by life insurance professionals who develop relationships with accountants.

Of greater interest to accountants is information on how to find and work with family businesses. This type of "how to" information will enable accountants to build their businesses. You, in turn, can benefit by their success.

Unique expertise: When you are recognized as an expert, accountants, as well as other advisors to family business owners, will happily refer business to you. A recognized unique expertise is like a magnet placed on a collection of iron fillings. Providing financial services or charitable estate planning to family businesses are two examples of a unique expertise.

Aside from accountants, there are other advisors to family business owners you can establish relationships with. Included here are attorneys, trust officers, and family business consultants.

Strategies To Use Selectively

The previous two approaches are rated by business owners as the most effective. Still, there are other very effective ways to gain access to family business owners. They are:

- High-quality seminars; and
- Public relations.

These approaches both have merit and should also be used when possible.

High-Quality Seminars

Brian Mathews has built his business providing financial and succession planning services to family businesses by using seminars. He recognizes that the most effective seminars don't just talk about services and products. Instead, they zero in on the needs of the participants.

Brian has a portfolio of seminars. While most of them share some elements, they are all targeted toward different types of family business owners. Brian, with the help of design professionals, has created five seminars to promote insurance to wealthy family business owners emphasizing different benefits. Without realizing it, he has created seminars which are built around the different motivations of family business owner personalities. He has created seminars for Loving Parents, Empire Builders, Status Seekers, Fortune Hunters, and Autocrats.

Furthermore, Brian is a talented speaker. He is able to get up in front of a group and communicate with clarity and conviction. Brian also wisely spends most of his seminar time lining up the right participants. And, he is excellent at following up after the seminar.

Principle: Seminars targeting the eight family business owner personalities can be successful in building a practice.

High-quality seminars can be tremendously influential in convincing the participants to use your services. However, you must make sure the "right" people are in the audience. The most effective seminars are highly focused. You want people attending who can use what you provide. Therefore, you should spend a good deal of effort making sure successful family business owners are in the audience.

Further, you need to spend a good part of your time following up with the seminar participants. Just because they all didn't rush you when you finished, doesn't mean they weren't interested. You have to follow up knowing that if you got the right people to attend and you did a good job on stage, you have sparked the interest of a fair number.

Public Relations

Getting your name in print is much more effective than advertising. As a way of getting who you are out to the most people possible, public relations is the best way to go. Leslie Brown found this out.

While the advertising campaign for the agency did little to produce new business, some of the public relations efforts proved profitable. A lot of the charitable projects of the agency have garnered a great deal of attention. Because of this attention, the local paper did a feature on the agency, and wealthy family business owners walked in the doors for weeks.

The feature talked about the agency's special programs for family businesses. The business owners who read about these programs wanted to learn more. So, they made contact with the agency.

Principle: You can capture the attention of successful family business owners through the skillful use of public relations.

The key to effective public relations is finding something that will interest the media. The story has to be newsworthy. When we discuss this point with life insurance professionals, they tend to think in terms of the *Wall Street Journal* or *Fortune.* This is a mistake. Instead, think in terms of your local newspapers and radio shows. They are always looking for interesting local items. You are able to provide one.

Helen Burns, for example, helped Bertrum Delallaney, a Status Seeker, set up a private foundation. Helen contacted the local media who were very interested in Bert and his new foundation. The local and regional newspapers did stories about the foundation and all the people involved, including Helen. Aside from Bert's pleasure with the attention, Helen picked up new family business owners as clients because they read about Bert.

Public relations based on significant things you do for clients is a good marketing approach. The clients need not all be Status Seekers. In fact, it is very likely that most family business owners would be happy to see their names in the paper associated with a worthy cause.

Another benefit to Helen is that the reporters have started to call her whenever they are doing stories on financial and estate planning issues. Thus, Helen is continuing to get her name in front of potential clients.

Avoid These Pitfalls

Financial service providers use a wide variety of approaches to making contact with successful businesses. Not all of them are particularly effective. The following widely-used approaches have not been identified by business owners as successful:

- Direct mail and advertising;
- Cold-calling; and
- Referrals from friends and family.

These approaches can be more effective if they are based on the psychology of family business owners. However, since current efforts do not incorporate their motivations, these approaches prove to be of limited value.

Direct Mail And Advertising: Leslie Brown is a relationship manager of the Gotham-King Agency. The agency sought to generate new business through a media-based campaign. They were focusing their efforts in two directions. One was based on direct mail and the other was an advertising campaign. Both approaches proved, after a cost of over $100,000, to not be able to produce new clients.

The question then becomes, "Are these approaches ineffective or did the agency fail to use them effectively?" Inherently, the approaches are not ineffective. Properly constructed direct mail pieces and advertising campaigns can potentially lead to contact with a family business owner. However, most life insurance professionals do not use these approaches effectively.

Principle: Only by carefully promoting products and services as solutions to problems based on the eight family business personalities will direct mail or advertising campaigns be effective.

Rarely are any of these marketing efforts based on the psychology of the family business owner. And this is where they stumble. Advertising can be effective if it is targeted at a particular family business owner personality.

Cold-Calling: Kim Preston works at a top-of-the-line insurance brokerage agency. She has been successful off-and-on in the past "dialing for dollars." When Kim was successful in getting a new client this way, she was picking up clients who were not particularly wealthy and were buying off-the-shelf products. More complex services like financial planning just weren't moving. Also, she was unable to get to speak with family business owners.

Principle: Cold calling is an ineffective approach to generating new family business owner clients. There is not a list in existence that someone else doesn't already have.

A list of family business owners that has not been used by other life insurance professionals is valuable. It is also, most probably, a rare thing. All the lists available have already been gone through by a number of life insurance professionals.

Referrals From Friends And Family: Nathan Malcolm, a high-income life insurance professional, at one time thought of using some of his country club connections to generate leads. He spent a lot of time at the country club talking up his agency. This proved to be completely ineffective. The people he was talking with at the club were not in a position to introduce him to the owners of the family businesses. The owners were busy running the family business and Nathan rarely, if ever, was able to "run into them" at the club.

At the same time Nathan was striking out with family connections, he was equally unsuccessful working through the friends of family business owners. At the club, the friends of wealthy family business owners were not in a position to recommend a financial services provider.

Principle: Do not focus your efforts on the family and friends of successful business owners. They are not effective in getting you to see the decision makers.

Family business owners are not very, if at all, receptive to the recommendations of friends and family concerning life insurance professionals.

Caveat: The ratings of these various ways of making contact with family business owners are based on what life insurance professionals are doing — and doing well. These ratings do not necessarily reflect prospecting approaches you can use with a great deal of effectiveness.

You shouldn't look at these approaches and think, "I should never advertise and only target accountants." What you should be doing is thinking about the value of these different sources of information for family business owners and what is likely to work best for you.

It is important to keep in mind what is likely to be most effective. In effect, you have to prioritize your marketing efforts unless you have unlimited resources. If you have a choice between producing high-quality seminars and putting an advertisement in the paper, you will probably be more successful with the seminar.

Everything works under the proper conditions. Advertising and direct mail can indeed be effective if they can readily tap into the psychology of the family business owner. In fact, everything will work better if it is based on the eight family business personalities.

Your Action Items

- Systematically assess your family business owner clients' current levels of satisfaction.
- For those family business owner clients who are highly satisfied, you are in an excellent position to solicit referrals.
- You are also now able to enhance the levels of satisfaction of those clients that you have concluded are less than highly satisfied. When you have raised their levels of satisfaction they will be prime referral sources.
- Identify advisors to family business owners who are amenable to working with you.

Richard carefully considers everything he has learned and decides to redouble his efforts with his own clients. This is where he has historically obtained most of his new business. He is putting together a marketing plan where all his best clients will be periodically asked for referrals.

He has also decided to develop a program that will permit him to target accountants. These people are interested in serving their clients and Richard understands that if he can help them do so, they will refer business to him. Richard is very careful to present himself as only interested in providing insurance services. By being highly focused when trying to network with other advisors to family businesses, Richard will not be encroaching on anyone else's turf.

Richard has also decided to begin developing seminars geared to the specific needs and concerns of the various family business personalities. He knows he can use his clients to help fill the seminars. And, this is an excellent way for him to cross-sell his services. In addition, he is likely to draw successful business owners who currently are not doing business with him.

CHAPTER 13
SELLING THEM

For Richard Bentley to be successful in marketing financial services to family businesses, he must understand them. Richard must know how to identify each of the eight family business personalities. He has to understand the positive and negative roles that shadow influencers play. Richard knows all this.

Currently, Richard is able to network effectively with family business owners. He is referred to them from other advisors, especially accountants, as well as satisfied clients. However, getting in front of them is only the first hurdle. Next he has to promote his services and products.

To do this effectively, Richard must know how successful business owners select life insurance professionals. He has to understand what it is best to emphasize and what does not require a great deal of effort.

A mistake made by many life insurance professionals targeting family businesses is that they fail to strategically position their services and products. What exactly does this mean?

Consider James Gary. Over the years he has developed a sales pitch that he uses without fail. Regrettably for Gary, it fails more often than not. Gary has thought about how he should modify his sales pitch and has regularly made changes to it. Gary's determination of what to change is based on what he thinks will do the trick.

To succeed you must base your approach to selling on what your market — in this case, family business owners — will respond to. Not only do you need to know what you should emphasize, you need to know what you shouldn't.

In this chapter we will be looking first at the critical selection criteria that family business owners use in deciding which life insurance professionals to work with. By concentrating on the selection criteria that family business owners are most responsive to, you will be in the best position possible to make a sale. We will also address several factors that are not extensively used by business owners in making their selections. Finally, we will examine the sales platform.

Why They Will Choose You

There are five critical selection criteria used by family business owners in determining which financial services provider they will purchase services and products from. The five criteria, in order of importance, are:

1. The care with which the financial services provider identifies their needs.
2. The degree to which they feel they can trust the financial services provider.
3. The financial services provider's philosophy surrounding the management of the family business owner's financial situation.
4. The discretion of the financial services provider.
5. The attentiveness of the financial services provider.

If you want to persuade family business owners to work with you, you must be certain to communicate exactly why and how you are the financial services provider who most closely matches their criteria.

Identifying Needs

Allen William, a Loving Parent, wasn't happy with any of his financial advisors until one of his suppliers introduced him to Panner Gelsey. William wanted to put in a 401(k) plan. Like all of the previous financial advisors, Gelsey had a basic fact finding session with William. However, Gelsey didn't stop there.

At the same time that Gelsey was putting the retirement program in place, she spent a good deal of time with William talking about how much the family business means to him because it lets him take care of his family obligations. Gelsey spent half a day seeing William work with his family in the business and loving it. This led to a long conversation about William's fondest wish of transferring the business to his sons.

In identifying William's needs, Gelsey wasn't looking at only the expressed needs - the 401(k) program. She was looking much deeper. Gelsey was talking to William about his needs as a Loving Parent. In this way, she was able to help William identify his other concerns. These concerns translated into other ways Gelsey was able to help. When they were finished, Gelsey set up a buy-sell arrangement for William in addition to the retirement program.

William, satisfied that Gelsey understands what he is about, has asked her to review his estate plan. Gelsey is also involved in working on the estate plans of some other family members.

Principle: The key in working with family business owners to identify their needs is knowing their family business personalities.

In identifying the needs of family business owners, you must concentrate first on those items that they specifically want to discuss. This is what prompted them to consider your services. However, in order to build a rewarding practice with family businesses, you must use your understanding of their family business owner personalities to go beyond the obvious.

Before reading on take a moment to complete Figure 13.01 and review the overriding primary needs (i.e., motivations) of each of the eight family business owner personalities.

Figure 13.01

PRIMARY MOTIVATIONS OF THE FAMILY BUSINESS OWNER PERSONALITIES	
Instructions: Write in a few key words that describe the primary motivations of each personality type.	
Autocrats	
Empire Builders	
Fortune Hunters	
Loving Parents	
Recruits	
Rebels	
Status Seekers	
Social Benefactors	

Building Trust

Jean Malley is an Autocrat. She finds it hard to delegate responsibility. Jean also finds it hard to not be involved in each and every detail of important decisions that affect the family business.

What made Erin Pales successful with Jean was her ability to build a trusting relationship. Erin is good at making people feel at ease. She is especially good at showing them she understands what is important to them. All of Erin's actions tell her clients that she is not only a very capable financial services professional, but a caring person who they can depend on.

Principle: You must communicate with your family business owner clients in a manner than engenders confidence in yourself and your abilities.

Building trust is based on being empathic and reliable. Empathy will let you build bridges to a wealthy family business owner. At the same time, you have to be responsible about delivering what you said you would. The best way to communicate to family business owners that they should put their trust in you is by skillfully using testimonials.

Your Business Philosophy

By being perceived as an expert on family businesses, you have a distinctive competitive advantage. In one-to-one dealing with family business owners, you must continue to convey evidence of that expertise.

Linder Small conveys evidence of her expertise by talking about her philosophy surrounding her financial planning practice. In particular, she highlights how she sees her services and products helping family businesses benefit the family. She is able to do this well because she shapes these conversations toward the family business personality of the owner she is speaking to.

Principle: Tell your family business owner clients how your business philosophy fits into their motivations for having a family business.

Many life insurance professionals have a mission statement. At least the company or agency they are associated with has a mission statement. Sometimes, financial services providers will use some of the key points from that mission statement in promoting themselves.

This is a good starting point, but we can do better. You want to let family business owners know your practice is geared toward helping them. The best way to do this is to have a position statement for each of the eight family business personalities.

A position statement explains why the prospect should work with you. Since you can accommodate selected financial services needs of family businesses and their owners, you are simply positioning your services to the usually unexpressed agenda of your prospects. In conversation with family business owners, you spell out why they should work with you. You tell them how you see your services and products helping them achieve their goals.

To begin this process, complete the exercise in Figure 13.02.

Bentley sat down and analyzed what he does as a professional life insurance agent. His version of the positioning exercise is in Figure 13.03.

Another component of conveying your philosophy is by letting them know how you can work together. One of the key factors here is letting them know how you make your money. While many times this will be obvious, make certain there aren't any misunderstandings.

Figure 13.02

TAILORING YOUR POSITIONING STATEMENT EXERCISE

Instructions: In the center of the circle, write your CORE positioning statement. Then modify that statement so that it appeals to each of the eight types of family business owners.

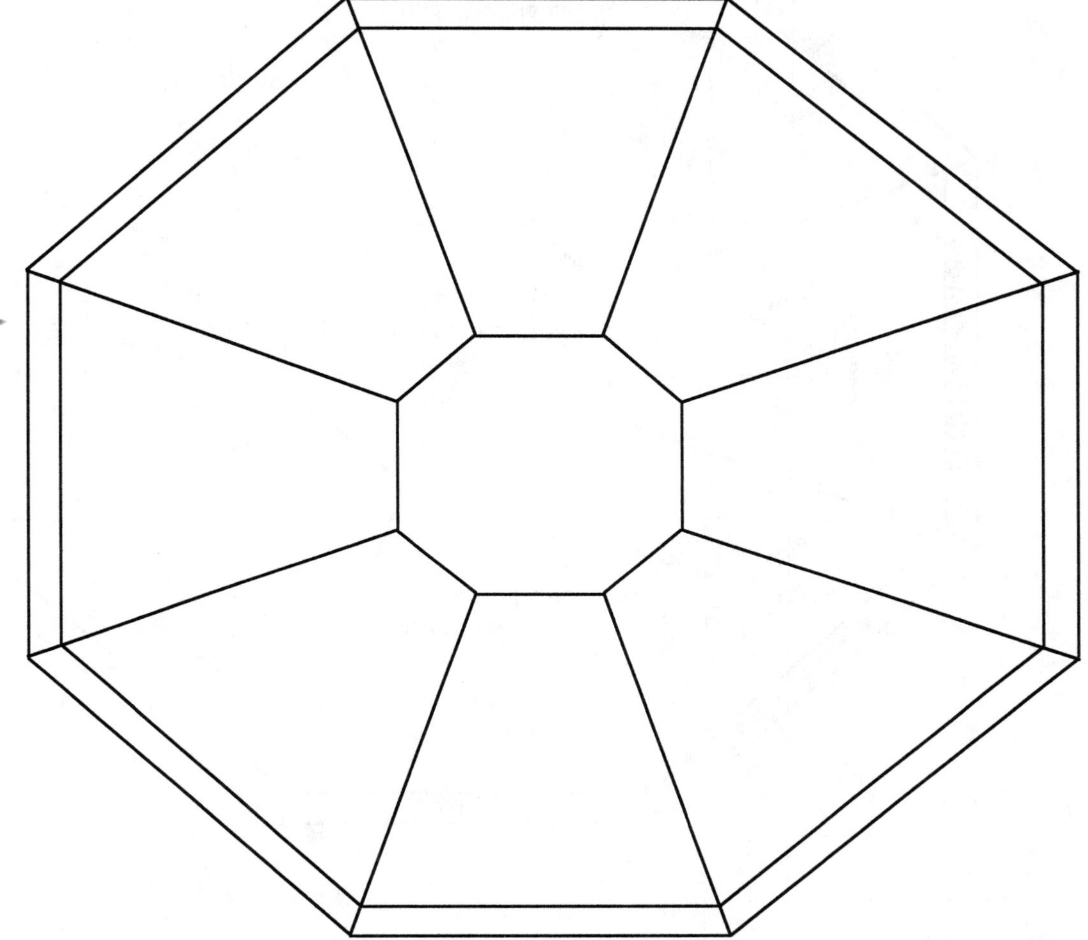

Figure 13.03

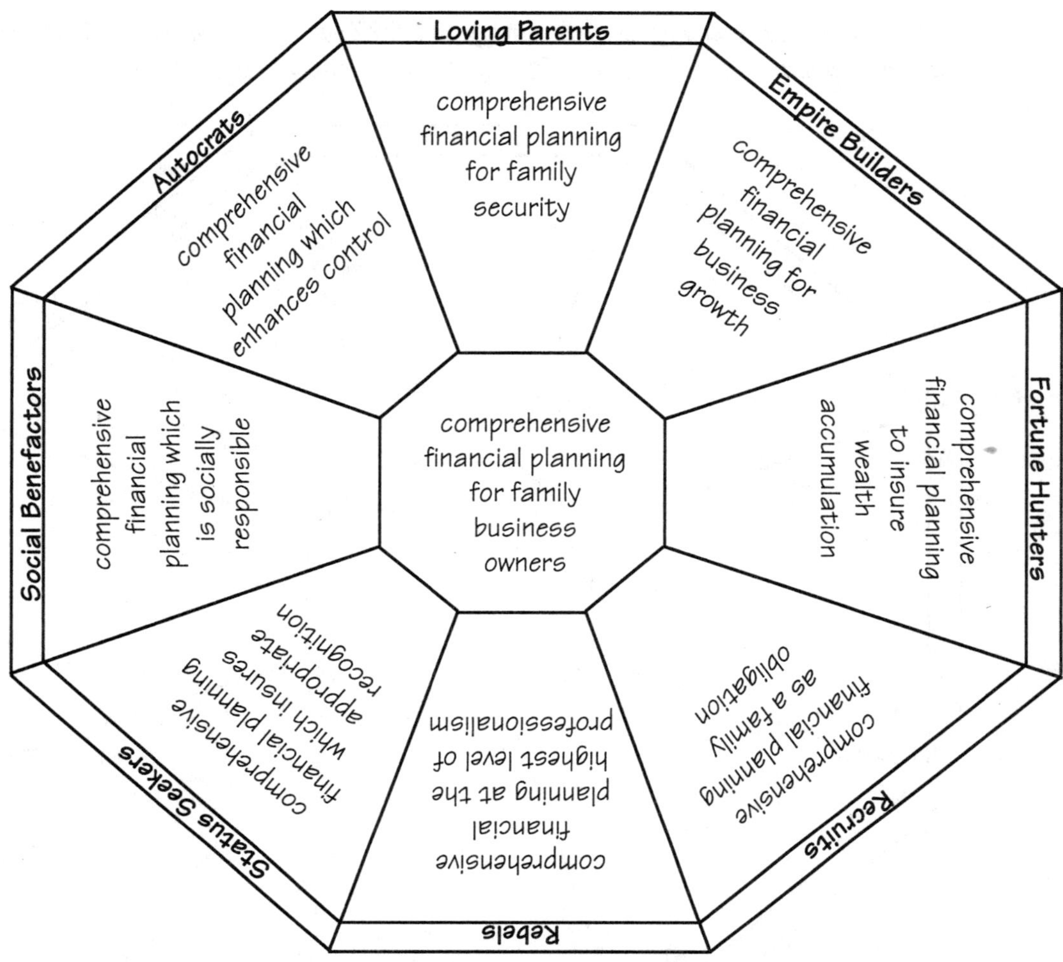

Discretion

Confidentiality is of enormous importance to family business owners. They do not want private information about themselves and their businesses disclosed. David Green, a Fortune Hunter, not only left his insurance agent but sued him once he found out the agent used his name — without permission — to help get other clients.

Principle: Family business owners must know that everything they tell you will be kept completely confidential.

At some point along the way you should explicitly state that everything you are told is confidential. This might sound a little silly, but it makes family business owners much more comfortable with you.

You should also talk about why some of your clients are happy to provide testimonials and referrals. You have to make sure that your prospects understand that some of your clients are delighted with your services and are more than willing to share this fact with others. You are not in any way being indiscreet.

One of the most effective techniques used in selling to family business owners is testimonials. These third-party endorsements validate your expertise and talents. Some of the most effective testimonials are letters written by highly satisfied clients. The intent is to selectively show them to family business owner prospects. This way you are reinforcing other word-of-mouth endorsements of you and your professionalism.

The critical thing is to amass a library of testimonials for each personality type. Thus, when you find a prospect of a specific type you can demonstrate your abilities in a way that he will almost immediately relate to.

The exercise in Figure 13.04 will help you begin to create your library of testimonials.

Attentiveness

Peatro Irwin knows his family business is very successful. He knows he is wealthy. And, in order to keep things that way, he knows he has to get high quality service and financial products. Irwin also knows that there are a lot of financial service providers eager to do business with him.

Irwin is an Empire Builder, but his expectation that life insurance professionals will be very attentive to his needs is characteristic of all family business owners. After seriously considering more than ten estate planning professionals, Irwin selected Neale Owen because Owen put in the most effort responding to Irwin.

Owen has been a financial planner for more than thirty years. He has a large well-established financial planning practice. Nevertheless, Owen is very much aware that if he wants to continue to grow his financial planning practice with clients like Irwin, he has to be exceedingly attentive to them - not only in order to get the business, but to keep it as well.

Principle: You must respect the wishes, needs, and wants of family business owners.

Being attentive to their needs is often an extension of identifying their needs. In many ways being attentive is demonstrated by communicating that you are trustworthy and that you will keep their secrets.

Figure 13.04

TESTIMONIAL EXERCISE		
Instructions: Create a list of 10 family business owners you have worked with. Each of them should be very satisfied with the services you provided. Then, specify the family business personality of the client. List three prospects to whom you would show the testimonial letter.		
Satisfied family Business Owners	**Owner Personality**	**Prospects**
1.		1. 2. 3.
2.		4. 5. 6.
3.		7. 8. 9.
4.		10. 11. 12.
5.		13. 14. 15.
6.		16. 17. 18.
7		19. 20. 21.
8		22. 23. 24.
9.		25. 26. 27.
10.		28. 29. 30.

Being attentive is also demonstrated when the financial services and products you suggest are the ones that clearly are solutions to the issues being confronted by the family business. Owen, for example, is known for providing innovative ways of dealing with financial concerns of family businesses. For Irwin he demonstrated how the use of dynasty trusts can meet many of his expressed as well as unexpressed desires. This is what sold Irwin on Owen over all the other professionals who were attentive to only the surface issues.

A Single Sound

In practice, these five selection criteria become intertwined. Conceptually they are distinct criteria. Novice life insurance professionals approach each of the criteria as a single issue. Meantime, experienced life insurance professionals bring them all into the picture at one time.

Principle: Work to blend the five critical selection criteria. All five should be a part of your communications with family business owners at all times.

For the inexperienced financial services provider, the critical selection criteria are each separate instruments. The audience sees them as such and hears them as such. In contrast, experienced life insurance professionals blend the sounds of the five critical selection criteria into an orchestra. The sound is not five sounds but one, as shown in Figure 13.05.

Figure 13.05

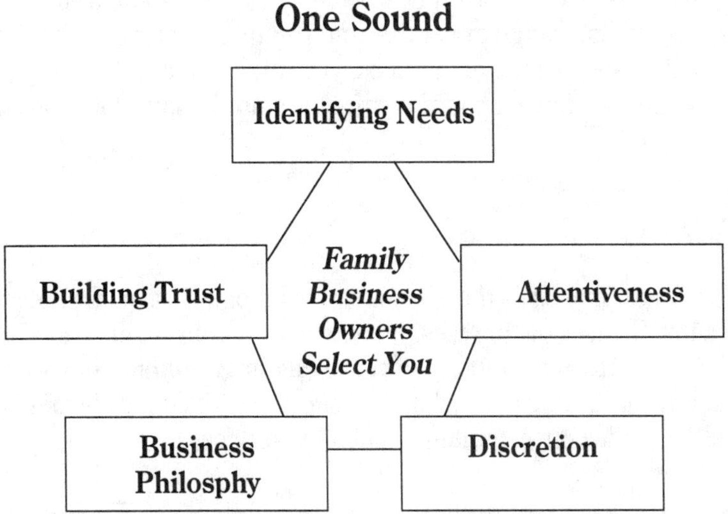

Separating The Wheat From The Chaff

In considering the competitive landscape, a significant number of life insurance professionals tend to emphasize two factors. They mistakenly believe these factors are meaningful to the selection decision of most family business owners. These two factors are:

- Range of services; and
- Cost of services.

It is important to understand that these two factors are not considered, at least not initially, by family business owners when selecting a financial services provider. Therefore, they shouldn't be emphasized by you when you are trying to sell. Let's look at both of them in greater detail.

Range Of Services

Erwin Kim works at one of the top insurance agencies in the state. Her insurance agency has created joint marketing ventures with other financial services providers such as trust companies. Therefore, when Kim talks to family business owners, she can offer them a complete menu of financial services and products. Unfortunately, this menu approach hasn't resulted in many initial sales. It also has not resulted in a great number of cross-sells.

Principle: Depth, not breath, appeals to family business owners. Concentrate on communicating your high level of focused expertise.

Family business owners are not looking for a Jack-of-all-trades. They tend to seek out specialists. A wide range of service and product offerings is not going to entice them. If you provide a wide range of services, you might eventually sell all of them to your family business clients. However, initially they are not looking for everything you may have on your shelves.

Cost Of Services

Paul King sees himself as the low cost provider of insurance and related financial services to the wealthy. He uses the phrases, "more value for your money" and "why pay more when you don't have to." He is attempting to convey an image of high quality without the need to pay exorbitantly for it. King has had limited success with family business owners even though he has had numerous opportunities to pitch his services.

Principle: Do not emphasize low cost. The cost of your products and services is not the issue. The value of your services and products is.

Family business owners are not concerned about the cost. Instead, they prefer to talk about value. Successful family business owners are willing to pay more if they think they are paying for services and products that will do what they want them to do. The price is not the issue. In fact, often higher cost is associated with higher value.

The Sales Platform

When you are attempting to sell your services and products to family business owners you are taking off from the sales platform. The sales platform consists of three components:

- The quality of the presentations;
- The quality of the proposal; and
- The quality of the promotional materials.

All three components are important in positioning the sale. While the five critical selection criteria are the concepts you need to communicate, the three components of the sales platform form the basis of how you communicate.

Quality Of The Presentations

John Kimberly is an excellent sales professional. He intuitively incorporates the five key selection criteria into his presentations to family business owners. Keep in mind that when we are talking about presentations, we are referring to all the meetings you have in the process of promoting your products and services. In effect, the presentation as we define it is the one-to-one sales process.

Kimberly has a true affinity for the various types of family business personalities. He believes this is a result of successfully working with them for more than 40 years. After all this time you either get to understand the motivations of the wealthy family business owners or you find another line of work. For those life insurance professionals without 40 years of experience to draw upon, the framework provided here is a shortcut to the same level of proficiency.

The key to the presentation is the process of selling financial services to business owners based on an in-depth understanding of what is important to them. You are leveraging your knowledge of the personalities in order to sell your services and products. Thus, the personality framework is essential to be effective.

Principle: Your ability to present is critical to your success in selling to family businesses.

The goal is to enable you to promote your services and products as solutions to problems. Your objective is to focus on what the business owner wants to accomplish. This is the opportunity he or she is providing you. Then you need to tailor your services and products to meet these wants. When this is done well, you have made a sale, usually a significant sale.

Leveraged selling results in you, not the competition, selling financial services and products to business owners. Moreover, it results in providing your clients with services and products they recognize that they need.

Leveraged selling is a three stage sales process that entails using insights into the buying psychology based on knowing the family business personality of the client. To this foundation, you add a knowledge of how to most effectively promote your services and products based on these insights. Then, you close the sale and communicate to the family business owner the value of what he just purchased. Formally, the three stages are:

- Stage 1: Assessment
- Stage 2: Personal sales strategy
- Stage 3: Justification

Stage 1: Assessment. This stage can be conceptualized as having two components which are evaluated simultaneously. The two components are:

- Identification of the family business owner's personality; and
- Specification of opportunities.

When working with a family business owner you need to determine the personality you are dealing with as quickly as possible. By knowing how they look at their family businesses, you are able to most effectively sell financial services to them. The easiest way to determine a business owner's personality is to use the Personality Assessment Tool explained in Chapter 5.

While you are determining the family business personality, you are simultaneously ascertaining the owner's wants. Specifically you are listening to his problems.

Business owners tend to talk about what they would like to have happen, that is, what the future "should" be. They talk about an "ideal state." It's your responsibility to translate this ideal state into solutions that are possible when particular financial products and services are purchased. Use the opportunity matrix in Figure 13.06 to begin outlining your selling strategies.

After you have determined what these problems are, it is essential that you confirm your assessment. All this means is that you explain to the business owners what you think they are saying. If you are right, aside from confirming that you are, you are enhancing your relationship by demonstrating your sensitivity. On the other hand, if you did not quite get it right, the business owners will readily correct you.

Stage 2: Personal sales strategy. Once you know the family business personality a well as the wants of the wealthy person with whom you are dealing, you are ready to leverage this information and strategically position your financial services and products. A personal sales strategy involves:

- Tying "themes" to your offerings;
- Employing responsive listening skills; and
- Involving shadow influencers.

Figure 13.06

OPPORTUNITY MATRIX			
Instructions: Identify 10 of your business owner clients. Specify each one's personality. Then identify his or her desired "ideal state." Make a note of related financial products and services. (See Chapters 6 through 11.)			
Family Business Owner	**Personality Type**	**"Ideal State"**	**Products and Services**
1.			
2.			
3.			
4.			
5.			
6.			
7.			
8.			
9.			
10.			

You have to communicate to business owners why your services and products are right for them. In effect, you have to show them that the services and products you are recommending will fulfill their expressed and unexpressed needs.

Themes are derived from the business owner personalities. Themes are an extension of what the business owner is seeking to accomplish. By focusing on themes, you are doing nothing more than showing how your recommended services and products meet their needs.

Responsive listening is your ability to be empathic. This is comprised of focusing in on the verbal as well as the nonverbal messages communicated by family business owners. The way to focus on verbal messages is to listen responsively, which means focusing on

Figure 13.07

TRIGGER WORDS AND PHRASES

Type	Trigger Words and Phrases
Loving Parents	Security Protection Generations Legacy Caring
Autocrats	Control Direction Power Authority In charge
Fortune Hunters	Wealth Money Assets Accumulation Riches
Empire Builders	Legacy Growth Expansion Development Increase
Rebels	Independence Autonomy Professionalism Freedom Liberation
Recruits	Duty Obligation Expectations Responsibility Commitment
Status Seekers	Recognition Acknowledgment Appreciation Acceptance Fame
Social Benefactors	Doing Good Ethics Caring Helping others Responsibility

what they are saying as opposed to preparing for your next statement. Nonverbal listening refers to reading body movements, gestures, and facial expressions.

You must not only understand the psychology of family business owners, you must communicate to them that you understand them. The best way to do this is to talk their language. You must talk in ways that tell them you know what's important to them. By using terms and phrases they readily use, you are letting them know you really understand them. The table in Figure 13.07 provides a short list of some of the terms and phrases commonly used by the different family business personalities.

It is also important to proactively include and refer to the "shadow influencers." This is something akin to a pre-emptive strike. They are going to get involved. By seeking their involvement you are, once again, demonstrating that you know how to work with family businesses.

One of the most effective ways of understanding the position and role of shadow influencers is by using sociometric schematics. Figure 13.08 shows an example of one such schematic for the Ivory family business.

Figure 13.08

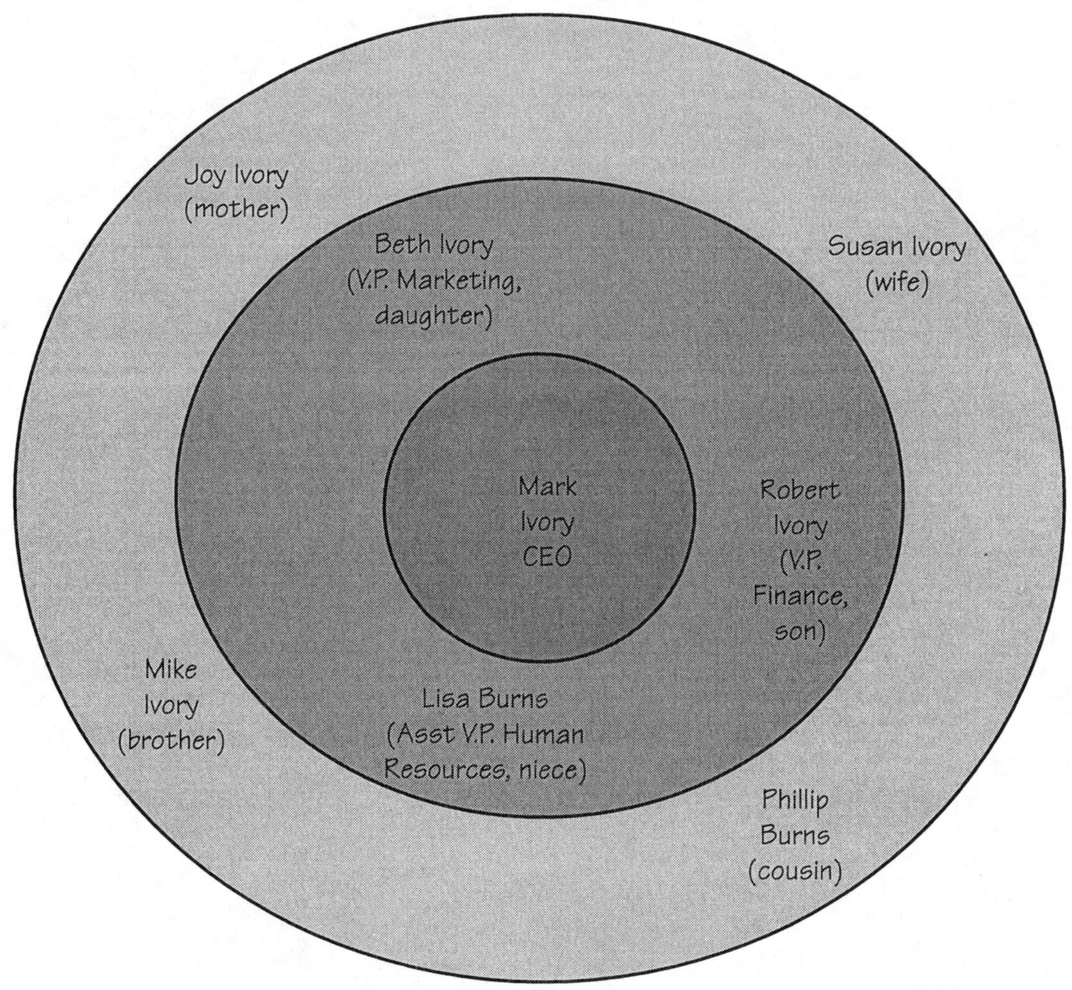

There are three steps in creating a shadow influencers sociometric schematic:

- Step 1: Write the name of the family business owner in the center circle.
- Step 2: In the next ring, write the names of those family members who are also in the business and who will exert an influence over the decision. Specify their titles in the business as well as their familial relationships to the owner. Also, put a star next to the heir apparent, if you know who he or she is.
- Step 3: In the outer ring, write the names of those family members who are not in the business, but exert influence over significant decisions. Also, note their relationships to the family business owner.

Take a moment to create a schematic for one of your clients in Figure 13.09.

Figure 13.09

SHADOW INFLUENCERS SOCIOMETRIC SCHEMATIC EXERCISE

Instructions: Take one of your family business clients. Pick one you have been thinking about and using in other exercises. Fill in the schematic.

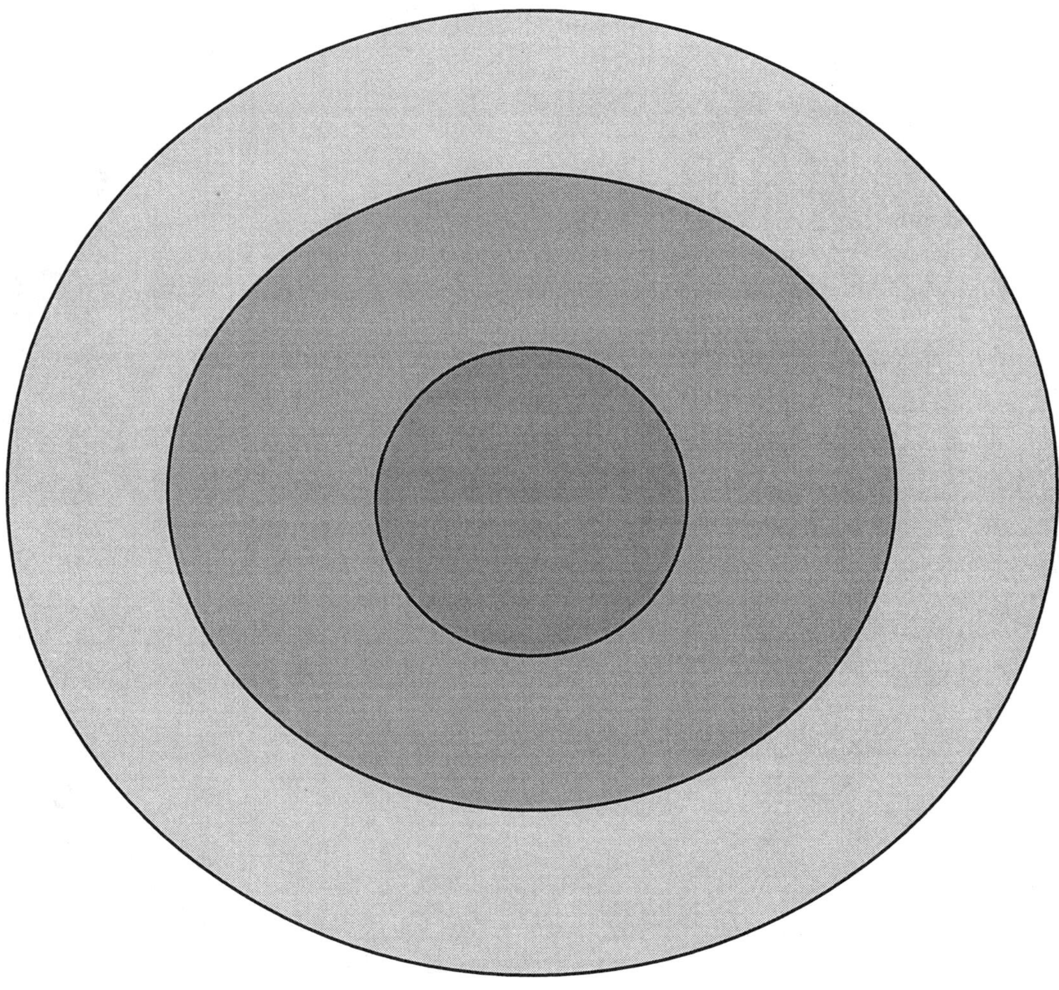

Step 3: Justification. Once you have made your points, you will have to reinforce them by repeating the logic of your proposal. This is best done by tying it back to the "ideal state" and the benefits of the products and services on which you focused.

Quality Of The Proposal

Ned Callow took the insurance proposal he was given by his insurance agent and showed it to his accountant and some of his family including key members of the company's management team as well as shadow influencers. Every day for nearly two weeks, Callow read and re-read the proposal until he had it memorized.

All the people who saw the proposal provided Callow with their opinions. The proposal was the best way for Callow to tell these important people just what the insurance agent was recommending. The proposal represented the conclusions of the insurance analysis and the action Callow should take. It also provided the financial justification for the recommendations.

The quality of the proposal had a tremendous effect on Callow's decision to purchase insurance. Generally his family thought the recommendations outlined in the proposal were good for the business and the family. Callow's accountant went over all the numbers and considered the recommendations to be based on a solid understanding of Callow's situation. All told, in this case the quality of the proposal was very important in closing the sale.

Principle: By making your proposals of the highest quality, you are making sure that others who are asked by the family business owner to review them will recognize you as an expert and recognize your recommendations to be beneficial to the family and the business.

The proposals you give to family business owners should be self-contained. They need to represent all your recommendations and the logic behind them. At the same time, the proposals cannot be overwhelming. You cannot overwhelm your prospect with numbers.

Bill Alder deals with this apparent paradox by giving two proposals. One is an executive summary. It's for the family business owner and the family members, including shadow influencers. The other is for those people who want to go through all the numbers. The accountants like the second proposal.

An essential part of both proposals is a call to action. They are explicit about the next steps that the family business owner needs to take, including why it is so important he or she take these steps now.

Quality Of The Promotional Material

The owners of the Malcolm Agency have spent an enormous amount of money and time on promotional materials for their agents to use with wealthy family business owners. First, they did a considerable amount of research. Using a focus group methodology, they did a great deal of concept testing.

They then hired one of the top design firms in the country to create the prototype materials. After the prototypes were produced, they once again called in the research company to test the materials. This process went back and forth between the design and research companies two more times.

When they were finished, The Malcolm Agency had some extremely impressive promotional material. Regrettably, even very high quality promotional material is not going to motivate a family business owner to purchase services and products. Unquestionably, it is important to have good handouts — materials you can leave behind with a prospect. However, the materials will not make the sale. Complicating the matter is the ease with which high quality promotional materials can be produced. A local rival firm to The Malcolm Agency saw the promotional materials and with some desktop publishing equipment was able to produce some high quality promotional material of its own using the same concepts.

Principle: High quality promotional materials are important. They will have the greatest effect if you design them incorporating your understanding of the eight family business personalities.

In all probability, promotional materials can be more effective than they usually are. The way to strike the proper cord with family businesses is for the materials to speak to their needs and wants. This means that your promotional materials must capitalize on your understanding of the eight family business personalities.

In focusing on what motivates family business owners, the promotional materials need to be concerned with the five critical selection criteria important to all the personalities.

Your Action Items

- You now need to create individual sales plans for family business prospects based on the five criteria we addressed.
- For each family business sales plan, develop the three stage selling model – assessment, personal sales strategy, and justification.
- Before executing each family business sales plan, make sure that your proposals and promotional materials are of appropriate content and quality.

Richard Bentley is sitting at his desk. On his PC, he opens his data base of his family business prospects. He selects the Ivory file for his upcoming presentation of retirement programs.

He has already determined that Mark Ivory is a Loving Parent. He customizes his opening remarks by incorporating the trigger words that Loving Parents will instinctively respond to.

As he reviews his presentation, he is pleased because he knows that two key shadow influencers will be in attendance — Susan Ivory the wife and Joy Ivory the mother. He is confident that they will be satisfied with his proposal and he knows they will be very supportive.

CHAPTER 14
KEEPING THEM

Richard Bentley is able to network through his own family business clients as well as accountants. These approaches to accessing the wealthy family business owner have turned out to be very effective for him.

He is also proficient at selling his services and products once he has made contact. He skillfully uses his knowledge of the critical selection criteria used by these business owners. He has a well-rehearsed collection of presentations. His proposals communicate that he understands them. And his promotional materials reinforce his image as an expert on family businesses.

Bentley is very much attuned to the shadow influencers. He is able to identify them and he works hard to win them over from the beginning.

Now, Bentley has to make sure that his new family business clients are very satisfied with his performance. The issue isn't the performance of the services and products he sold, although this is a concern. Bentley is concentrating on making certain he is properly managing the relationship.

All too often, life insurance professionals think that once the sale is made, they're done. While they might talk about on-going efforts to manage the relationship and be responsive to the client, more often than not this is just lip service. It sounds good, but in practice it dramatically falls short.

In examining the relationship management behavior of the financial services industry, it appears that only the better life insurance professionals really understand what it's all about. Calvin Berman is called, by his friends, a one- hit wonder. He is able to make the big sale and then he moves on. He doesn't do a very good job of creating a long-term relationship with his clients.

Berman realizes that this is not going to work for him over the long run. He wants to do a better job of relationship management but readily concedes that he doesn't quite know what to do. He points out that he takes his clients to lunch often, but that doesn't seem to do it.

Berman mistakes taking a client to lunch for relationship management. Relationship management is not just taking a family business owner out to lunch. Relationship management is not a series of transactions.

Relationship management is composed of those behaviors which make your clients want to stay with you and happy to refer other family business owners to you. We are not talking about mushy or touchy-feely things here. To the contrary, we are talking about specific behaviors that build the loyalty of family businesses.

The Importance Of Satisfied Clients

We cannot impress upon you the value of having satisfied clients. Not only are we concerned with the critical importance of doing what's right by them, but it is without question your responsibility to deliver the highest-quality service possible. Moreover, there is a twofold economic value of having highly satisfied clients:

- Client retention; and
- Client referrals.

Client Retention

Bart James is a Fortune Hunter. He says his entire essence is geared for only one purpose — to make money. Lewis Fredricks manages his considerable mutual fund investment portfolio. In some years, Fredricks has done an exceptional job of picking funds. In other years, things have not gone nearly as well. The portfolio has even lost money in an up stock market.

You might think that when times got rough, James would have left Fredricks and found another advisor. Under most conditions, James would have done just that. However, the situation is not all that usual. James stays with Fredricks even when he loses money. What magic does Fredricks have to keep a money- minded person loyal as money is lost?

Fredricks is very good at creating client satisfaction. Client satisfaction isn't only about the quality of financial services or products. In this case the investment performance is the service which would not be up to standards, yet James was still a satisfied client.

Principle: Family business clients will remain clients even when services and products are below acceptable levels if the relationship is skillfully managed. By handling the interpersonal aspects of the relationship you can retain clients even when the services and products perform poorly.

This switching investment managers as soon as they perform poorly is characteristic of affluent investors unless the investment manager has done an excellent job of managing the relationship. Investment management is not the only financial product or service that can send a business owner running if it doesn't work as expected. Retirement programs, insurance, actually every financial service or product that doesn't work as promised can destroy a relationship.

When financial products and services don't work as promised, the situation can be much worse than just losing a client. Sidney Banks put a deferred compensation program in place at a family business. The deferred compensation program did not live up to the promises made. Banks pulled all his business from the insurance agent who put in the deferred compensation program. Banks then made sure everyone he knew and everyone they knew learned about the insurance agent who is a "total screw-up." Banks wasn't done yet. He sued the insurance agent and the insurance company.

No doubt there will be times when the financial services and products do not deliver as expected. By effectively managing the relationship, you are able to retain clients even during these difficult times. Retained clients also do not generally tell others of your shortcomings.

Client Referrals

Even when his investment portfolio was losing money, James referred other wealthy family business owners to Fredricks for investment management services. Once again, the importance of a satisfied client is clear. James has such confidence in Fredricks' investment skills that even if his portfolio is currently not doing well, he will tell his associates that they should take advantage of Fredricks' expertise.

Principle: Family business clients will refer other business owners to you if they are highly satisfied.

Client referrals are the primary way to make contact with potential family business clients. By ensuring clients are highly satisfied they will readily refer other people to you.

Creating Satisfied Clients

Client satisfaction is a function of two factors:

- Providing high quality financial services and products; and
- High quality relationship management skills.

As far as the high-quality financial services and products are concerned, clearly you should do your best to ensure you are doing the right thing for your clients. You are no doubt adept in your chosen field and, therefore, are capable of selecting the services and products which are best.

The point of distinction between successful and exceptionally successful life insurance professionals is not necessarily in the financial services and products themselves. Actually, when you get down to it, all financial services and products are commodities. No, the difference is in their ability to do a first class job of managing relationships.

The research supplemented by the experiences of truly exceptionally life insurance professionals points out some of the behaviors you can use to create highly satisfied family business owner clients. High quality relationship management is not an excuse to do a poor job providing financial services and products. Relationship management is what's important to create the kind of relationship that supports family business owners. It also is key in letting you effectively grow your business.

Meetings, Lots of Meetings

Dale Cummins, a Status Seeker, is greatly comforted by the considerable attention he receives from Jon Hiller, his insurance agent. Hiller is very interested in meeting with Cummins as often as Cummins wants to meet.

Hiller always asks Cummins when he would like to meet. However, he does more than that, he recommends that they meet often. And Cummins is very receptive to these suggestions.

Principle: Find out from your clients when they would like to meet and exceed their expectations. Meet often with your family business clients.

A clear demonstration of your concern is the number of times you are interested in meeting with your family business clients. This is how they interpret your desire to see them often.

Meeting with them often to review their situations will not necessarily lead to a new sale each time. However, it does build trust and enhance the quality of your relationship. It keeps you in the forefront of their thoughts when financial services and products are discussed. This makes it much more difficult for another financial services provider to approach your clients.

Previous research has shown that three or more meetings per client results in the highest level of retention. Holding three or more meetings is also associated with increased business from the client as well as client referrals.

Highly successful life insurance professionals instinctively meet with their clients often. Even though three times has empirically been shown to be powerful, based on your individual practice, you might be able to achieve the same results with fewer meetings. On the other hand, it might require more meetings. The way to determine how many meetings you should be setting is by determining your "personal benchmark" in Figure 14.01.

Using An Agenda To Add Direction To The Meetings

Meeting often with your family business clients is a goal, but it's not enough. The meeting must have value. When Hiller meets with his clients, he always tries to provide an agenda for the discussions. Of course, his agendas are not carved in stone. He is very flexible. All he is trying to do is make sure he will deal with some important issues at the meeting.

Principle: You can effectively provide direction for a meeting by using an agenda. The agenda can be nothing more than telling the family business owner the concerns you have and want to discuss.

Figure 14.01

PERSONAL BENCHMARK FOR MEETINGS FREQUENCY

Instructions: Randomly select 10 representative family business owner clients. For each one note the number of face-to-face meetings you have had with them in the last 12 months. Then check the appropriate box indicating how satisfied they are in your judgment. Subsequently, fill in the blanks below and calculate your personal benchmark.

Family Business Owner	*Number of Meetings*	*Satisfaction*
1.	_____	❑ High Satisfaction ❑ Medium Satisfaction ❑ Low Satisfaction
2.	_____	❑ High Satisfaction ❑ Medium Satisfaction ❑ Low Satisfaction
3.	_____	❑ High Satisfaction ❑ Medium Satisfaction ❑ Low Satisfaction
4.	_____	❑ High Satisfaction ❑ Medium Satisfaction ❑ Low Satisfaction
5.	_____	❑ High Satisfaction ❑ Medium Satisfaction ❑ Low Satisfaction
6.	_____	❑ High Satisfaction ❑ Medium Satisfaction ❑ Low Satisfaction
7.	_____	❑ High Satisfaction ❑ Medium Satisfaction ❑ Low Satisfaction
8.	_____	❑ High Satisfaction ❑ Medium Satisfaction ❑ Low Satisfaction
9.	_____	❑ High Satisfaction ❑Medium Satisfaction ❑ Low Satisfaction
10.	_____	❑ High Satisfaction ❑ Medium Satisfaction ❑ Low Satisfaction

Number of highly satisfied family business owner clients: _____

Average number of meetings per highly satisfied clients _____

Your Personal Benchmark

Caveat: This exercise is only the starting point. It provides some insight into the process you should use. The limited sample may not yield reliable data. Thus, the larger the sample, the more accurate you will be.

Alan Simon is an Empire Builder. When Hiller meets with him, he usually starts by asking Alan what he would like to discuss. Simon always has some matters he wants to deal with. Hiller is careful to move at Simon's pace. He makes suggestions about what the meeting can be about but he makes sure Simon is the one determining the agenda.

This is another way of setting an agenda. Here the business owner is determining the importance of the issues from the very beginning. Hiller thoughtfully makes certain that he and Simon attend to any pressing issues.

Encourage Clients To Be Involved

Hiller doesn't see himself as running the show. It is more the other way around. He works for his clients and is always conscious of this fact. He knows that the best way to make sure he is doing what they want is to get them involved.

Hiller does this in a number of ways. Some of his most effective ways include:

- Encouraging them to ask questions freely.
- Encouraging them to express their opinions often.
- Encouraging them to talk about why things are important to them.

He is direct when it comes to getting his family business clients involved. He tells them right from the start that they should ask questions, give their opinions, and make sure the conversations are about matters of importance to them.

Principle: Involvement is important in building a high quality relationship. You can involve your clients by making certain they are not sitting back and just shaking their heads. You must get them to participate in the process.

Fostering involvement is a crucial way of strengthening your relationships with your family business owner clients. You need not be as forthright as Hiller to benefit from his recommendations. Sally Brenner sells a great deal of insurance by encouraging her wealthy family business clients to actively participate.

You might think that all family business owners would just state their points of view. However, this isn't the case. Sometimes the way they communicate is with their feet. What you always want to do is work with them as a partner helping them meet their financial needs. You can guarantee this by encouraging them to express themselves.

Creating involvement must be done in the context of the personality types of the business owners. There are a number of sales tracks that can be used with different family business owners. It is essential that you are conversant with all of them. Of course, modifications will be required based on the particular family business owner with whom you are talking. Nevertheless, the core message is the same.

Complete Figure 14.02 before reading on.

Figure 14.02

INVOLVEMENT EXERCISE

Instructions: For each of the three ways to involve family business owners, write the appropriate sales track. Two examples are provided.

Encourage Family Business Owners to Ask Questions Freely — Sales Track:

"Because your family is very important to you, as we go through this, it would be a great help if you bring up questions that your wife and son might have as well as the ones that occur to you."

Which of the eight types is this sales track appropriate for:____________

"As we go through the planning process, I want you to think of questions you may have as to how my recommendations will support the growth and expansion of your company. Whenever you have a question be sure to bring it up."

Which of the eight types is this sales track appropriate for:____________

For the remaining six family business owner personalities, write a sales track that encourages them to ask questions.

Recruits:

____

____

____

____

Autocrats:

____

____

____

____

Fortune Hunters:

____

____

____

____

Rebels:

____

____

____

____

Status Seekers:

____

____

____

____

Social Benefactors:

____

____

____

____

Encourage Family Business Owners to Express Their Opinions Often — Sales Track

"You couldn't have become such a recognized manufacturer in this community without knowing what you're doing. So whenever I make a recommendation, I'm going to ask for your reaction."

Which of the eight types is this sales track appropriate for:____________

"You understand your business better than anybody else. And I've designed this plan to give you the greatest degree of control possible. Every time I hit on an aspect of the plan that makes sure you're in charge, I'm going to check with you to see if this works for you."

Which of the eight types is this sales track appropriate for:____________

For the remaining six family business owner personalities, write a sales track that encourages them to ask questions.

Recruits:

____

____

____

____

Loving Parents:

Fortune Hunters:

Rebels:

Empire Builders:

Social Benefactors:

Encourage Family Business Owners to Talk About Things That Are Important To Them — Sales Track

"From everything you've told me so far, I understand you're primarily interested in wealth accumulation. For me to be able to customize investment alternatives to meet your needs, I need to understand your vision of retirement and your vision of the quality of life you expect to have."

Which of the eight types is this sales track appropriate for:____________

"Running the company is a big responsibility for somebody responsible for the family. I need to hear more about what your family expects in the way of executive and retirement benefits."

Which of the eight types is this sales track appropriate for:____________

For the remaining six family business owner personalities, write a sales track that encourages them to ask questions.

Rebels:

____

____

____

____

Autocrats:

____

____

____

____

Loving Parents:

____

____

____

____

Empire Builders:

____

____

____

____

Status Seekers:

Social Benefactors:

Make Sure They Understand

Another way Hiller gets them to participate is by making sure they understand just what he is doing. He wants to take the mystery out of the process of buying insurance. He strives to lay everything out as simply as possible.

Hiller likes to regularly ask if his clients need anything explained. To get over client resistance for fear of looking foolish, he would say, "Would you like me to go over this again, I realize it's very complicated?" He gives them a justification for asking him to explain something.

Additionally, Hiller tries to have them explain to him what he is doing and how the financial services and products will meet their needs. Too often, Hiller has lost cases because his clients failed to really understand what he was proposing. By having them explain it to him, he is able to correct any misconceptions. Thus, his clients know what they are getting and why.

Principle: To be sure they understand, frequently ask if your family business owner clients want anything explained. Also, get them to explain it to you.

Confusion is a certain killer of relationships. When your family business clients have expectations that are out of line with reality, reality wins and you lose. You can avoid this potentially disastrous situation by arranging to look at the situation in the same way. Jon's approach to doing this is particularly effective.

Involve The Shadow Influencers

We know how powerful shadow influencers can be in making decisions about purchasing financial services and products. They are just as powerful anytime financial services and product are being promoted.

Hiller keeps the shadow influencers involved from the beginning. When he first meets with family business owners, he begins to identify and evaluate the impact of shadow influencers. Hiller continually updates his assessment of shadow influencers and encourages family business owner clients to consult with important family members — always by name — who may not be directly involved in the business.

Principle: Always encourage family business owners to involve shadow influencers. Specifically, recommend that they talk to family members about the products and services you are providing.

Shadow influencers are a distinctive part of family businesses. They have a tremendous impact on the way family businesses buy financial services. While they pose some difficulties, they can be a great asset. You should therefore look at them as an asset and work with them.

In addition, by encouraging the family business owner to consult with shadow influencers, you are demonstrating that you really understand their world. A world where family and business interests overlap. The family business owners as well as the shadow influencers will recognize and appreciate your understanding, helping you to build a better relationship.

Involve Other Advisors

Hiller is careful to get his client's other advisors in on the decision making process as quickly as possible. Somewhere along the line, they are going to get involved at the request of the family business owner. All Hiller is doing is showing he realizes that his expertise is only one piece; other advisors bring additional skills and knowledge. Making sure that all the client's advisors are working together is the only way to insure that the right thing is done for the client.

Accountants, attorneys, and other advisors appreciate Hiller recommending that they be called in. This way Hiller is doing what's best for his client while building bridges to other influential advisors to his clients. These good relationships endear Hiller to the client and the advisors who have been recommending new family business clients to him for insurance services.

Principle: Always encourage family business owners to involve their other advisors as quickly as possible. By doing so, you will be avoiding problems down the road.

As with the shadow influencers, family business owners will turn to their other advisors. For instance, many family business owners will turn to their accountants to evaluate insurance proposals, retirement programs, and so forth. By getting them involved early in the process, you are making them allies and not adversaries to your recommendations.

Your Action Items

- When working with family business owners you need to meet with them often. Thus, you need to create your own relationship marketing benchmarks.
- It is imperative to encourage family business owner involvement by using the involvement techniques detailed above.
- Make sure to involve the appropriate shadow influencers and advisors.

Bentley puts a great deal of effort into relationship management. Not only is this a good practice from the point of view of building and maintaining his insurance business, it is the ethical way to work with clients.

Bentley is rewarded for all his efforts at relationship management. He knows that one of the best ways of getting new clients is through referrals from current highly-satisfied clients. Because of all his effort at managing the relationship, Richard consistently gets at least one hot lead from each of his current clients. This is how he is able to continue to grow his business at such an amazing rate.

APPENDIX A
RESEARCH BASIS OF THE BOOK

The research program on which this book is based has extended over ten years. Two sets of studies in particular were used as the source for many of the statistics provided.

Psychographic Segmentation Study

Psychographic segmentation has been used with considerable success in markets where face-to-face interaction between buyer and seller typifies the exchange. The market of family business owners as served by life insurance professionals is one such market.

Psychographics refers to the attitudes, beliefs, and needs of buyers in relation to the category of products being considered. In this instance, we were interested in the attitudes, beliefs, and needs of family business owners as they considered insurance and financial products.

Interviews with many family business owners, a review of the literature, and conversations with several panels of insurance and financial service professionals all contributed to the construction of the psychographic battery. This battery and eight pages of additional questions was administered to a national sample of 971 family business owners.

Psychographics: Motivations and Goals

Although strategies differ, the objectives of publicly-held corporations usually are centered around the theme of increasing shareholder wealth. However, there has been long-standing acknowledgment of variance in the objectives of individual managers due to values, beliefs, and ideologies. Some managers seek greater individual power, others value personal wealth, still others want to insure security for their families or to contribute in a meaningful way to their communities. An important task for executives in large publicly-held corporations is to blend the personal objectives of individual managers to serve the overall business objective.

However, in family businesses (i.e., the ones that are inclined to produce private wealth), ownership is private, not public. As a result, the objective of increasing shareholder wealth is not necessarily the objective of the business enterprise. Instead, because the CEO is often the controlling, or at least a dominant, shareholder family business owners display a wider range of objectives in a manner similar to individual managers. Further, their personal objectives become business objectives.

For industrial marketers, a close understanding of the objectives of family businesses has become important because of the economic impact of this sector of the economy. Family firms are the most prevalent form of enterprise in the United States; some 90% or more of all enterprises are thought to be family businesses. Family businesses employ an estimated 50% of all workers in the United States and contribute a projected 50% of the country's gross national product. By extension, family businesses may account for as much as half of all industrial purchasing in the country.

It is important for business-to-business marketers to know whether or not family business CEOs act out of family as well as business motivations and whether these motivations affect organizational buying behavior. The research documents the breadth of family business CEO motivations as assessed through psychographic segmentation and explores the impact of these motivations on organizational buying behavior.

Exploring Family Business Owner Motivations

Although norms, rules, and established procedures typify organizational buyer behavior, organizational buyers are known to be influenced by both rational and emotional motivations. Rational motives include such economic factors as cost, quality and service while emotional motives are more subjective and might include status, security and risk avoidance.

Much of the family business literature has focused on documenting motivations for the enterprise which are family-oriented and which distinguish family from non-family firms. Findings to date indicate that buyer motivations in a family firm appear to include some which have both a rational and emotional loading primarily because they are linked to long-term family well-being. Primary motivations identified in the literature include insuring family security, spending time with the family, attaining personal goals, contributing to local communities, and achieving personal power.

Insuring Family Security. Family firms are highly motivated to achieve financial stability and security for the owner and the family. There are several means by which family security can be assured. Some of the methods identified include creating a sustainable, multi-generational business, hiring family as employees in the firm and providing professional training for family members. However, it has been established that such family-oriented motivations can be counter-productive to business success in some instances.

Spending Time With the Family. Many family business owners are motivated to structure the business in such a way that they can spend more time with family members – usually by employing them in the business. In some family businesses, control motivations dominate. In others, motivations are more inclusive. These family style patterns influence the relative formality and informality of decision-making processes.

Attaining Personal Goals. Family business owners often express goals of personal growth and challenge such as attaining significant financial success and personal wealth or the creation of a new technology. Within the family business field there are many anecdotes of new business initiatives started to provide employment and experience for a family member or to fulfill some set of personal goals on the part of an individual family member.

Contributing to Local Communities. A close relationship between family businesses and the communities in which they do business has been frequently observed. Owners of family businesses are often motivated to make the family name well known in the community for business and philanthropic reasons. Family firm owners often count community support among their personal and business goals and successful family businesses are observed to generally be good citizens.

Achieving Personal Power. Heads of family firms tend to concentrate personal power. They do so through a distinctive set of attributes which includes distrust of other authority figures, self reliance, rejection of advice from others, exercise of power in seemingly arbitrary and capricious ways, domination and control of both business and family activities, reluctance to delegate, and development of a philosophy that is followed explicitly.

Segmenting Industrial Markets

Segmenting business markets on the basis of CEO objectives for the business, such as those described above, is an extension of currently available methods for segmenting. There are at least sixteen bases for segmenting industrial markets. These have been classified into macro and micro approaches, although combination, or nested, approaches are increasingly common.

Macro-segmentation approaches involve dividing the market into subgroups based on overall characteristics of customer organization such as ownership, size, application, and geographic location. Macro-segmentation approaches have the advantage of being relatively easy to implement for marketing management because the data by which firms may be classified are relatively available. However, one limitation of macro-segmentation approaches is that they do not provide much insight into organizational buyer behavior. Although some work has been done on distinguishing family businesses from non-family businesses on the basis of macro-segmentation, it does not provide direct insight into organizational buyer behavior processes.

Micro-segmentation approaches have been developed to fill this gap. Micro-segmentation approaches divide markets on the basis of aspects of their organizational buyer behavior. Examples of micro-segmentation approaches include segmentation on the basis of buying criteria, benefits sought, attitudes towards the purchase, organizational innovativeness and benefits. Because micro-segmentation approaches profile customers in terms of how they view products and the process of their procurement, these methods are particularly useful in personal selling situations.

The most significant disadvantage of micro-segmentation is implementability. Often, the data by which customer organizations are segmented are usually not available from any external source but must be developed by the firm. This occurs, increasingly, through data base marketing.

The micro-segmentation approach of psychographic segmentation was selected as the framework for this research because the array of reported family and business objectives is so extensive. Psychographic segmentation creates homogeneous groupings of customers based on the objectives, values and benefits they seek to fulfill.

Although developed for consumer marketing, the method has been revealing in industrial market contexts. It was used, for example, to identify four types of data terminal buyers: the

Hardware Buyer, the Brand Buyer, the People Buyer, and the One-Stop Shopper. More recently, the authors used the approach to create three types of commercial banking services customers: the Return Seekers, the Relevance Seekers and the Relationship Seekers.

Psychographic segmentation is best used when the opportunity for direct interaction between buyer and seller allows the seller to classify the buyer according to the framework. By understanding the values of a potential purchaser and buying organization, an industrial salesperson can tailor a selling strategy to fit the particular needs and objectives of the organization.

Especially in a rapidly-changing economy, a psychographic segmentation of family business owners would enable industrial marketers to:

- Determine which sub-segments of the family business population have the greatest potential;
- Create product positionings relevant to the objectives of each segment;
- Shape their tactics to optimize impact; and
- Enable them to plan for productive relationships with the segments.

Data Collection

Sample. The sample of family business CEOs was recruited through a national network of nine professional services firms. In order to avoid some of the potential biases of cluster sampling, three accounting firms, three insurance brokerages and three law firms were enlisted in the sampling and data collection effort. Managing partners or the equivalents in these firms supervised the process of identification of suitable respondents and developed procedures for inviting their participation.

Defining the Family Business. All respondents were screened to be CEOs of firms in which they controlled at least 51% of the ownership, in which other family members were involved in management and who indicated the intention to pass the business to heirs within the family. These criteria were set on the basis of the family business literature.

To date, various definitions of the family firm have been offered. Among them are definitions based on the degree of ownership by family members, the degree of family involvement in the management of the business, and the intention to pass the business to the next generation. Multiple indices of family firm status are now preferred and were used by the authors. In addition, all firms participating in the study had to employ at least 50 people. This latter criterion served to exclude very small businesses and entrepreneurial firms.

Limitations. A limitation of the study is the non-probability basis of data collection. As there are no national statistics on the characteristics of family business owners, it is not possible to assess the adequacy of this sample on the basis of known characteristics. As will be discussed in the analysis section, however, steps were taken to assure reliability of the results.

Measures of Motivation. A representative list of motivations and objectives for owning a family business was collected through a comprehensive search of the family business case study literature and in-depth interviews with twenty family business owners. From this archive, forty statements were created reflecting the range of goals and needs. The statements were refined through pre-tests.

Measures of Procurement Processes. In order to evaluate the adequacy of the segmentation framework for marketing strategy development, respondents were also asked questions about procurement. In order to obtain reliable data, the decision was made to explore aspects of professional services purchasing. Professional services such as legal and accounting services are known to be nearly universally procured by businesses. They are also known to trigger non-employee family involvement in the buying process.

Analysis

Hierarchical cluster analysis based on nearest centroid sorting was performed on split samples of the data set. The results of the two procedures were compared on a number of factors including the fusion coefficients revealed in the dendrogram results, the distribution of sample among the clusters and the descriptive appeal of the results and their conformance with theory.

On this basis, the eight group solution was selected and the samples recombined for final analysis. Descriptive statistics for these eight clusters were calculated on the remaining variables (not used in the clustering) to generate a data-based profile for each family business segment.

Profile

These family business owners share characteristics of family business owners nationally as to their business size, industry distribution, and personal demographics. For example, the businesses included in this research represent successful businesses with at least fifty employees, as shown below.

NUMBER OF EMPLOYEES

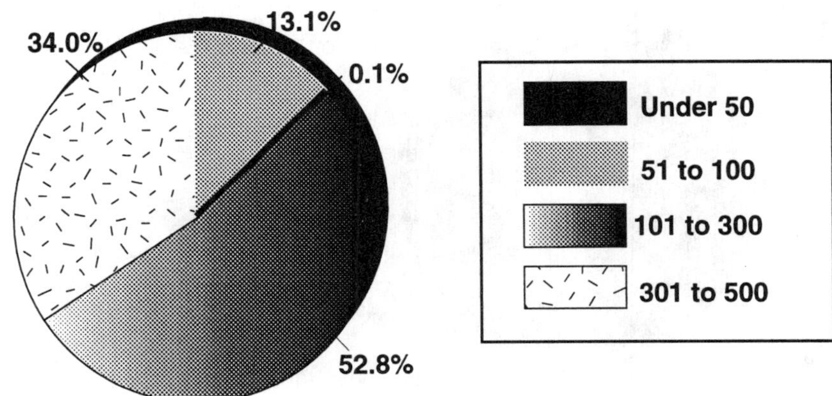

Number of Family Business Owners = 971

Four broad industry classifications were used. The results show that family business owners encompassed all four industries, as illustrated below. The largest concentration is in wholesale businesses, which is consistent with the family business literature which shows family businesses to be concentrated in distribution industries such as beer and soda distributors and auto parts.

INDUSTRY CLASSIFICATION

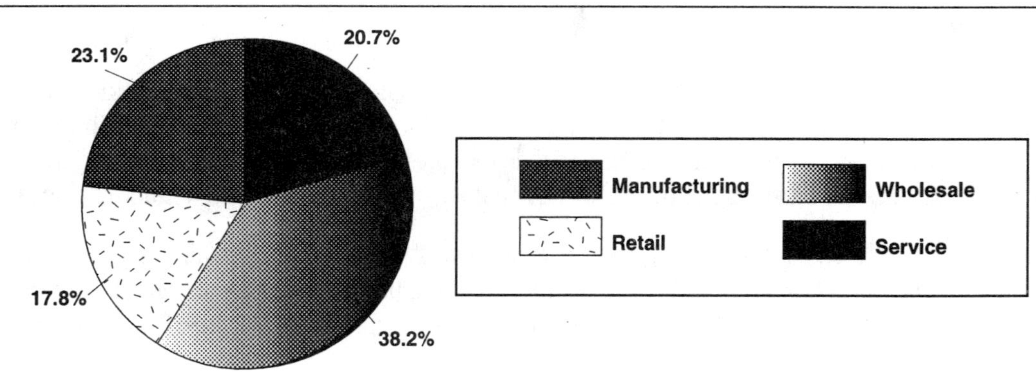

Number of Family Business Owners = 971

As shown below, almost half of family business owners are between 35 and 49 years old. Slightly less are between 50 and 64 years of age. Only 3.5% are over 65 and even fewer are younger than 35.

AGE OF FAMILY BUSINESS OWNERS

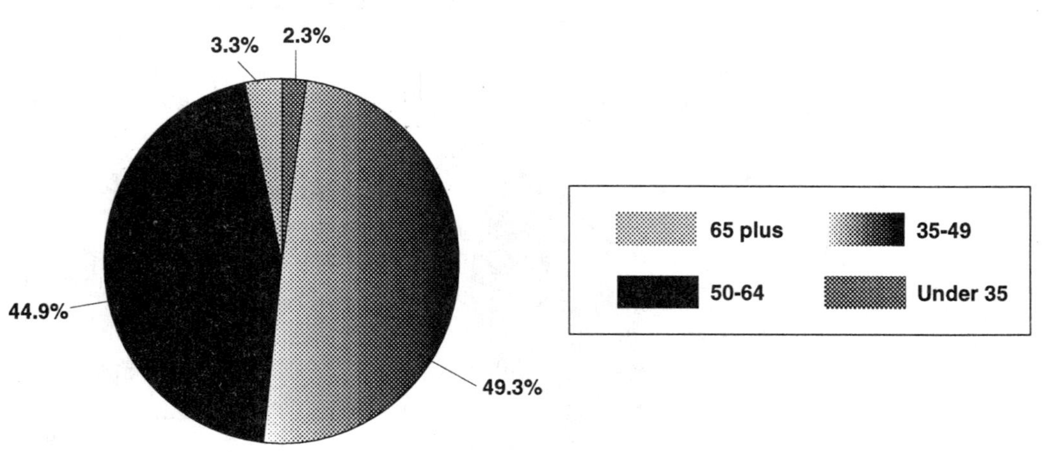

Number of Family Business Owners = 971

More than three quarters of the sample are male, as shown below. Few large family businesses are led by women but their numbers are increasing as more women start their own businesses.

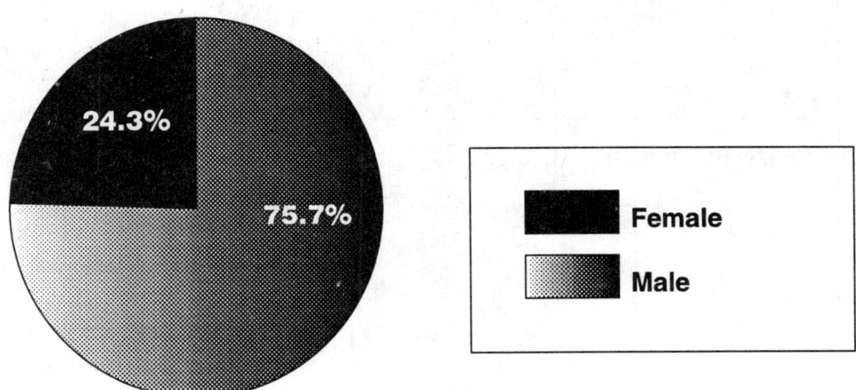

Number of Family Business Owners = 971

Product Positioning Study

A second research program was conducted in order to explore the relationships between psychographic segment and the benefits associated with major financial products. The difficulty with this research was that the family business owners did not often think in terms of products in the way that the financial service industries often do. To compensate for this differing perspective, product classes were the focus of the research. Nevertheless, within the product classes, individual products were addressed.

Over 3,000 interviews were conducted with individuals who had purchased insurance products related to each of these product classes within the last 24 months. Six product classes were explored in depth, as illustrated below.

PRODUCTS AND PRODUCT CLASSES EXPLORED IN THE STUDIES

Product class	Products
Executive benefits (Chapter 6)	• Health insurance • Life insurance • Disability insurance • Corporate car • Restricted stock or stock options • Severance pay plans • Medical expense reimbursement plans
Retirement planning (Chapter 7)	• Employees share in gains and losses • Flexible contributions • Salary deferrals for employees • Large benefits for older employees • Predictable retirement benefits • Fixed contributions
Business succession and estate planning (Chapter 8)	• Formal (written) succession plan • Life insurance to pay estate taxes • Buy-sell agreements • Trust services • Formal training program for heirs
Asset protection planning (Chapter 9)	• Off-shore trusts • Property and casualty insurance • Personal liability insurance • Officers and directors insurance • Use of trusts to protect assets
Investment management (Chapter 10)	• Mutual funds • Variable products • Discretionary investment accounts • Wrap accounts
Charitable estate planning (Chapter 11)	• Charitable bequests • Private family or corporate foundation • Charitable remainder trusts • Donor advised funds • Charitable lead trusts • Pooled income funds • Charitable gift annuities • Life insurance

APPENDIX B
FAMILY OFFICES: THE MEGA-WEALTHY

A very special case of family businesses is the family office. The descendants of Eugene Grace, the legendary Bethlehem Steel chairman, have established a family office currently being managed by Charles Grace. The name of their family office is the Ashbridge Corporation which, at present, manages the wealth of eight families. In total, the family office is responsible for more than $250 million dollars.

Very affluent families have historically established "offices" for themselves. A principal purpose of these "offices" is to manage their wealth. All in all, there are between 2,500 and 3,000 family offices in the United States today.

A family office is established when a wealthy family decides to provide financial and related advisory services to members of the family. When they create a formal structure to do this, you have a family office. The concept of the family office pre-dates the formal formation of the financial services industries. These organizational arrangements, initially re-invigorated by the industrial revolution, have seen significant growth due, in part, to the tremendous creation of wealth in the 1980s.

The formal family office structure was originally intended to serve the needs of only the wealthy family. However, as the number of heirs have grown and the family wealth has been stretched, many family offices have opted to provide their services to non-family affluent individuals and family groups. Hence, these family offices are not only managing the wealth of the founding family but the wealth of similarly mega-wealthy families as well as other affluent individuals.

The Mega-Wealthy

What constitutes mega-wealthy? It varies. To justify creating a family office — putting in place a formal organization to manage the family's wealth — a good minimum would be family assets of at least $50 million. There are family offices where the asset level is slightly lower. At the same time, there are many more family offices where the asset level is substantially greater, often reaching into the hundreds of millions.

A study of the country's 150 richest families with $100 million or more in assets was conducted on behalf of Graystone Partners, a Chicago-based advisor to family offices. The sample for the study was drawn from the client relationships and prospects of Graystone Partners.

How The Mega-Wealthy View Society And The Future

This research focused on the interrelation between the mega-wealthy's view of society and the future and their needs and uses of numerous financial and related services and products.

More than many other affluent individuals, the mega-wealthy are strongly focused on the future. With respect to their financial decisions, their expectations of what will happen impacts the financial and related professionals they work with as well as the services and products they need and want.

Some of the key findings concerning their expectations for the future follows. Overall, two-thirds of the mega-wealthy foresee that:

- The US trade balance will continue to worsen;
- The portion of the national budget allocated to entitlements will continue to rise;
- The national debt will balloon upward;
- Tax incentives for successful individuals will be eliminated; and
- To ensure their personal safety, they will have to rely on their own resources.

Just because the majority believe these scenarios doesn't mean they will come about. However, it does mean that the mega-wealthy will be basing their financial decisions on them.

Four Family Office Personality Types

Not all of the mega-wealthy estimate the probability of various trends in the same way. Indeed, there are significant differences among family offices in terms of their attitudes about the future.

THE MEGA WEALTHY

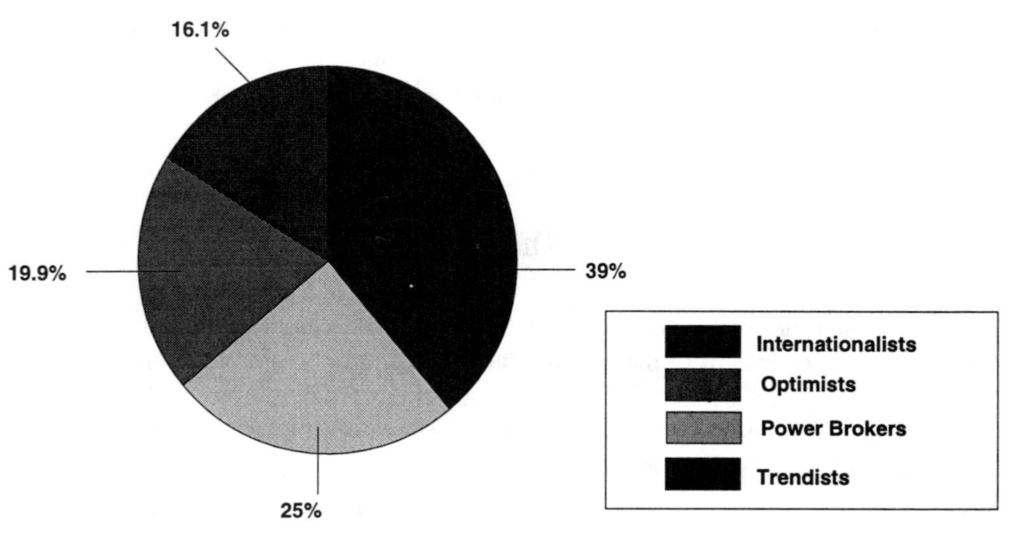

Just as there are eight unique family business owner identities, there are four distinctive personality types of family offices. Each family office personality has a clearly different perspective of the future and is currently acting on that perspective when making financial and related decisions.

As shown below, the four family office personality types are:

- Trendists;
- Power Brokers;
- Optimists; and
- Internationalists.

Trendists

Members of this group tend to attach a considerable amount of importance to trends that have garnered public attention. Moreover, they are inclined to act based on these commonly-held beliefs.

Trendists espouse current trends and are unlikely to anticipate changes or to prepare for change. Their attitudes are likely to be revealed in the negative — in the attitudes they do not share — with other groups.

They tend to see the world in straight line terms. That is, the future is the rationalized extension of the present.

Additionally, Trendists are the least likely of the four family office personality types to be proactive. Instead, they are inclined to respond to changes as those changes become apparent.

Power Brokers

This group seeks to align itself with other wealthy people to affect public policy favorably. Moreover, they believe they have the combined influence to do so. The objective is to create a favorable environment for themselves and their families.

Power Brokers have strong concerns about the future of the United States. At the same time, they are extremely focused on the United States and are intent on working within the system to improve it. They strive to employ their financial, political, and interpersonal resources to assist in setting aspects of the national agenda.

This orientation also results in the formation of affinity groups. Through these like-minded associations of the mega-wealthy, Power Brokers work to empower themselves.

Optimists

This group is largely up-beat about economic conditions in the United States. Furthermore, they believe that society has the ability to overcome challenges.

While having a generally positive view of the future, Optimists are quite conservative. They are openly supportive of the system, feeling that the United States government is able to effectively deal with the problems it confronts. Admittedly, they recognize this might not all go smoothly. Nevertheless, their faith in the system is very strong.

Internationalists

This group has a pessimistic attitude concerning the economic environment in the United States. In fact, they envision a declining future for the United States.

Internationalists are distinguished by their high levels of skepticism about the future of the US economy. This, in turn, results in their determination to protect their families and their assets by adopting a globally-oriented investment strategy.

Moreover, they are most inclined to utilize more esoteric means of protecting their wealth. For example, Internationalists are most likely to make use of off-shore trust arrangements.

Areas of Competence

Family offices are not adept in all areas of financial and related services. They cannot necessarily address the total range of issues affecting their mega-wealthy family members and other clients. Many of the family offices we studied are not focused or have not accessed the resources to deal with a variety of concerns and opportunities.

Areas Relevant to Insurance Professionals

While 16 areas were evaluated, three were particularly relevant to insurance professionals, as shown below.

COMPETENCY OF FAMILY OFFICES

Slightly more than half of the family offices saw themselves as extremely competent in providing financial and estate planning services. Less than a third believe themselves to be extremely competent in property and casualty insurance planning. About a quarter of the family offices considered themselves especially adept with respect to life insurance planning.

Area Expertise By Family Office Personality

The four family office personalities differ to the extent they are extremely competent in these areas, as shown below. In targeting and working with family offices insurance professionals must understand and appreciate these differences.

Internationalists are the most proficient when it comes to financial and estate planning. Slightly more than half of the Trendists identify this area as one where they are especially proficient. Half of both the Optimists and Power Brokers report this area to be one in which they are extremely competent. Of the 16 areas examined, financial and estate planning was the one identified by more family offices as an area of extreme competence.

AREA EXPERTISE BY FAMILY OFFICE PERSONALITY

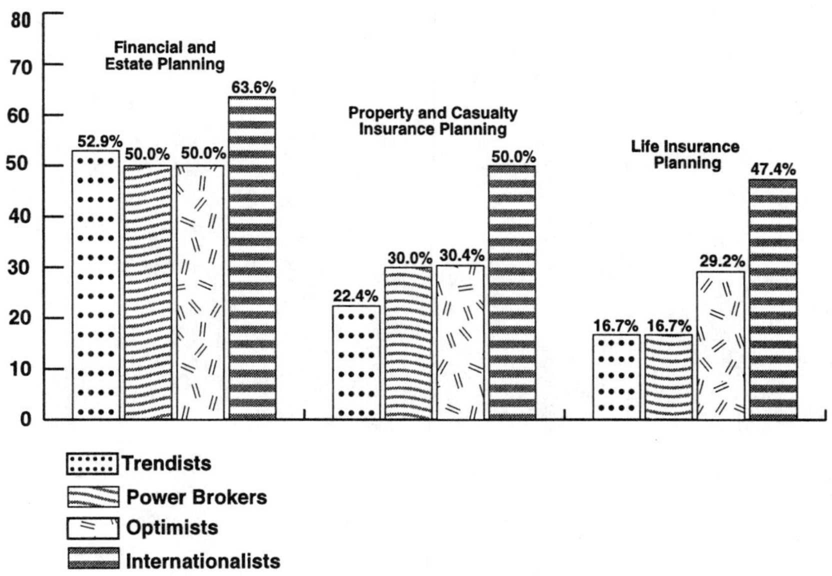

Internationalists boast the greatest relative expertise in property and casualty insurance planning. Less than a third of Optimists and Power Brokers say the same thing. Slightly more than a fifth of Trendists feel this way.

Approximately half of the Internationalists are very competent with respect to life insurance planning. Optimists are next in line. Relatively fewer of the Trendists rate themselves as being very adept. The same percentage of Power Brokers claims expertise in life insurance planning.

Implications

- The mega-wealthy in the form of family offices can be divided based on the way they perceive the future. This has resulted in the identification of four distinct family office personalities.
- When working with the mega-wealthy it is essential to be cognizant of these unique groups. Thus, you will be able to establish and build the high-quality relationship that is fundamental in working with the mega-wealthy.
- With respect to three areas of competence of particular interest to insurance professionals, family offices claim not to be particularly competent. A lack of expertise in these areas means that the family offices are going outside of their own organizations for these services. More than three-quarters of them will need to turn to life insurance professionals in order to provide life insurance planning and other related services and products.
- This situation provides tremendous opportunities to insurance professionals who can create viable relationships with these family offices and provide a high level of expertise coupled with highly customized insurance products.

APPENDIX C
THE PRINCIPLES

Section I:
The Family Business Market

Chapter 1:
The Ten Trillion Dollar Market

Principle: Affluent family businesses are the primary source of private wealth throughout the world.

Principle: The attractiveness of the family business market is drawing numerous competitors.

Chapter 2:
What You Must Know About Family Business Dynamics

Principle: In most family businesses, family goals are more important than business goals.

Principle: Succession drives the need for professional expertise.

Chapter 3:
How Family Businesses Buy Insurance

Principle: Shadow influencers can dramatically affect the decision-making process because they focus on family-oriented criteria instead of business-oriented criteria.

Principle: Shadow influencers will become involved when your services and products will impact the financial status of the family.

Principle: It often takes much more time for affluent family business owners to purchase financial services when the family will be affected.

Principle: When shadow influencers are involved, greater demands are placed on financial services providers.

Principle: Affluent family business owners are much more loyal clients. Loyalty is the payoff for addressing all the challenges they create.

Section II:
Eight Family Business Owner Identities

Chapter 4:
The Eight Family Business Owner Identities

Principle: An affluent family business personality is a characterization of the needs, wants, and desires that encapsulate the very reason for the existence of the family firm at this point in time.

Section IV:
Marketing to Family Businesses

Chapter 12:
Finding Them

Principle: The most effective way to get family business owners as new clients is by getting referrals from existing satisfied clients.

Principle: Accountants are the most influential advisors to successful family businesses.

Principle: Seminars targeting the eight family business owner personalities can be successful in building a practice.

Principle: You can capture the attention of successful family business owners through the skillful use of public relations.

Principle: Only by carefully promoting products and services as solutions to problems based on the eight family business personalities will direct mail or advertising campaigns be effective.

Principle: Cold calling is an ineffective approach to generating new family business owner clients. There is not a list in existence that someone else doesn't already have.

Principle: Do not focus your efforts on the family and friends of successful business owners. They are not effective in getting you to see the decision makers.

Chapter 13:
Selling Them

Principle: The key in working with family business owners to identify their needs is knowing their family business personalities.

Principle: You must communicate with your family business owner clients in a manner than engenders confidence in yourself and your abilities.

Principle: Tell your family business owner clients how your business philosophy fits into their motivations for having a family business.

Principle: Family business owners must know that everything they tell you will be kept completely confidential.

Principle: You must respect the wishes, needs, and wants of family business owners.

Principle: Work to blend the five critical selection criteria. All five should be a part of your communications with family business owners at all times.

Principle: Depth, not breath, appeals to family business owners. Concentrate on communicating your high level of focused expertise.

Principle: Do not emphasize low cost. The cost of your products and services is not the issue. The value of your services and products is.

Principle: Your ability to present is critical to your success in selling to family businesses.

Principle: By making your proposals of the highest quality, you are making sure that others who are asked by the family business owner to review them will recognize you as an expert and recognize your recommendations to be beneficial to the family and the business.

Principle: High-quality promotional materials are important. They will have the greatest effect if you design them incorporating your understanding of the eight family business personalities.

Chapter 14: Keeping Them

Principle: Family business clients will remain clients even when services and products are below acceptable levels if the relationship is skillfully managed. By handling the interpersonal aspects of the relationship you can retain clients even when the services and products perform poorly.

Principle: Family business clients will refer other business owners to you if they are highly satisfied.

Principle: Find out from your clients when they would like to meet and exceed their expectations. Meet often with your family business clients.

Principle: You can effectively provide direction for a meeting by using an agenda. The agenda can be nothing more than telling the family business owner the concerns you have and want to discuss.

Principle: Involvement is important in building a high-quality relationship. You can involve your clients by making certain they are not sitting back and just shaking their heads. You must get them to participate in the process.

Principle: To be sure they understand, frequently ask if your family business owner clients want anything explained. Also, get them to explain it to you.

Principle: Always encourage family business owners to involve shadow influencers. Specifically, recommend that they talk to family members about the products and services you are providing.

Principle: Always encourage family business owners to involve their other advisors as quickly as possible. By doing so, you will be avoiding problems down the road.